MICROFINANCE

Microfinance has become an important component of development, poverty reduction and economic regeneration strategy around the world. By the early twenty-first century tens of millions of people in more than 100 countries were accessing services from formal and semi-formal microfinance institutions (MFIs). Much of the initial attention on microcredit came through work on Bangladesh's much-lauded Grameen Bank but there are now many different 'models' for microfinance and many countries have substantial microfinance sectors.

This timely book, written by one of the major players in the UK in development economics, explores, amongst others, topics such as:

- microfinance and poverty reduction
- microfinance, gender and social development
- microinsurance
- regulating and supervising microfinance institutions.

Topical and insightful, this important text examines what has become a vast global industry employing hundreds of thousands of people and attracting the attention of large numbers of governments, banks, aid agencies, non-governmental organizations and consultancy firms.

David Hulme is Professor of Development Studies at the Institute for Development Policy and Management, Associate Director of the Brooks World Poverty Institute and Director of the Chronic Poverty Research Centre at the University of Manchester.

Thankom Arun is Reader in International Finance at Lancashire Business School, University of Central Lancashire and Honorary Senior Fellow of the School of Environment and Development at the University of Manchester.

ROUTLEDGE STUDIES IN DEVELOPMENT ECONOMICS

ECONOMIC DEVELOPMENT IN THE MIDDLE EAST
Rodney Wilson

MONETARY AND FINANCIAL POLICIES IN DEVELOPING COUNTRIES
Growth and stabilization
Akhtar Hossain and Anis Chowdhury

NEW DIRECTIONS IN DEVELOPMENT ECONOMICS
Growth, environmental concerns and government in the 1990s
Edited by Mats Lundahl and Benno J. Ndulu

FINANCIAL LIBERALIZATION AND INVESTMENT
Kanhaya L. Gupta and Robert Lensink

LIBERALIZATION IN THE DEVELOPING WORLD
Institutional and economic changes in Latin America, Africa and Asia
Edited by Alex E. Fernández Jilberto and André Mommen

FINANCIAL DEVELOPMENT AND ECONOMIC GROWTH
Theory and experiences from developing countries
Edited by Niels Hermes and Robert Lensink

THE SOUTH AFRICAN ECONOMY
Macroeconomic prospects for the medium term
Finn Tarp and Peter Brixen

PUBLIC SECTOR PAY AND ADJUSTMENT
Lessons from five countries
Edited by Christopher Colclough

EUROPE AND ECONOMIC REFORM IN AFRICA
Structural adjustment and economic diplomacy
Obed O. Mailafia

POST-APARTHEID SOUTHERN AFRICA
Economic challenges and policies for the future
Edited by Lennart Petersson

FINANCIAL INTEGRATION AND DEVELOPMENT
Liberalization and reform in sub-Saharan Africa
Ernest Aryeetey and Machiko Nissanke

REGIONALIZATION AND GLOBALIZATION IN THE MODERN WORLD ECONOMY
Perspectives on the Third World and transitional economies
Edited by Alex E. Fernández Jilberto and André Mommen

THE AFRICAN ECONOMY
Policy, institutions and the future
Steve Kayizzi-Mugerwa

RECOVERY FROM ARMED CONFLICT IN DEVELOPING COUNTRIES
Edited by Geoff Harris

SMALL ENTERPRISES AND ECONOMIC DEVELOPMENT
The dynamics of micro and small enterprises
Carl Liedholm and Donald C. Mead

THE WORLD BANK
New Agendas in a changing world
Michelle Miller-Adams

DEVELOPMENT POLICY IN THE TWENTY-FIRST CENTURY
Beyond the post-Washington consensus
Edited by Ben Fine, Costas Lapavitsas and Jonathan Pincus

STATE-OWNED ENTERPRISES IN THE MIDDLE EAST AND NORTH AFRICA
Privatization, performance and reform
Edited by Merih Celasun

FINANCE AND COMPETITIVENESS IN DEVELOPING COUNTRIES
Edited by José María Fanelli and Rohinton Medhora

CONTEMPORARY ISSUES IN DEVELOPMENT ECONOMICS
Edited by B.N. Ghosh

MEXICO BEYOND NAFTA
Edited by Martín Puchet Anyul and Lionello F. Punzo

ECONOMIES IN TRANSITION
A guide to China, Cuba, Mongolia, North Korea and Vietnam at the turn of the twenty-first century
Ian Jeffries

POPULATION, ECONOMIC GROWTH AND AGRICULTURE IN LESS DEVELOPED COUNTRIES
Nadia Cuffaro

FROM CRISIS TO GROWTH IN AFRICA
Edited by Mats Lundal

THE MACROECONOMICS OF MONETARY UNION
An analysis of the CFA franc zone
David Fielding

ENDOGENOUS DEVELOPMENT
Networking, innovation, institutions and cities
Antonio Vasquez-Barquero

LABOUR RELATIONS IN DEVELOPMENT
Edited by Alex E. Fernández Jilberto and Marieke Riethof

GLOBALIZATION, MARGINALIZATION AND DEVELOPMENT
Edited by S. Mansoob Murshed

PROGRAMME AID AND DEVELOPMENT
Beyond conditionality
Howard White and Geske Dijkstra

COMPETITIVENESS STRATEGY IN DEVELOPING COUNTRIES
A manual for policy analysis
Edited by Ganeshan Wignaraja

THE AFRICAN MANUFACTURING FIRM
An analysis based on firm surveys in sub-Saharan Africa
Dipak Mazumdar and Ata Mazaheri

TRADE POLICY, GROWTH AND POVERTY IN ASIAN DEVELOPING COUNTRIES
Edited by Kishor Sharma

INTERNATIONAL COMPETITIVENESS, INVESTMENT AND FINANCE
A case study of India
Edited by A. Ganesh Kumar, Kunal Sen and Rajendra R. Vaidya

THE PATTERN OF AID GIVING
The impact of good governance on development assistance
Eric Neumayer

NEW INTERNATIONAL POVERTY REDUCTION STRATEGIES
Edited by Jean-Pierre Cling, Mireille Razafindrakoto and François Roubaud

TARGETING DEVELOPMENT
Critical perspectives on the Millennium Development Goals
Edited by Richard Black and Howard White

ESSAYS ON BALANCE OF PAYMENTS CONSTRAINED GROWTH
Theory and evidence
Edited by J.S.L. McCombie and A.P. Thirlwall

THE PRIVATE SECTOR AFTER COMMUNISM
New entrepreneurial firms in transition economies
Jan Winiecki, Vladimir Benacek and Mihaly Laki

INFORMATION TECHNOLOGY AND DEVELOPMENT
A new paradigm for delivering the internet to rural areas in developing countries
Jeffrey James

THE ECONOMICS OF PALESTINE
Economic policy and institutional reform for a viable Palestine state
Edited by David Cobham and Nu'man Kanafani

DEVELOPMENT DILEMMAS
The methods and political ethics of growth policy
Melvin Ayogu and Don Ross

RURAL LIVELIHOODS AND POVERTY REDUCTION POLICIES
Edited by Frank Ellis and H. Ade Freeman

BEYOND MARKET-DRIVEN DEVELOPMENT
Drawing on the experience of Asia and Latin America
Edited by Makoto Noguchi and Costas Lapavitsas

THE POLITICAL ECONOMY OF REFORM FAILURE
Edited by Mats Lundahl and Michael L. Wyzan

OVERCOMING INEQUALITY IN LATIN AMERICA
Issues and challenges for the twenty-first century
Edited by Ricardo Gottschalk and Patricia Justino

TRADE, GROWTH AND INEQUALITY IN THE ERA OF GLOBALIZATION
Edited by Kishor Sharma and Oliver Morrissey

MICROFINANCE
Perils and prospects
Edited by Jude L. Fernando

THE IMF, WORLD BANK AND POLICY REFORM
Edited by Alberto Paloni and Maurizio Zanardi

MANAGING DEVELOPMENT
Globalization, economic restructuring and social policy
Edited by Junji Nakagawa

WHO GAINS FROM FREE TRADE?
Export-led Growth, Inequality and Poverty in Latin America
Edited by Rob Vos, Enrique Ganuza, Samuel Morley, and Sherman Robinson

EVOLUTION OF MARKETS AND INSTITUTIONS
A study of an emerging economy
Murali Patibandla

THE NEW FAMINES
Why famines exist in an era of globalization
Edited by Stephen Devereux

DEVELOPMENT ETHICS AT WORK
Explorations - 1960–2002
Denis Goulet

LAW REFORM IN DEVELOPING AND TRANSITIONAL STATES
Edited by Tim Lindsey

THE ASSYMETRIES OF GLOBALIZATION
Edited by Pan A. Yotopoulos and Donato Romano

IDEAS, POLICIES AND ECONOMIC DEVELOPMENT IN THE AMERICAS
Edited by Esteban Pérez-Caldentey and Matias Vernengo

EUROPEAN UNION TRADE POLITICS AND DEVELOPMENT
Everything but arms unravelled
Edited by Gerrit Faber and Jan Orbie

MEMBERSHIP BASED ORGANIZATIONS OF THE POOR
Edited by Martha Chen, Renana Jhabvala, Ravi Kanbur and Carol Richards

THE POLITICS OF AID SELECTIVITY
Good governance criteria in world bank, U.S. And Dutch development assistance
Wil Hout

ECONOMIC DEVELOPMENT, EDUCATION AND TRANSNATIONAL CORPORATIONS
Mark Hanson

ACHIEVING ECONOMIC DEVELOPMENT IN THE ERA OF GLOBALIZATION
Shalendra Sharma

SUSTAINABLE DEVELOPMENT AND FREE TRADE
Shawkat Alam

THE IMPACT OF INTERNATIONAL DEBT RELIEF
Geske Dijkstra

EUROPE'S TROUBLED REGION
Economic development, institutional reform and social welfare in the Western Balkans
William Bartlett

WORK, FEMALE EMPOWERMENT AND ECONOMIC DEVELOPMENT
Sara Horrell, Hazel Johnson and Paul Mosley

THE CHRONICALLY POOR IN RURAL BANGLADESH
Livelihood constraints and capabilities
Pk. Md. Motiur Rahman, Noriatsu Matsui and Yukio Ikemoto

PUBLIC-PRIVATE PARTNERSHIPS IN HEALTH CARE IN INDIA
Lessons for developing countries
A. Venkat Raman and James Warner Björkman

RURAL POVERTY AND INCOME DYNAMICS IN ASIA AND AFRICA
Edited by Keijiro Otsuka, Jonna P. Estudillo and Yasuyuki Sawada

MICROFINANCE
A reader
Edited by David Hulme and Thankom Arun

MICROFINANCE

A reader

Edited by David Hulme and Thankom Arun

Routledge
Taylor & Francis Group
LONDON AND NEW YORK

First published 2009
by Routledge
2 Park Square, Milton Park, Abingdon, Oxon, OX14 4RN

Simultaneously published in the USA and Canada
by Routledge
270 Madison Avenue, New York, NY 10016

Routledge is an imprint of the Taylor & Francis Group, an informa business

Typeset in Times New Roman
by Pindar NZ, Auckland, New Zealand
Printed and bound in Great Britain
by CPI Antony Rowe, Chippenham, Wiltshire

British Library Cataloguing in Publication Data
A catalogue record for this book is available from the British Library

Library of Congress Cataloging-in-Publication Data
Hulme, David.
Microfinance: a reader / David Hulme & Thankom Arun.
p. cm. — (Routledge studies in development economics ; 69)
ISBN 978-0-415-37532-0 (hardback) — ISBN 978-0-203-88276-4
(ebook) 1. Microfinance. I. Arun, Thankom. II. Title.
HG178.3.H85 2009
332—dc22
2008033546

ISBN 13: 978-0-415-37532-0 (hbk)
ISBN 13: 978-0-203-88276-4 (ebk)

ISBN 10: 0-415-37532-0 (hbk)
ISBN 10: 0-203-88276-8 (ebk)

This book is dedicated to the hundreds of microfinance managers and field staff who have spared their time over the years to show us their programs, tell us about their ideas and introduce us to their clients and colleagues. May your repayment rates be high, your clients happy and head office far away.

CONTENTS

ILLUSTRATIONS

Boxes

Figures

Tables

CONTRIBUTORS

Thankom Arun is Reader in International Finance at the University of Central Lancashire. He is also a Honorary Senior Fellow at the University of Manchester and was a Visiting Professor at the University of Rome, 'Sapienza'. He has worked largely on the industrial and financial sectors in the context of globalization, the wider discussion on the purposeful reorientation of development objectives, and the functions of institutions to enhance the competitiveness of the global system.

Warren Brown is a seasoned Product Development professional with experience in developing and launching products in microfinance, mainstream financial services and the computer software industries. Warren's background in microfinance includes the Research group at Calmeadow (where this article was written) and the R&D group at ACCION International. In addition to microinsurance, he has also researched and supported the development of micro-housing products in Latin America and Africa.

Monique Cohen is the Founder-President of Microfinance Opportunities and a leading international expert on financial services for the poor and client assessment in microfinance. Dr Cohen designed and led the AIMS (Assessing the Impact of Microfinance Services) project at the United States Agency for International Development, where she served as Senior Technical Advisor in the Office of Microenterprise Development. She has published extensively on microfinance and teaches at the University of Southern New Hampshire's Microenterprise Development Institute and the Microfinance Training Program, in Boulder, Colorado.

David Hulme is Professor of Development Studies at the University of Manchester, Associate Director of the Chronic Poverty Research Centre and Associate Director of the Brooks World Poverty Institute. He currently holds a Leverhulme Senior Research Fellowship. His current research interests focus on integrating time into poverty analysis, the concept and practice of global poverty reduction, combining quantitative and qualitative research approaches, understanding poverty dynamics (Bangladesh), the role of social protection in poverty reduction strategies (global), natural resource management and livelihoods (Africa) and microfinance.

Naila Kabeer is a Professorial Fellow at the Institute of Development Studies, Sussex. She has worked extensively on gender, poverty and social policy issues. Her main areas of research have been in South and South East Asia. She has also been active in developing frameworks and methodologies for integrating gender concerns into policy and planning and has substantial experience of training and advisory work with governments, bilateral and multilateral agencies and NGOs. She is on the Ford Foundation's Global Impact Evaluation of Microfinance Programmes.

Imran Matin is the Director of the Research and Evaluations Division, BRAC, Bangladesh. He has a Masters degree in Development Economics and a PhD in Economics from the University of Sussex. His research interests include livelihoods, microfinance, enterprise development and extreme poverty.

Jonathan Morduch is Professor of Public Policy and Economics at the University of New York, Wagner. He has worked extensively on access to finance, social investment and insurance in the context of international development. He is co-author of *The Economics of Microfinance* (MIT Press, 2005) and directs the Financial Access Initiative, a research consortium based at New York University.

Paul Mosley is Professor of Economics at the University of Sheffield. His research interests include international aid and finance, political economy and development, the welfare state and poverty, market failure and economic history. He is the editor of the *Journal of International Development* and has worked for a number of organizations including the United States Agency for International Development, United Nations Conference on Trade and Development, the World Bank and UK Department for International Development.

Marguerite Robinson is an independent consultant and author. She served as Professor of Anthropology and Dean of the College of Arts and Sciences at Brandeis University before joining the Harvard Institute for International Development (1978–2000). She served for many years as adviser to the Indonesian Ministry of Finance and to Bank Rakyat Indonesia (BRI) on the development of BRI's microbanking system – now the largest financially self-sufficient microfinance system in the world. She is author of *The Microfinance Revolution*, published by the World Bank and Open Society Institute.

Stuart Rutherford is an Honorary Senior Fellow at the Brooks World Poverty Institute at the University of Manchester and Founder-Director of SafeSave, a microfinance organization that works in the slums of Dhaka. He originally trained and worked as an art historian and architect and later became Field Director for ActionAid in Burundi and Bangladesh. His passion for understanding how poor people manage their money led him into action research on microfinance. His publications include *The Poor and Their Money* (Oxford University Press, New Delhi).

PREFACE

The origins of this collection lie in the demands from our students at the Institute for Development Policy and Management (IDPM) at the University of Manchester for a textbook on microfinance. We struggled to find the time to write such a book, and we doubted our intellectual ability to achieve such an ambitious goal, so we settled on editing a set of readings. In this book we try to help students who are relatively new to microfinance, and practitioners looking for an entry point into the vast academic literature, to become acquainted with the main ideas and debates about microfinance. The book is the outcome of screening more than 400 published books and papers on this topic.

In the text that follows we have sought to introduce the student and/or practitioner to some of the best known writers on microfinance, to the ideas that have shaped the growth of today's 'microfinance industry' and to provide some coverage of the major regions of the developing world. Inevitably we have had to leave out many papers that have been seminal to our own understanding of the theory and practice of microfinance. There are many authors, papers, issues, institutions and country case studies that we have been pained to omit.

The papers have been selected so as to be accessible to undergraduate and graduate students in the social sciences and to the practitioners of microfinance who come from very varied backgrounds. We have not included the recent burgeoning econometric literature on microfinance. This is partly because they are often incomprehensible to folk who have not undertaken postgraduate studies in econometrics; partly because some of them draw conclusions that are based on highly dubious assumptions (sometimes hidden away in small print); and, partly because some of them ask foolish questions. To a university-based econometrician with a dataset, asking 'Is group lending better than individual lending?' may seem sensible. But, as any practitioner will explain, both models are excellent … wherever they work well. The evolution of the microfinance industry has depended on specific institutions developing products that meet client needs at a reasonable cost in specific contexts and not on the identification of laws of development economics.

Many people have helped to assemble this collection. First and foremost we must express our gratitude to the contributors and to the publishers of their original papers and books. We are especially grateful to David Clark, Leonith Hinojosa,

Karen Moore, Lemmy Manje and Maneesha Chadha for support in listing and selecting articles, seeking permissions and research assistance. Thanks also to Stuart Rutherford and Graham Wright for comments on Chapters 10 and 14. At the Brooks World Poverty Institute, University of Manchester, our particular thanks to Denise Redston for coordinating and delivering the final manuscript.

Finally, our thanks to Shoba and Georgina for supporting us through this project, and many others, and putting up with our absences overseas.

David Hulme, Manchester,
July 2008

Thankom Arun, Preston/Manchester
July 2008

ACKNOWLEDGEMENT TO PUBLISHERS

We would like to express our thanks to the publishers for allowing us to reproduce the following articles.

Edward Elgar Publishing Ltd

Thankom Arun, David Hulme, Imran Matin and Stuart Rutherford (2005) 'Finance for the Poor: The Way Forward?' in *Finance and Development, Surveys of Theory, Evidence and Policy*, edited by C. J. Green, C.H. Kirkpatrick and V Murinde.

Elsevier Ltd

T. Arun (2005) Regulating for Development, *The Quarterly Review of Economics and Finance*, 45 (2–3), pp. 345–57.

D. Hulme (2000) Impact Assessment Methodologies for Microfinance: Theory, Experience and Better Practice, *World Development*, 28 (1), pp. 79–98.

N. Kabeer (2001) Conflicts Over Credit, *World Development*, 29 (1), pp. 63–84.

I. Matin and D. Hulme (2003) Programs for the Poorest, *World Development*, 31 (3), pp. 647–65.

J. Morduch (2000) The Microfinance Schism, *World Development*, 28(4), pp. 617–29.

P. Mosley and D. Hulme (1998) Microenterprise Finance: Is there a Conflict between Growth and Poverty-alleviation?, *World Development*, 26 (5), pp. 783–90.

Oxford University Press

S. Rutherford (2000) *The Poor and Their Money*.

World Bank

Marguerite S. Robinson (2001) *The Microfinance Revolution: Sustainable Finance for the Poor*.

John Wiley

M. Cohen (2002) Making Microfinance More Client Led, *Journal of International Development*, 14 (3), pp. 335–50.

ITDG Publishing

W. Brown (2001) Microinsurance – The Risks, Perils and Opportunities, *Small Enterprise Development*, 12 (1), pp. 11–24.

1

INTRODUCTION

Thankom Arun and David Hulme

Since the 1980s microfinance has become an important component of development, poverty reduction and economic regeneration strategies around the world. By the early twenty-first century tens of millions of people in more than 100 countries were accessing services from formal and semi formal microfinance institutions (MFIs). It has become a vast global industry involving large numbers of governments, banks, aid agencies, non-governmental organizations (NGOs), cooperatives and consultancy firms and directly employing hundreds of thousands of branch-level staff.

Much of the initial excitement about microfinance centered on Bangladesh's much lauded Grameen Bank, which talked of the transformation of economic and social structures through microenterprise loans and group formation. It propounded a 'bottom-up' approach that made the social mobilization of marginalized communities, and particularly women, a main focus. How times have changed. There are now many different 'models' for microfinance, many countries have substantial microfinance sectors and the main activity is on providing microfinancial services rather than the grander goal of social transformation. Microfinance today is about drawing the benefits of contemporary capitalism down to those with low incomes rather than promoting alternatives to capitalism. It is part of the post-Washington Consensus (Stiglitz, 1998) and not an alternative to the orthodoxy.

Access to financial services can be seen as a public good that is essential to enable people to participate in the benefits of a modern, market-based economy – analogous to access to safe water, basic health services, and primary education (Peachey and Roe, 2004). Microfinance initiatives have emerged as an alternative to the well documented failures of government rural credit schemes to reach small farmers (Hulme and Mosley, 1996) and the formal banking sector to provide services to low-income households. They pay close attention to the incentives that drive efficient performance (Morduch, 1999) in the context of small transactions and large numbers of clients. Many MFIs use group-based lending approaches and thus reduce the administrative costs (or transfer them to clients) of gathering information, contract design and enforcement of credit transactions, including loan recovery. Over time the microfinance sector has become less the domain of NGOs and non-profits and more the domain of commercial organizations. There were 3,316 microcredit institutions reported reaching 133,030,913 clients at the end of 2006 (Daley-Harris, 2007). According to Daley-Harris, nearly 70 percent of the clients were among the poorest when they took their first loan, but some observers query this claim. In terms of the financial size of the organizations, in Bangladesh, the Grameen Bank and the Bangladesh Rural Advancement Committee (BRAC) have a cumulative disbursement of over US$4.7 billion and US$2.2 billion respectively (Hulme and Moore, 2008). However, the phenomenal growth of the sector has brought out the issues of poor management and inadequate corporate governance among MFIs (Lascelles, 2008).

A vast printed and electronic literature has grown around microfinance but it is dispersed across many professional and academic journals (in economics, development studies, small enterprise development, banking, finance, sociology, social policy and management), books, agency reports and websites. This structured reader presents 12 articles, carefully selected from a review of more than 400 publications to provide a comprehensive overview of microfinance from an interdisciplinary perspective, and a conclusion. These readings cover the key debates in microfinance – such as poverty, gender, client-led products, regulation and impact assessment – along with case studies from a carefully selected range of countries. The early chapters examine the evolution of microfinance and review broad sets of issues. Later chapters focus on more narrowly defined issues and/or specific case studies, such as the Grameen Bank.

The first article, by Thankom Arun, David Hulme, Imran Matin and Stuart Rutherford (Chapter 2), examines a number of key issues about the demand of poor people for microfinancial services and the informal and formal ways in which these have been met. It argues that neither an emphasis on 'supply' (as occurred in the 1960s and 1970s) nor on 'demand' (as assumed by the neo-liberals of the 1980s) is sufficient to provide services to the poor. The key is balancing supply and demand by supporting the development of MFIs and products that have a capacity to understand the preferences of clients and provide services that match these preferences at affordable prices.

In Chapter 3 Jonathan Morduch, a development economist with long-term interests in poverty and vulnerability as well as microfinance, explores the schism between those who see 'good banking' as the best way forward for microfinance and those who focus on social impacts. He warns that there is no 'win-win' situation in which an MFI can get the best of both sides of this debate. He argues for proponents of microfinance to directly address the schism through further innovation and more rigorous monitoring of achievements.

Rutherford, a long time scholar-practitioner of microfinance who has inspired many analysts of this sector, examines the 'need to save' that he has encountered in poor and near poor people in Bangladesh and other parts of the world in Chapter 4. His argument focuses on the need for poor people to create 'usefully large lump sums' (to meet life cycle events, emergency situations and economic opportunities) out of small and irregular daily and weekly earnings. They can do this by 'saving up' (conventional saving), 'saving down' (borrowing a lump sum and then repaying it by making small, daily or weekly savings in their consumption behavior) or 'saving through' (joining clubs that involve making regular savings and getting a lump sum at some stage during the savings cycle). He concludes that poor people have insufficient opportunities to engage in 'basic personal financial intermediation' – effective microfinance can help remedy this situation.

In Chapter 5 Marguerite Robinson, who spent many years studying and advising on microfinance in Indonesia, looks at the 'absurd gap' between supply and demand in microfinance. She identifies two main approaches to microfinance – 'poverty lending' and 'financial systems'. The former seeks to reduce the poverty of its clients using foreign aid supplied subsidies. The latter focuses on developing savings and lending services that meet the needs of poor and non-poor households and that are profitable – so that they can be expanded on regional and national scale without needing donor subsidies. Her argument is detailed, so we have had to shorten some sections. It makes a powerful case for MFIs to pursue a 'financial systems' approach.

Paul Mosley and Hulme explore an aspect of Robinson's analysis in Chapter 6. Drawing on their empirical research in several countries (Hulme and Mosley, 1996), they argue that microenterprise credit has a more significant impact on the incomes of the non-poor than the poor. At the time they wrote this piece it confronted the dominant discourse about microcredit that was used to develop the microcredit summits – 'microcredit always works'. They argue that their finding occurs because the poor have a greater need to divert microenterprise loans to consumption, are more likely to have to sell assets because of adverse shocks and have a more limited range of investment opportunities than better-off people. On a more positive note they identify product design features that can help improve the poverty impacts of microcredit. The findings of this paper have been influential but its methods of analysis, and conclusions, have been challenged in recent times (Morduch, 2008).

Chapter 7 (by Matin and Hulme) looks at one of the schemes that have been designed to help very poor people in Bangladesh reach an economic and social position that will permit them to take advantage of microfinance, and other economic opportunities. Matin is Head of BRAC's Research Department and Hulme has studied BRAC since 1992. BRAC is a major provider of microcredit but in the 1990s it realized that its microfinance schemes where not reaching the poorest. Using the knowledge it had gained from food aid programs it developed a 'Targeting the Ultra Poor' (TUP) program that provides a cash stipend, social development and business training and an asset transfer (often cows, goats, ducks or chickens) to very poor women. Many of the women participating in TUP have subsequently joined BRAC and other microfinance schemes. For a more detailed review of TUP see Hulme and Moore, (2008).

In Chapter 8 Naila Kabeer explores the reasons why recent evaluations of the empowerment potential of credit programs for rural women in Bangladesh have arrived at very conflicting conclusions. Kabeer is at the Institute of Development Studies, University of Sussex and has spent many years researching issues on poverty, gender, and social policy. Although the evaluations use somewhat different methodologies and have been carried out at different points of time, the paper argues that the primary source of the conflict lies in the very different understandings of intra household power relations which the different studies draw on. It supports this argument through a comparative analysis with the findings of a participatory evaluation of a rather different credit program in Bangladesh in which the impact of loans was evaluated by women loanees themselves.

Monique Cohen opens up the debate on the need for a client-led focus in microfinance in Chapter 9. The solutions to the concerns on competition and dropout are defined in terms of more responsive products, the creation of new products, and the restructuring of existing ones in line with the client-led agenda. Appropriate products will not only benefit the operations of an institution they will also have a positive impact on the wellbeing of the client, reducing the risk of borrowing and the poor's vulnerability.

Several iconic institutions have been exceptionally influential in the evolution of microfinance. While Bank Rakyat Indonesia (BRI) and Bolivia's BancoSol are discussed by Robinson in Chapter 5, Chapter 10 reviews the evolution and present status of the world's best known MFI – the Grameen Bank. It is an original paper specially written for this volume by Hulme as the bulk of the literature on the Grameen Bank fails to note that it has transformed its organizational goals and business model since 2001. The paper argues that the Bank has put aside its 'poverty lending' approach (Grameen I) and adopted a 'financial systems' approach (Grameen II). It is no longer in danger of financial collapse, as was the case in the late 1990s, and is one of Bangladesh's fastest growing MFIs with more than 6 million clients. However, its claims to being a bank for the poorest are now rather tenuous.

In Chapter 11, Warren Brown explains the microinsurance products which have gained prominence recently. Microinsurance refers to financial services that use risk pooling to provide compensation to low-income individuals or groups that are adversely affected by a specified risk or event. However, he questions whether the majority of MFIs have the expertise required to support insurance products, such as pricing, and whether the target clients actually want insurance or other risk-managing financial products.

In recent years most countries in which microfinance has become significant have been examining their regulatory systems. Arun, in Chapter 12, reviews the issues of supervision and regulation for MFIs. There is an argument that MFIs are unlikely to achieve their potential unless they are in an effectively regulated environment. Many MFIs have looked to deposit mobilization as the primary source of funds for their growing loan portfolios. The incentive for MFIs to be regulated is the legal right regulation gives to accept deposits for on-lending, and thereby to expand the scale of their programs. How effective is it to license these institutions when the majority of them are dependent on the continuing availability of subsidies is the real issue. Issues of self-regulation, rating agencies, cost of supervision and the role of prudential versus non-prudential regulation are also important in MFIs.

However, regulatory and supervisory issues in microfinance should lead to better organizational structures, legitimacy, independence and market growth.

Evaluating microfinance programs remains a major activity as the industry still attracts donor support and many funders and NGOs have asked (and are asking) whether microfinance should be prioritized or whether there are other types of program that are a greater priority. In Chapter 13 Hulme reviews the approaches and methods that can be used for microfinance impact assessment. It contrasts the market-based perspective (if microfinance meets client needs and covers its own costs then it is successful) with the more demanding poverty-impact perspective (the direct and indirect impacts of microfinance must be measured and compared with the costs incurred – economic and social). Further, Hulme contrasts the high 'scientific' approaches preferred by econometricians (now promoted by MIT's 'The Abdul Latif Jameel Poverty Action Lab') with the more organizationally focused moderate cost impact assessments that are the base of most evidence about microfinance. He believes that high quality scientific evaluations will be relatively few and that there is a real danger of those that seek 'laws' of development economics not understanding that microfinance has to be context specific and that MFIs usually evolve and learn – they are not designed and then implemented as naïve, normative theory promises.

In the concluding chapter (Chapter 14) we speculate on the 'Future of Microfinance', particularly on the ways in which the sector may evolve over coming years as a set of services that raises the prospects for low-income households. It has been widely accepted that microfinance is not a magic bullet that automatically lifts poor people out of poverty through microenterprise. The trends of commercialization in microfinance benefits consumers in terms of lower prices, product and service innovations, improved product and service quality and technological advancements. The microfinance sector seems set to continue to expand and diffuse through different forms such as specialist MFIs and formal banks. However, the speed and nature of these processes is still unclear and we may need to continue the efforts to provide access to financial services to those people and regions who still have very limited access to finance.

References

Daley-Harris, S. (2007), *State of the Microcredit Summit Campaign Report 2007*, Washington, DC: Microcredit Summit Campaign.

Hulme, D. and Moore, K. (2008), 'Assisting the Poorest in Bangladesh: Learning from BRAC's "Targeting the Ultra-poor" Programme', in A. Barrientos and D. Hulme (eds), *Social Protection for the Poor and Poorest: Concepts, Policies and Practices*, London: Routledge.

Hulme, D. and Mosley P. (1996), *Finance Against Poverty*, London: Routledge.

Lascelles, D. (2008), *Microfinance Banana Skins 2008: Risk in a Booming Industry*, Center for the Study of Financial Innovation (CSFI), New York. http://www.microfinancegateway.org/files/47464_file_CSFI_Microfinance_FINAL.pdf (accessed June 12, 2008).

Morduch, J. (1999), 'The Microfinance Promise', *Journal of Economic Literature*, 37(4), pp. 1569–614.

—— (2008), 'Another Look at Winners and Losers in Finance Against Poverty', *Financial Access Initiative Working Paper*, New York, New York University.

Peachey, S. and Roe, A. (2004), *Access to Finance: A Study for the World Savings Bank Institute*, Oxford: Oxford Policy Management.

Stiglitz, J. (1998), 'More Instruments and Broader Goals: Moving Toward the Post Washington Consensus', Helsinki: 1998 WIDER Annual Lecture, January 7.

2

FINANCE FOR THE POOR

The way forward?

Thankom Arun, David Hulme, Imran Matin and Stuart Rutherford[1]

2.1 INTRODUCTION

Since the 1980s, microfinancial services have generated considerable interest among academics, donors and development practitioners as an alternative to the documented failures of government rural credit assistance to reach low-income households (Hulme and Mosley, 1996; Johnson and Rogaly, 1997).The failures are attributed to causes such as urban-biased credit allocation, higher transaction costs, interest rate restrictions, high default rates and corrupt practices. The reasons for poor loan recovery are related to inappropriate design features, leading to incentive problems, and politicization that made borrowers view credit as political largesse (Lipton *et al.*, 1997). These failures stimulated a set of innovative financial institutions in several corners of the world which began to prosper and attract attention, especially in Bolivia, Bangladesh and Indonesia. These microfinance institutions (MFIs) share a commitment to serving clients that have been excluded from the formal banking sector.

The development of the microfinance sector is based on the assumption that the poor possess the capacity to implement income-generating economic activities but are limited by lack of access to and inadequate provision of savings, credit and insurance facilities. This approach also breaks from the directed credit strategies by reducing the government involvement and by paying close attention to the incentives that drive efficient performance (Morduch, 1999). The developments in microfinancial services have been based on a prototype delivery model that is considered the best answer to capture financial needs of the poor in various socioeconomic and institutional systems. However, after two decades of experience, a better understanding of the financial service preferences and behaviours of the poor and poorest is still needed to expand the scope of microfinance initiatives in addressing the concerns about welfare implications of MFIs (Morduch, 2000; Matin and Sinha, 1998; Gulli, 1998; Rutherford, 1999).

Following the Introduction, Section 2.2 of this chapter explores the fallacy of the misconceptions regarding the poor and savings. Section 2.3 reviews the role of informal providers and mutual finance in relation to saving by the poor. Section 2.4 explores the recent microfinance initiatives in the formal sector, with the distinctiveness of MFIs and the possible welfare impacts of MFIs being discussed in Section 2.5. Section 2.6 draws out the main conclusions of the chapter and highlights the importance of matching demand and supply initiatives in microfinance.

2.2 THE POOR AND SAVINGS

The popular conception about the inability of the poor to save is not true. The nature of the 'Lilliputian economy' in which the poor operate involves high levels of insecurity and risk that lead to the use by the poor of savings and credit mechanisms as substitutes for insurance (Platteau and Abraham, 1984; Alderman and Paxson, 1994; Fafchamps, 1995). The poor may save money as it goes out (keeping a few coins back from the housekeeping money) as well as when it comes in (deducting savings at source from wages or other income). Also *reciprocal lending*, which is very common among the poor, making up the bulk of financial transactions for poor people (Matin and Sinha, 1998; Dreze *et al.*, 1997), demonstrates the poor's capacity and willingness to save. However the idea behind savings is to get a large lump sum, which is not possible through their daily patterns of living. The interconnectedness of the roles of savings, credit and insurance leads one to think about the motivation behind savings which can be expected to be in broadly three categories of life cycle needs, emergencies and opportunities.

Life cycle needs such as childbirth, education, marriage, home-building, old age, funeral expenses, festivals and the desire to bequeath a lump sum to heirs vary from region to region. These can be anticipated as they require relatively large sums of money to be amassed. The amount of cash needed to meet such expenses is much larger than can normally be found in the household. Emergencies also create a sudden and unanticipated need for a large sum of money. Idiosyncratic emergencies such as sickness or injury, the death of a breadwinner, the loss of employment and theft, or the covariant emergencies such as war, floods, fires and cyclones, create a sudden need for more cash than can normally be found at home. There may be opportunities to invest in an existing or new business, to buy land or other productive assets, or to pay a bribe to get a permanent job.

Other than savings, the poor can obtain lump sums through selling assets, and through mortgage and pawn. In a large number of cases, poor people sell in advance assets that they do not currently have but expect to hold in the future, such as the sale of crops. The second method, mortgage and pawn, enables poor people to convert assets into cash and back again, which may not always be realized. However, both these methods require the user to have a stock of wealth in the form of an asset of some sort, of which poor people often have very few. The saving method enables the poor to convert the small savings into lump sums through a variety of mechanisms such as savings deposit, loans and insurance. The savings strategy helps the poor to develop an asset base to protect against risks and shocks in the future. However the success of this strategy depends on the understanding of the informal arrangements that the poor themselves innovate and use varies from region to region.

The financial diaries[2] prepared by poor households in urban and rural areas in Bangladesh and in India reveal that the respondents patch together a wide array of informal financial arrangements with semi-formal and formal services. All households in the samples engage in money-managing practices and on average the Bangladeshi households push or pull through financial services and devices each year a sum of money (US$839) equivalent to two-thirds of their annual cash income. In the Indian case, households enter a fresh financial arrangement (with a moneylender, money guard, savings club or formal provider, among others) on average every two weeks. In Bangladesh, among 42 households, 33 types of service or device have been used. These households see financial services as a day-to-day activity, neither as a right or privilege nor as a reward or enticement for engaging in some form of approved behaviour. These diaries reveal that poor people want reliable, convenient and flexible ways to store and retrieve cash and to turn their capacity to save into spending power, in the short, medium and long term on a continuing basis (Morduch and Rutherford, 2003).

This experience shows the fallacy of the prevalent conception that the poor in general cannot save. This leads to an overemphasis on the promotional role of financial services as credit for investment. The better conceptualizations of the poor as a heterogeneous group, of vulnerable households with complex livelihoods (Carney, 1998; Scoones, 1998; Ellis, 2000), explores the need for microfinancial services to be redesigned as client-centred organizations to help the poor to be more likely to achieve the goals that they seek to achieve.

2.3 MUTUAL FINANCE, INFORMAL PROVIDERS AND SAVINGS

Credit can be provided in different forms and varied institutional arrangements such as standard loan or through different informal channels. Informal providers are a mixed group, such as moneylenders, pawnbrokers and traders, who have in common the fact that they provide unregistered sources of credit. The main sources of informal financial credit services are (i) lending by individuals on a non-profit (and often reciprocal) basis; (ii) direct but intermittent lending by individuals with a temporary surplus; (iii) lending by individuals specializing in lending, whether on the basis of their own funds or of intermediated funds; (iv) individuals who collect deposits or 'guard' money; and (v) group finance (for a detailed discussion on these various categories, see Matin *et al.*, 2002). Informal providers are ready to accept collateral in different forms that are unacceptable to formal providers. They are part of a localized scale of financial intermediation and have much better information regarding the activities and characteristics of borrowers.

The type of informal finance that makes the greatest contribution to additive savings[3] is mutual finance: group-based or reciprocal financial services. Other than the mutual finance schemes, the level of intermediation is either absent or very localized for informal finance. Moneylenders normally rely on their own funds and do not accept receipts (Binswanger and Rosenzweig, 1984). The major attractions of mutual finance arrangements as effective financial intermediaries are (i) reciprocity, or the inbuilt provision of borrowing at short notice which serves as a kind of access to a liquidity-guaranteeing function which is especially important to business; (ii) being able to save in small instalments; (iii) provision of disciplined environment for saving; (iv) convenience and absence of formalities; and (v) meeting liquidity preferences by permitting savings to be hidden away from the demands of friends and relatives.

Getting access to a useful lump sum through building mutual savings is central to informal group finance schemes. In such arrangements, groups of individuals pool their savings and lend primarily to each other. The credit extended by group finance arrangements is the financial product which incorporates the functions of savings and insurance, which the poor households tend to use to a greater extent than the non-poor. The two main methods of group financing are savings services provided by rotating savings and credit associations (ROSCAs[4], where the case rotates evenly between all the group members), and accumulating savings and credit associations (ASCRAs, where some members borrow and others do not).

In ROSCAs, the equal periodic savings of every member are pooled together and given to each member in turn. The number of poolings depends on the number of members and the cycle comes automatically to an end when each member has taken their turn. In an ASCRA, the pooled savings of the members may accumulate until such time as one or more members are willing to take them on loan. ROSCAs are often classified under informal credit and considered predominantly a means of acquiring indivisible consumer durables (Besley *et al.*, 1990). ASCRAs lack the clarity of ROSCAs, which demand more management skills to succeed. However, ASCRAs can be put to uses like insurance more easily than ROSCAs, and manage intermediate savings over longer periods of time. The continuing prevalence and growth of these arrangements have negated the apprehension about the viability of these arrangements in the long run and Brink and Chavas (1991) show that these institutions are built on sound microeconomic foundations.

As mentioned elsewhere, credit often serves as an insurance substitute in informal finance.[5] However a substantial number of households, particularly the most poor, appear ill-equipped to handle risks even to smaller extent (Alderman and Paxson, 1994; Morduch, 1997). Many of the risks faced by low-income households are insurable and it has been proved that well designed insurance products can have a significant development impact (Brown, 2001). Many of these mechanisms are costly: for insurance, in rural India, households may sacrifice as much as 25 per cent of average income to reduce exposure to shocks. However insurance products which could reduce the vulnerability of poor people to negative income shocks, a salient dimension of vicious circle in which the poorest are trapped, are a priority area for experiment and innovation (Mosley, 2001).

2.4 MICROFINANCE AND THE FORMAL PROVIDERS

The increasing levels of transaction costs in small-size loans have an impact on formal sector institutions in financing the poor, while the charging of a standardized price makes the transactions unattractive to the poor as well. However in many countries (for example, Kenya, Malawi and Sri Lanka) the post offices run savings schemes that are widely used by low-income households, and in some countries (such as Sri Lanka and the Philippines) formal banks engage in pawnbroking. Recently certain examples emerging from different countries indicate that the formal sector is trying to develop new methods to link with microfinance initiatives. Here we review three such schemes form Indonesia, Bangladesh and India.

2.4.1 The Bank Rakyat Indonesia's unit desa (UD) scheme

The Bank Rakyat Indonesia (BRI) is notable for its success in delivering conventional banking services to low-income clients. In 1984, BRI established the unit desa (UD) or village bank system to reach the rural clientele. The scheme operates as a separate profit centre and has received a high degree of autonomy of operation from BRI. The scheme has developed products that have enabled it to work profitably with low-income households and it is more convenient for bank clients. The flexibility in saving services is an important aspect of the UD scheme, which offers convenient banking hours, a friendly atmosphere, unconstrained withdrawals and a range of incentives including bonuses and raffles. Deposit mobilization has been very successful under this scheme which relies on agents who have extensive knowledge about borrowers and local systems. A client may also take out loans with a range of convenient terms and repayment frequencies. The UD scheme also proved highly resilient to the shock of Asia's financial crises in the late 1990s.

2.4.2 The Gona Bima (popular insurance) scheme of Bangladesh

In Bangladesh, Delta Insurance, a large private insurance company, launched a Gona Bima (popular insurance) in 1994. It markets a life insurance product that has been designed to reach the poor in large numbers and has clearly benefited from the experience of MFIs like Grameen Bank. The product is a 10-year contractual savings account with fixed monthly premium payments leading to a one-time lump sum payout at maturity, along with accumulated interest.

The insurance element is provided by the guarantee that the death of the insured at any time during the term will trigger a full payout as if the term has been completed. The bureaucratic procedures such as medical examinations are minimal in the delivery mechanism of this scheme. Gona Bima rents simple office accommodation in rural and urban centres staffed by field workers who collect the premium from customers arranged in groups in the villages and slums. The smallest monthly premium accepted is about two US dollars. The office then relends the premium income to its customers in loans whose terms are similar to those of the Grameen Bank. However the scheme is now facing major problems because of administrative problems that threaten its financial viability.

2.4.3 Self-help groups (SHGs) in India

The SHG programme in India, a distinctive microfinance programme which is based on the existing banking network in delivering financial services to the poor, is a recent phenomenon (Arun and Mosley, 2003). The Reserve Bank of India (RBI) has instructed all commercial banks to participate and extend finance to SHGs, extending this to regional rural banks (RRBs) and cooperative banks in 1993. As in most group lending, peer pressure operates among the members and no group member may receive a loan while any member is in default on their loan instalments. Also the members are aware that, to obtain loans from banks, they have to produce evidence of credit history which could develop through the repeated rotations of savings to mutual credit among the members. The groups themselves, however, clearly build on the traditional institution of the ROSCA, and provide access to both savings and credit for the asset-less poor. Such groups are eligible for loans from banks, usually accompanied by training, after six months of savings and credit operations.

The formal financial institutions extend loans to highly performing SHGs[6] in certain multiples (mostly in the range of one to four times) of the accumulated savings of each SHG. The RBI has allowed banks to decide on the interest rates to be charged to the SHGs. These loans are sanctioned to the SHG as a whole and do not contain any instructions on disbursement among the members. The groups will prioritize the purposes for which loans are to be given to its members, which vary from emergency and consumption needs to acquisition of income-generating assets. The group is collectively responsible for the repayments as well. The individual members maintain their own accounts with SHG; banks of non-governmental organizations (NGOs) do not have direct contact with individual members.

2.5 WELFARE IMPACTS OF MFIS

MFIs are different from small-scale commercial and informal financial institutions and from large government-sponsored schemes. MFIs are independent of government and/or have a high degree of autonomy from bureaucrats and politicians. The primary clientele of these institutions are those who face severe barriers in gaining access to financial services. There is also an acceptance that what households need is access to credit, not cheap credit. Some of these MFIs are financially successful, boast repayment rates above 95 per cent and constantly check the levels of subsidy and inefficiency. The real innovations in these schemes are the concepts such as a group lending contract and incentives for loan repayments. Repayment incentives may include several devices, such as larger repeat loans, access to loans for other group members and cashback facilities for clients who repay on time. Many MFIs permit people to acquire useful lump sums through loans and allow borrowers to repay the loan in small, frequent and manageable instalments, further supported by quick access to larger repeat loans. The flexibility in repayment options is an important feature of MFI operations which allows borrowers to repay out of existing income, freeing the borrower to invest the loan according to their needs.

The studies have shown the positive impacts of microfinance initiatives on socio-economic variables such as children's schooling, household nutrition status and women's empowerment (Johnson and Rogaly, 1997). The ways in which financial services affect household welfare and food security can be grouped into income generation, cost efficient management of assets and liabilities, and diversion of use for immediate consumption needs (Zeller, 1996). Income generation decreases the cost of income smoothing by allowing households to engage in more risky but also more profitable activities. However some studies have argued that there is a significant difference between income generation and reducing poverty (Wright, 1999). The use of which income is put is an important variable in determining the poverty which is neither linear nor static. The second and third methods are related to decreasing the cost of consumption smoothing through allowing households to hold and retain better combinations of assets and liabilities or through increasing liquidity for direct consumption smoothing.

However there are apprehensions about the capacity of MFIs to provide services and products for the poorest of the poor category (Hulme and Mosley, 1996). The real challenge in serving them is to identify the beneficiaries from various categories, such as financial services alone, non-financial services along with finance, and non-financial services before participating in market-oriented finance (Meyer, 2002). Hulme (2000) has further argued that, outside Bangladesh, MFIs have not even scratched the surface of poverty. The exclusion of the poorest is probably driven by the emphasis on credit delivery by MFIs, which pay little attention to the needs of the poorest regarding savings.

2.6 THE WAY FORWARD: BALANCING SUPPLY AND DEMAND

Although the microcredit developments of the 1970s and 1980s contributed to the understanding of poverty reduction, the emphasis is shifting from the microcredit-poverty alleviation equation to one that recognizes the intrinsic importance of building sustainable financial systems that offer a wide-ranging menu of financial services, including savings and insurance, to poor people. For instance, in Bangladesh, studies have identified the limitations of the horizontal expansion of a single service which leaves a large range of other needs of existing clients and new markets unmet (Chaudhury and Matin, 2002). Along with the loan provision, opportunities for opening savings accounts and deposit services are especially important for the poor. As we explained earlier, the mobilization of the savings of the poor requires an understanding of the nature of such savings, which may be tiny and temporary surpluses that accrue to the household with high frequency and seasonality.

The failure of MFIs to attract the poorest of the poor may be due to their limited understanding of the limitations of their current products and the possible innovations which could be made to make products relevant to the need of the poorest. The majority of studies have focused on the demand-side forces and found that not all categories of the poor can make good use of the services. However the demand-side constraints are to be seen along with the supply-side limitations, such as the limited nature of the service provision (Arun and Hulme, 2003). It could be argued that better product design and delivery methods would alter demand in ways that deepen outreach. The Consultative Group to Assist the Poorest (CGAP) has assessed the relative emphasis that existing MFIs place on (a) identifying and reaching the poor, (b) attracting the poor and (c) discouraging or excluding the non-poor (CGAP 1998). The study shows that most emphasis is placed on identifying and reaching the poor and the least on attracting the poor, which lies at the centre of the financial service outreach arguments.

Diverse and flexible financial services can provide positive incentives to attract the poorest and reduce the likelihood of their exclusion.[7] It is argued that the provision of a wide range of financial services will fulfil the needs of clients, improve outreach depth, and enhance the access to sources of funding. The first microfinance revolution took a supply-side perspective and showed that the poor are bankable. The second revolution highlighted demand-side concerns to meet the complex livelihood-needs of the poor. It is also important to recognize the enhanced interest among the formal sector to engage in microfinance provisions, at least in certain countries. There is a need to improve the design and outreach of MFIs on a continuous basis and to put these institutions in a perspective which matches demand and supply concerns.

Notes

1 The main ideas presented in this paper are based on two earlier works: I. Matin, D. Hulme and S. Rutherford (1999), 'Finance for the poor and poorest: deepening understanding to improve provision', Finance and Development Working Paper No. 9, IDPM, University of Manchester; I. Matin, D. Hulme and S. Rutherford (2002), 'Finance for the poor: from microcredit to microfinancial services', *Journal of International Development*, 14, 273–94.

2 These financial diaries were collected by researchers from the Institute for Development Policy and Management (IDPM), University of Manchester in 1999–2001. Financial

diaries, each covering a full year, were prepared by poor, very poor and near-poor households through the help of two-weekly visits by researchers.

3 Additive savings are savings which would not have been mobilized by the formal sector in the absence of the informal.

4 The four main ways in which ROSCA users can decide the order in which a lump sum is taken are by prior agreement, by agreement at each round, by lottery and by bidding for the lump sum.

5 Morduch (1997).

6 The performance of SHGs who have been in existence for at least six months has been evaluated on the basis of a set of factors identified in the checklist of the National Bank for Agriculture and Rural Development (NABARD), such as loan recoveries, nature and participation of group meetings, accumulated savings and maintenance of accounts.

7 In Sri Lanka, for example, the Federation of Thrift and Credit Cooperatives' (SANASA) poorest clients use savings services more than credit services (Hulme and Mosley, 1996) and small, high-cost emergency loans more than larger, lower-cost investment loans.

References

Alderman, H. and C. Paxson (1994), 'Do the poor insure? A synthesis of the literature on risk sharing institutions in developing countries', *International Economic Association Moscow Conference*, 4.

Arun, T. and D. Hulme (2003), 'Balancing supply and demand – the emerging agenda for microfinance institutions', *Journal of Microfinance*, 5(2).

Arun, T. and P. Mosley (2003), 'SHGs in India – a magic bullet for poor rural women', paper presented to the ESRC seminar series on Finance and Development, 30 October, University of Manchester.

Besley, T., S. Coate and G. Lowry (1990), 'The economics of ROSCAs', Center for International Studies, discussion Paper No. 149, Princeton University.

Binswanger, H. P. and M. R. Rosenzweig (1984), *Contractual Arrangements: Employment and Wages in Rural Labour Markets in South Asia*, New Haven: Yale University Press.

Brink, R. and J. P. Chavas (1991), 'The microeconomics of an indigenous African Institution', Cornell Food and Nutrition Policy Program, Working Paper 15, Ithaca, New York.

Brown, W. (2001), 'Microinsurance – the risks, perils and opportunities', *Small Enterprise Development*, 12(1), 11–24.

Carney, D. (1998), *Sustainable Rural Livelihoods: What Contribution Can We Make?* London: DFID.

CGAP (1998), *How Microfinance Providers Target the Poor?*, Washington, DC: PACT Publications.

Chaudhury, I. and I. Matin (2002), 'Dimensions and dynamics of microfinance membership overlap – a micro study from Bangladesh', *Small Enterprise Development*, 13(2), 46–55.

Dreze, J., P. Lanjouw and N. Sharma (1997), 'Credit transactions in a North Indian village', mimeo, Delhi School of Economics.

Ellis, F. (2000), *Rural Livelihoods*, Oxford: Oxford University Press.

Fafchamps, M. (1995), *Risk Sharing, Quasi-Credit and the Enforcement of Informal Contracts*, Stanford University.

Gulli, H. (1998), *Microfinance and Poverty*, Washington, DC: Inter-American Development Bank.

Green, C. J., Kirkpatrick, C. H. and Murinde, V. (eds) (2005) *Finance and Development, Surveys of Theory, Evidence and Policy*, Cheltenham: Edward Elgar Publishing Ltd.

Hulme, D. (2000), 'Is microdebt good for poor people? A note on the dark side of microfinance', *Small Enterprise Development*, 11(1), 26–8.

Hulme, D. and P. Mosley (eds) (1996), *Finance Against Poverty*, vols 1 and 2, London: Routledge.

Johnson, S. and B. Rogaly (1997), 'Microfinance and poverty reduction', Oxfam Poverty Guidelines, Oxford.

Lipton, M., A. de Haan and S. Yaqub (1997), 'Credit and employment for the Poor', *Politica Internazionale*, 5(Sept.–Oct.), 153–66.

Matin, I and S. Sinha (1998), 'Informal credit transaction of microcredit borrowers', *IDS Bulletin*, 29(4).

Matin, I., D. Hulme and S. Rutherford (2002), 'Finance for the poor: from microcredit to microfinancial services', *Journal of International Development*, 14, 273–94.

Meyer, R. L. (2002), 'Track record of financial institutions in assisting the poor in Asia', Asian Development Bank Institute Research Paper, 49, ADB Institute, December.

Morduch, J. (1997), 'Between market and state: can informal insurance patch the safety net?', mimeo, Princeton University.

Morduch, J. (1999), 'The microfinance promise', *Journal of Economic Literature*, XXXVII(December), 1569–614.

Morduch, J. (2000), 'The microfinance schism', *World Development*, 28(4), 617–29.

Morduch, J. and S. Rutherford (2003), 'Microfinance: analytical issues for India', paper submitted for the World Bank, South Asia Region.

Mosley, P. (2001), 'Insurance against poverty? The "new generation" agricultural micro insurance schemes', *Small Enterprise Development*, 12(1), 51–8.

Platteau, J. P. and A. Abraham (1984), 'An inquiry into quasi-credit contracts: the role of reciprocal credit and interlinked deals in small scale fishing communities', *Journal of Development Studies*, 23(4).

Rutherford, S. (1999), *The Poor and Their Money*, New Delhi: Oxford University Press.

Scoones, I. (1998), 'Sustainable rural livelihoods: a framework for analysis', *IDS Working Paper*, 72, IDS, Brighton.

Wright, G. (1999), 'Examining the impact of microinsurance services – increasing income or reducing poverty?', *Small Enterprise Development*, 10(1), 38–47.

Zeller, M. (1996), 'Rural finance for food security for the poor: implications for research and policy', Food Policy Review no.4, IFPRI, Washington, DC.

Reprinted from J. Green, C. H. Kirkpatrick and V. Murinde (eds) (2005), *Finance and Development*, Cheltenham: Edward Elgar, pp. 304–14.

3

THE MICROFINANCE SCHISM

Jonathan Morduch[1]

3.1 INTRODUCTION

Few recent ideas have generated as much hope for alleviating poverty in low-income countries as the idea of microfinance. Microfinance promises both to combat poverty and to develop the institutional capacity of financial systems through finding ways to cost-effectively lend money to poor households.[2] Poor households are typically excluded from the formal banking system for lack of collateral, but the microfinance movement exploits new contractual structures and organizational forms that reduce the riskiness and costs of making small, uncollateralized loans. Microfinance programs have also demonstrated that even poor households can save in substantial quantities. Success stories are being written around the world, from Jakarta to Dhaka to Nairobi to La Paz. Advocates have broadcast these successes widely, and donors have been quick to pledge billions of dollars to support the expansion of programs in the next decade.

Much of the enthusiasm rests on an enticing 'win-win' proposition: microfinance institutions that follow the principles of good banking will also be those that alleviate the most poverty. By eventually eschewing subsidies and achieving financial sustainability, microfinance institutions will be able to grow without the constraints imposed by donor budgets. In the process, according to the argument, these institutions will be able to serve more poor people than can be served by programs fueled by subsidies. A key tenet is that poor households demand *access* to credit, not 'cheap' credit. Thus, programs can charge high interest rates without compromising outreach. If the argument is right, much poverty alleviation can be achieved at no cost to governments and donors – or perhaps even at a small profit. The vision has been translated into a series of 'best practices' circulated widely by the Consultative Group to Assist the Poorest (CGAP; a donor consortium housed within the World Bank), the US Agency for International Development, the United Nations Development Program, and other key donors.

While some find the win-win argument to be self-evident, most practitioners appear to be convinced by only part of the message. Despite keen awareness of 'best practices,' nearly all programs remain substantially subsidized. This is especially so for those with explicitly social objectives. For example, the most careful and comprehensive recent survey shows that the programs that target the poorest borrowers generate revenues sufficient to cover just 70 percent of their full costs (MicroBanking Bulletin, 1998).[3] While subsidy rates will surely fall as more programs gain age and scale, even many older, larger programs are far from being able to make ends meet with their own revenues. Some donors believe that little more than 5 percent of all programs today will be financially sustainable ever.[4]

Why are programs not raising interest rates and moving over to 'best practices' more quickly? Much of the answer is that the win-win proposition turns out to be far more complicated than it would seem at first. It rests on a series of empirical assumptions and logical connections that do not generalize easily and which have yet to be demonstrated through careful empirical studies. Almost no studies provide comparable and reliable evidence on attributes as basic as the incomes, occupations, or loan uses of clients – and of comparable non participants (the Hulme and Mosley, 1996, studies are an important exception). So while advocates continually trumpet the advantages and successes of one program or another, practitioners concerned with *who* they serve have inevitably discounted the success stories for fear that someone else's oranges are being compared to their apples.

By far, loan size has been the predominant metric for comparison of outreach. But loan size is a rough and indirect measure (Hatch and Frederick, 1998). A poverty focused nongovernmental organization (NGO) in Nepal or Malawi will be understandably reluctant to assume that lessons can be learned directly from the experience of say, the Badan Kredit Desas (BKDs) of Indonesia – a series of village based financial facilities that are financially self-sufficient despite serving clients with an average loan balance of just US$38 (relative to US$101 for the Grameen Bank; Christen, Rhyne, Vogel and McKean, 1995). The practitioners are probably right. The main clients of the BKD system are petty traders or owners of small service enterprises like restaurants and tailor shops, typically making high margin, quick turnaround investments. As a result, the clients are capable of paying real interest rates approaching 50 percent per year on 3–4 month loans (as is true for clients of Bolivia's well known BancoSol).[5] Elsewhere, in contrast, the best available investments of many microfinance clients involve longer-term loans for moderate return activities like livestock raising, handicrafts, and agricultural processing. Programs fear that increasing the costs of borrowing will put these investment opportunities beyond the reach of their target clients. Not surprisingly, donor exhortations to follow the full slate of 'best practices' have frustrated many NGOs. Until recently, consideration of *who* is being served has been almost entirely absent from the 'best practices' conversation.

Instead, socially minded practitioners have had to contend with the assertion that those clients that cannot pay the kinds of charges required for programs to break even then certainly must be destitute, in need of direct health and education programs (or simple charity) rather than credit (e.g. Gonzalez-Vega, 1998). But socially minded practitioners argue that their target group of clients is somewhere between destitute households and richer households. These target households (termed here the 'core' poor) can potentially benefit from microfinance services, even if average loan sizes are too small to allow the kinds of economies of scale that have delivered financial sustainability for well known programs such as BancoSol and Bank Rakyat Indonesia's (BRI) unit desa (UD) system.[6]

Confronting the schism between rhetoric and action – and between financially minded donors and socially minded programs – will first require that both donors and practitioners pay greater attention to who is being served (Woller, Dunford and Woodworth, 1999; Rhyne, 1998). Constructing profiles of clients by occupation, loan use, and income level is an important first step. The call to best practices will only be convincing if backed by a series of well documented examples of institutions that are (truly) breaking even financially while serving clients with profiles very close to those served by socially minded NGOs. Bangladesh's Association for Social Advancement (ASA) provides one promising example, as do some programs built on the village banking model. But these cases need to be expanded upon and more carefully documented with an eye to cross-country comparisons.[7]

Second, much could be gained by focusing more sharply on the mechanisms through which financial services are delivered, as well as the menu of services provided. Best practices have centered on important but general aspects of institutional performance, such as maintaining financial transparency, standardizing products, and achieving scale. A high level of generality has been natural given the diversity of contexts and programs at issue. But, spurred by win-win optimism, one result has been widespread replications of standard models (especially the Grameen Bank model and the Foundation for International Community Assistance's (FINCA) village banking model) in a wide diversity of economies. Many of these direct replicates appear however to do far better in terms of outreach than financial sustainability.

Instead, programs like Dhaka's SafeSave have found that it has been necessary to go back to the drawing board and create new financial services products that can be sold at interest rates high enough to allow the institution to break even while maintaining – or even improving – outreach.[8] SafeSave has found it necessary to depart from standard models in Bangladesh and make safe and flexible savings accounts, including the possibility of daily deposits, a key part of their services. In this they have drawn on lessons from informal institutions in Dhaka's slums, as well as on successful experiences with deposit mobilization in Indonesia (Rutherford, 1997). Bangladesh's ASA has similarly departed from Grameen's model to develop a simple management structure and accounting system that have reduced costs substantially, making it possible to approach financial sustainability without imposing excessively high costs on clients (Rutherford, 1995). Other programs, such as the village banks initiated by Freedom from Hunger, have found substantial benefits in bundling financial services with client education (MkNelly and Dunford, 1996 and 1998).

These examples show that mechanisms clearly matter. But the power of the win-win vision – that clients demand credit access at whatever the cost – has hindered the broader encouragement of experimentation, innovation, and the exchange of experiences that can lead to (a) new financial products for which the 'core' poor are willing and able to pay relatively high charges and (b) cheaper ways to deliver financial services to poor clients.

Third, the most important lessons to be learned from the failures of subsidized credit programs of the past are the need for efficiency, transparency, and appropriate management incentives. Although excessive subsidies were a large part of the problem, these key program attributes can be achieved with or without full financial sustainability. For some programs, ongoing subsidization can be an important means through which social missions are achieved.

If such programs lose access to government or donor funding, they will have no option but to close down, attempt radical cost cutting innovations, or attempt to cross-subsidize. But it is not clear why the starting point for so many is the belief that, as a matter of course, funding will be pulled away from programs, even those able to demonstrate sustained social effectiveness. Moreover, there has never been a general presumption that the most effective poverty alleviation programs can be – or should be – self-financing. Despite early optimism to the contrary, the microfinance experience so far presents little to change that view.

The aim of this paper is not to argue for one type of program over another. To the contrary, evidence suggests that achieving the richness of programs appropriate for broad and changing populations will require a diversity of programs at varying levels of outreach and financial sustainability. The aim is to help clarify discussions, to examine the logic of critical arguments, and to highlight salient tensions. The next section briefly reviews lessons and inferences from subsidized credit programs of the 1960s and 1970s. The following section takes apart the arguments underlying the win-win proposition. The final section puts forward an agenda for research on issues at the heart of the microfinance schism.

3.2 THE SUBSIDY TRAP

All sides agree on the importance of avoiding mistakes of the past. Earlier attempts to address gaps in financial markets focused on a now familiar set of problems: first, banks face high transactions costs per loan when lending at small scales; second, determining the riskiness of potential borrowers and monitoring the progress of clients is particularly difficult when clients are poor and in the informal sector; and third, many low-income households lack assets to put up as collateral.

The early programs recognized that many households could generate high returns if given credit and that, by starting small enterprises, the households could earn enough income to exit poverty, expand their businesses, and improve the quality of their lives. As a result, governments subsidized banks' loans to poor households, providing incentives to overcome banks' reluctance to lend. Recognizing the social mission of the project, interest rates were also kept below market clearing levels.

Despite the promise, the subsidized credit programs of the last three decades failed nearly universally, and disaster stories are well catalogued (Adams, Graham and von Pischke, 1984). The costs of these programs mounted quickly and, since no way was found around the collateral problem, default rates ballooned, with many borrowers expressing ambivalence about defaulting on government-backed loans, especially when most everyone else was doing so. Either the programs quickly ran out of money or they drained government accounts.

Moreover, because banks were losing money so steadily on the lending side but were amply capitalized by governments, they had little incentive to mobilize savings: deposit mobilization is costly and re-lending the deposits would just lead to greater losses. Instead, saving accounts were weighed down with restrictions and downward pressure was put on interest rates on deposits, generally to keep interest rates paid to depositors below the rates charged to borrowers. The result was that real rates on deposits fell to zero or below and savers had little incentive to build up accounts. Ultimately, little saving was generated, and money stayed under mattresses or was moved into nonfinancial assets.

Government involvement had another negative consequence. Loans often ended up subsidizing well off, politically connected entrepreneurs rather than poor households, and few mechanisms were in place to stem the leakages. The ultimate result was high costs and little benefit for the intended beneficiaries.

The new programs have set out to avoid these traps. Foremost, they have seen the importance of maintaining high repayment rates. By employing contractual innovations like group lending and by exploiting dynamic incentives, many programs have achieved repayment rates above 95 percent (Christen *et al.*, 1995; MicroBanking Bulletin, 1998). They have also kept an arm's length from government involvement, and most programs are run by NGOs.

The successes have bred three false generalizations, however. The first is that subsidization, inefficiency, and limited scale necessarily go hand in hand. The second is that government involvement means trouble. The third is that effective savings mobilization is incompatible with subsidized credit. As described below, none of these ideas is fully consistent with logic or experience. The challenge is to draw appropriate lessons from both the mistakes of the past and the successes of the present.

3.3 THE LOGIC OF THE WIN-WIN PROPOSITION

The win-win proposition has been a powerful piece of rhetoric, and it has kept many programs from repeating past disasters. But if it was fully convincing, the microfinance landscape would look very different from its present state – where subsidized programs far outnumber sustainable programs. Why has it not been fully convincing?

The win-win proposition rests on a series of supporting arguments. The most important is the argument that households require access to credit, not cheap credit. This is joined by eight principal claims. First, that raising the costs of financial services does not diminish demand. Second, that due to their scale, financially sustainable programs can make the greatest dent in poverty. Third, that financial sustainability will give programs access to commercial financial markets. Fourth, that since they come at no cost to donors, financially sustainable programs are superior weapons for fighting poverty. Fifth, that subsidized programs are inefficient and thus bound to fail. Sixth, that subsidized credit most often ends up in the hands of the nonpoor. Seventh, that successful microfinance programs must be nongovernment programs. And, eighth, that subsidizing credit undermines savings mobilization.

Not all of those who believe in the importance of financial sustainability will accept each claim. But the claims are often heard together, and they form a core set of ideas. Each is rooted in the experience of some programs in some places and at some times. But as general propositions they each rest on problematic logical extrapolations, inappropriate assumptions, or misreadings of evidence. In taking them apart, my objective is not to push for subsidized credit at all costs. Rather, it is to illustrate the 'disconnect' – i.e. why these arguments have not translated into action.

a) Interest insensitive credit demand

Claim: Raising interest rates does not substantially diminish demand for loans.

In Las Vegas, pawnshop owners charge borrowers effective annual interest rates of 120 percent, while in the gambling town of Biloxi, Mississippi, typical rates are 300 percent per year (*The New York Times*, December 13, 1997). Demand remains high in both settings.

But no one would argue that the typical small entrepreneur in the United States can repay loans at those rates. This, though, is the sort of argument that is commonly made in the microfinance context – that since moneylenders charge high interest rates, microfinance programs can too. But while poor households in low-income countries may borrow from moneylenders at rates above 100 percent per year, they are generally doing so to meet short-term consumption needs, not to make long-term productive investments.

Moreover, the distinction between which poor households are served by microfinance programs is obscured by observations that financially sustainable programs reach *some* poor households. For example, it is asserted in CGAP (1996; prepared by Richard Rosenberg):

> CAN microborrowers pay high interest rates?… [Microfinance institutions] charging very high interest rates almost always find that demand far outstrips their ability to supply it. Most of their customers repay their loans, and return repeatedly for new loans: this pattern demonstrates the customers' conviction that the loans allow them to earn more than the interest they have to pay. …Thus, there is abundant proof that poor people's tiny businesses can often pay interest rates that would strangle a larger business. Still, this proposition strikes many as counterintuitive.

The argument above makes the point that there are poor households that are able to pay high rates. The concern of many subsidized programs, however, is that there are also many borrowers who cannot pay high rates. (This has been a particular concern in South Asia.) These latter households tend to be poorer and harder to reach with traditional programs, and they constitute a large fraction of client bases. They are not the petty traders that can repay at rates above 50 percent per year. If these programs raised interest rates, they might not suffer for lack of demand either. But that is not the point. The programs fear losing much of their current client base, including the particularly vulnerable and underserved segments of poor populations that appear to be served well by moderately subsidized microfinance programs versus other economic development initiatives. Programs inevitably point to anecdotal evidence to support their claims, but even without harder data, it is clear that considering only aggregate demand is inadequate for programs seeking to maximize social welfare.

The argument is allied to another logical stretch. The assertion above implicitly invokes the principle of declining marginal returns to capital as a defense of charging high interest rates to poor clients while charging lower rates to richer clients.[9] The idea is that there are a limited number of great projects in which to invest. The first units of capital go to the best projects and subsequent units go to projects with increasingly lower returns. The principle is generally right, but its application is wrong. The basic principle applies to a single firm, holding all else fixed. It does not necessarily hold across firms (or across household microenterprises) as in the application here. Producing and selling goods requires more than capital. It requires skills, other materials, information, connections, transportation, etc. Since richer households tend to have more of these inputs, marginal returns to capital are often far higher for them than for poorer households. These richer households will thus be willing to pay far higher interest rates than poorer households. (In fact, the basic principle is unclear even when controlling for other inputs, since scale economies alone can yield higher marginal returns to later increments of capital than earlier increments.)

The ability to pay high interest rates is thus an empirical issue, dependent on the amount of capital being used, as well as the amount of all other inputs available. It cannot be inferred that because one group of poor households can pay high rates then even poorer households can pay those interest rates as well. Moreover, sensitivity to the costs of financial services is not likely to be common across economies. For example, practitioners argue that sensitivity tends to be much greater in South Asia than in Latin America. But careful studies have yet to demonstrate this in either context.

b) Advantages of scale

Claim: Financially sustainable programs can achieve greater scale than subsidized programs. Thus, they can make a bigger dent in poverty. The diversity within poor households is similarly obscured by common arguments on the advantages of achieving a broad scale of operations. Again, the argument is put well in CGAP (1996):

> Some people treat [the question of how high to set interest rates] as if it comes down to a value judgement: which do you care more about – poor people or profits (or financial system, or neoliberal ideology). To avoid any such confusion, let's assume that the only objective we care about is maximizing benefit to poor people. From this perspective, the argument for high interest rates is straightforward. In most countries, donor funding is a limited quantity that will never be capable of reaching more than a tiny fraction of those poor households who could benefit from quality financial services.

The argument has greatest power if concern with poverty rests exclusively with minimizing the *number* of people below the poverty line (making no distinction between groups within the working poor population). But it loses power if we also consider the distribution of income below the poverty line – and this makes value judgements paramount. Value judgements cannot be so easily swept away.

Consider tradeoffs in scale and outreach when the objective is to minimize a poverty measure that is sensitive to the distribution of incomes below the poverty line. Since clients in subsidized credit programs tend to be much poorer than those in sustainable programs, for illustration assume that the typical client in a subsidized program has an income of, say, 50 percent of the poverty line, while the typical client of a sustainable (high interest rate) program has an income of 90 percent of the poverty line. To focus the comparison, assume that borrowers receive identical net returns (after repaying loans with interest).[10]

One metric of social welfare is the poverty rate as measured by a distributionally sensitive index like the Watts measure or 'average exit time' of Morduch (1998). By this measure, raising the poorer borrower's income by one US dollar has 1.8 times greater impact than doing the same for the less poor borrower. The same calculation for the commonly used 'squared poverty gap' of Foster, Greer and Thorbecke (1984) gives a ratio of 5 to 1. The 'cubed poverty gap' yields a ratio of 25 to 1.

The numbers can be put in perspective by comparing the required scale of subsidized and sustainable programs that would have equivalent impacts on measured poverty. Say that the sustainable program has 75,000 clients (roughly the size of Bolivia's BancoSol). How large would the subsidized program need to be to have an equivalent impact (under the assumptions above)? When measuring poverty with the Watts measure, the subsidized program would need to reach at least 42,000 clients. When measuring poverty with the squared poverty gap, the subsidized program would need to reach 15,000 clients. It would also need to serve just 3,000 clients as measured by the cubed poverty gap.

The exact comparison is a matter of value judgement – which poverty measure best captures the social value of poverty reduction? The initial claim above makes sense only under specific assumptions about objective functions, relative outreach, and the elasticity of credit demand with respect to interest rates. Under plausible assumptions, the claim could hold, but it is not a general proposition. Well targeted programs can often do more for poverty reduction than much larger programs reaching mainly better off households.

c) Access to commercial finance

Claim: Financial sustainability is critical for institutions as it is the route to being able to access capital from commercial financial markets rather than donors. The argument in CGAP (1996) continues:

> We can hope to reach most of those households only if [microfinance institutions] can mobilize relatively large amounts of commercial finance at market rates. They cannot do this unless they charge interest rates that cover [total costs].

This claim also requires re-examination. This step in the argument goes beyond the untethering from donor strings. The vision described is one in which the equity of programs is multiplied through access to commercial finance – i.e. the creation of leverage. The vision opens up exciting prospects, but as Conning (1999) argues, they are not likely to be shared as amply by programs focused on poorer households – even if the programs charge 'market rates.'

The scenario parallels that of a poor borrower unable to obtain loans from formal sector banks for lack of collateral (e.g. Banerjee and Newman, 1994). The story is well known: banks are reluctant to lend because it is difficult to identify the truly reliable borrowers, to then monitor borrowers' behaviors, and, if needed, to implement effective punishments. Combating this phenomenon has been the driving impetus for the microfinance movement.

The same kinds of difficulties emerge when the microfinance program itself seeks commercial funds, since it lacks collateral to back its portfolio. As the borrowers found, merely being able to generate positive expected returns is not enough to secure commercial credit. Thus, even financially sustainable banks will not necessarily be able to gain sufficient access to wider capital markets. As Conning argues, banks focused on poor borrowers are likely to face the greatest difficulties in creating leverage since their portfolios are likely to appear that much riskier to capital suppliers. Relying on commercial finance can thus lead to further reductions in the depth of outreach.

As a point of economic logic, of course, it is not incompatible to both subsidize interest rates charged to clients and to obtain commercial finance. The Grameen Bank, for example, has sold bonds (guaranteed by the government) while not passing all costs on to clients. While there is debate about whether the price of the bonds is at market rates, the principle remains that subsidization does not rule out tapping commercial finance for partial funding. The chief constraint is not subsidization *per se* but the ability to limit perceived riskiness.

d) Irrelevance of cost-benefit comparisons

Claim: Since sustainable programs do not require outside funding, consideration of costs and benefits is irrelevant. There are no costs borne by governments or aid agencies – there are only benefits. Sustainable programs are thus superior to subsidized programs.

The idea of cost free poverty alleviation is appealing, but consider this simple analogy. When diners go to a restaurant, they have the option of drinking water or purchasing a beverage. The water is free and adequate, but most diners also buy wine, beer, or soft drinks to complement their meal. To them, the zero cost option is not always the one that leads to the greatest satisfaction, and the same logic holds here. When funding is available, subsidizing credit beats the zero cost option as long as benefits outweigh costs.

A problem with the 'best practices' approach is that it proceeds as if there has to be just *one* interest rate policy and one sort of program in an area. Sustainable programs may have advantages in achieving scale. Subsidized programs appear to have advantages in outreach. Just as all diners are not forced to drink the same beverages, general social welfare perspectives suggest that it can make sense to support multiple programs within the same region, some focusing on scale and others on outreach.

e) Subsidies reduce efficiency

Claim: Subsidized credit programs are inefficient and ultimately bound to fail. A much sharper criticism of subsidized credit programs is that they cannot survive over the long term. Nancy Barry of Women's World Banking (CGAP, 1995) asserts, for example, that 'few low income entrepreneurs end up benefiting from subsidized programs, because these programs fail before they reach significant numbers.' She argues further that 'microenterprise financial intermediaries have learned that they cannot depend on governments and donors as reliable, long term sources of subsidized funding.'

Barry's assertion evokes the lessons of past failures. But microfinance advocates have argued strenuously that the new programs are radically different from those of the past. Subsidized programs like the Grameen Bank and Bangladesh Rural Advancement Committee (BRAC) together, for example, have together reached around four million borrowers and face substantial competition from other groups like the ASA and Proshika. Barry's first assertion is hard to reconcile with the experience in Bangladesh to date.

The second issue is whether subsidized funding will dry up. Since donors and governments remain committed to poverty alleviation as a top priority, advocates are not unreasonable in arguing for allocating some poverty alleviation funds to support innovative and effective microfinance programs over the long term. How this will play out exactly is a matter of speculation, but there is no reason to think that concern with poverty alleviation will quickly whither. Nor is there reason to think that support for subsidized microfinance programs will whither – as long as they remain vigilant in containing costs and maximizing outreach.

A third issue is whether subsidized programs can be efficient. Barry (CGAP, 1996), for example, argues that 'efficient financial intermediaries need to charge high rates to cover the costs of making small loans.'

Typically, judging institutional performance by profitability gives managers the right incentives. But appropriate incentives can also be provided in nonprofit enterprises. Maintaining 'hard' budget constraints is the key, not maximizing profits. The two mechanisms are often confused, but it is the former that is critical for efficiency, not the latter. If budget constraints are soft and performance criteria are not carefully specified, managers can expect to be bailed out after poor performances. If constraints are kept hard and performance criteria are made clear, managers must cope with failures, and efficiency can be maintained, even in non-profit programs.

One important mechanism for achieving efficiency in subsidized programs is to use socially determined transfer prices and to be rigid in evaluating performance according to those prices. Transfer prices are the internal prices used by institutions to value capital and determine relative performance at branch levels. In a profit making enterprise, the transfer prices reflect the full value of capital, a system used very effectively by the BRI's UD program. In a subsidized program, they are shadow prices, adjusted downward so that prices reflect the social gains delivered by lending. The transfer prices can be used to calculate shadow profits. Thus, while bank managers may not be able to lend at an actual profit, they may be able to lend at a net social gain, and efficiency can be achieved by tying their compensation to performance on the basis of transfer prices and shadow profits.

Translating the theory into practice takes creativity and experimentation, but the basic idea can be implemented with simple rules of thumb. This is not an academic dream: most universities and many hospitals run on a not-for-profit basis with purely social objectives. Managers of not-for-profit microfinance institutions can learn from their weaknesses and build on their successes.

f) Subsidies lead to mistargeting

Claim: Subsidized credit most often ends up in the hands of nonpoor households.

A common experience in the credit programs of the 1960s and 1970s was that subsidized credit was often diverted away from poor households. Since the subsidies were valuable, politically powerful groups, usually not poor, muscled their way in and managed to grab a share. The problem was compounded by the fact that most programs were government run, providing further incentives for misfeasance as the granting of loans was often partly a political payoff (this is discussed further below).

These problems are fully avoided when subsidies are eliminated. But the problems may also be greatly reduced by just partial elimination of subsidies. The concern with targeting introduces a floor to interest rates – it does not mean that interest rates need be at break even rates. The floor is determined by the rates at which others (the politically powerful, say) can get loans.

Consider a program lending exclusively to poor borrowers. It would have to charge, say, 30 percent per year in order to break even. In contrast, a formal sector program aimed at richer borrowers could break even when charging, say, 15 percent per year since it can more easily take advantage of returns to scale. Loans at 5 percent per year will seem appealing to all households when the alternative, formal sector sources charge 15 percent. Nearly without fail, such *absolutely* cheap credit has led to subsidy traps.

Loans around 20 percent will seem however much less appealing to the richer households. Rates around 20 percent provide meaningful subsidies for poor households, and are not seen as gifts. The loans are cheap relative to full costs, but they are not absolutely cheap. Mistargeting has thus not been a major concern for those programs providing moderate sized subsidies. The lesson from the failures of the 1960s and 1970s is to avoid excessive subsidies. The lesson is not to avoid subsidies altogether. Discussions of interest rates in microfinance programs often equate subsidized credit with cheap credit, and this has created considerable confusion. Absolutely cheap credit is typically the problem. Relatively cheap credit can, in principle, work.

g) Minimal role of government

Claim: Microfinance has been and should continue to be a movement with minimal government involvement.

Governments in low-income countries have played very little direct role in the microfinance movement, and this has been no accident. The movement is fundamentally an NGO movement, free of many of the political biases of earlier subsidized programs. This creates its own problems, of course. There are good and bad NGOs and often little apparatus for effective oversight, but so far the microfinance track record has allayed most fears.

Governments, though, have played critical indirect roles. Indonesia's BRI and Thailand's Bank of Agriculture and Agricultural Cooperatives, for example, are state-owned although run as standard commercial banks. The Grameen Bank, which sometimes finds itself at odds with Bangladeshi politicians, nonetheless has obtained loans at concessional rates from the Bangladesh Bank (and began as a special project of the Bangladesh Bank).[11] The spread of microfinance in China will also of necessity proceed with heavy government involvement, at least in the near term (Morduch, Park and Wang, 1997).

While sustainable programs can afford to eschew government involvement, subsidized programs cannot. Subsidized programs need NGOs, foundations, international donors, or their own governments for funding. If subsidized programs are to continue at current funding levels, they will likely need to rely increasingly on their own governments. Rather than backing away from governments, subsidized programs will need to build constructive relationships. Lessons from past failures suggest that this will require a clear understanding of the (sharp) limits to direct government involvement and a commitment to the transparency and accountability of programs.

h) Subsidies limit savings mobilization

Claim: Mobilizing savings is not likely to make sense for subsidized credit programs.

Household welfare can be greatly improved through the chance to mobilize savings. Early microfinance programs were not effective in mobilizing savings and showed little interest in doing so. Partly, it was thought that poor households were too poor to save. One of the lessons from the recent microfinance experience, however, is that even poor households are eager to save if given appealing interest rates and/or flexible accounts. Indonesia's BRI, for example counted over 16 million low-income depositors by the end of 1996.

Incorporating savings mobilization in microfinance programs makes sense for a number of reasons (Robinson, 1995). First, it can provide a relatively inexpensive source of capital for re-lending. Second, today's depositors may be tomorrow's borrowers, creating a natural client pool. Third, savings deposits offer important advantages to low-income households, allowing low-income households to build up assets to use as collateral, to reduce consumption volatility over time, and to self-finance investments rather than always turning to creditors (Wright, Hossain and Rutherford, 1997).

Thus, a savings program may be an essential feature of both subsidized and sustainable programs. It has been sustainable programs however, that have been most aggressive in mobilizing savings, partly because mobilization can greatly aid the financial bottom line. Subsidized programs have tended to focus on 'forced saving' programs, forcing borrowers to put aside a fixed percentage of borrowed money to draw upon in case repayment difficulties arise, rather than mobilizing voluntary savings.

Maintaining savings deposits can be expensive for programs, and when programs are losing money in their lending operations, they have little incentive to mobilize deposits if capital can be obtained more cheaply from donors. This was part of the subsidy trap described above. If, however, programs can generate capital from depositors more cheaply than donors can generate capital, it can be in all parties' interests to encourage programs to mobilize savings. One way to do so is to split the difference between programs' costs of generating capital and donors' costs of obtaining capital. For every dollar that programs mobilize, donors can then reduce their loans to the programs by one dollar. The arrangement can reduce costs for both donors and programs and at the same time encourage savings mobilization.

For example, the Grameen Bank obtained funds from the Bangladesh Bank at just 5–6 percent in the mid 1990s while alternative sources of funds would have cost 12–15 percent. If Grameen could have mobilized savings at a cost below the Bangladesh Bank's opportunity cost of funds, the social cost of subsidization could have been reduced. Under early, failed credit schemes, everyone lost out through savings mobilization. Under the proposed scheme, however, everyone can benefit.

Practical constraints to savings mobilization must be worked out, though. The most important constraint is that NGOs are not chartered to hold savings deposits. Prudence dictates that only tightly regulated institutions are given the privilege and responsibility of holding savings. This thus creates a problem for microfinance programs (except those that are fully chartered banks). One answer is that fully chartered savings banks could operate independently but alongside NGOs engaged in lending. A contractual link to exploit the rebate opportunity above could still be used to reduce costs of subsidization on the lending side.

Both the rebate proposal and the savings bank/microcredit partnership proposal are straightforward in principle but require careful, transparent contracts to work well. The ideas are speculative but suggest that there may be creative ways around roadblocks.

3.4 THE CHALLENGE AHEAD: A RESEARCH AGENDA

The arguments above suggest holes in the win-win logic that help to explain why 'best practices' have not been adopted more widely. But subsidization raises its own tensions, particularly surrounding issues of governance. Among the key questions are: Can new product development and program design sufficiently improve financial performance without compromising outreach such that subsidies are not needed? If not, are the costs of subsidies typically justified by the social benefits of programs? Can innovations be implemented to help subsidized programs maintain efficiency and effective targeting? Which groups among the poor are best served by which types of programs? Can social benefits be easily and reliably measured on an ongoing basis? Can funding be sustained over the long run?[12]

The socially oriented programs should have careful economic and social evaluations at the top of their research list. The Grameen Bank and BRAC have been pioneers in this area, with a large, comprehensive survey completed in 1991–92 and a follow up survey underway. The key to this survey has been use of a sample frame that incorporates stratified randomization and the collection of data on both participants and nonparticipants, including random samples from villages not served by any program.[13] The survey, though, has been expensive, and devising ways to complete cheap, ongoing surveys is the next step.

The role of competition is an additional issue of growing importance. Practitioners need to know much more about problems that arise when multiple programs – some subsidized, some not – coexist. Here, the issue is a supply elasticity: how sensitive is the performance of financially sustainable programs to the presence of targeted, subsidized programs?

Another set of questions surrounds the functioning of specific program features. All types of programs may be able to learn from studies that explore the effectiveness and costliness of various lending mechanisms – for example, weekly versus bi-weekly versus monthly payment schedules, lending to individuals versus lending to groups, intensive versus minimal group lending operations, and increasing loan size quickly or slowly with successful repayment. Systematic experimentation and evaluation with household level data can be critical along these lines.

3.5 CONCLUSIONS

The optimism of the win-win vision has generated much energy for the microfinance movement, and it has helped to discourage repetitions of the costly mistakes of the past. But the past decade shows that it has also discouraged constructive dialogues and the sorts of serious empirical studies that can help to resolve continuing debates. As a result, the empirical agenda remains wide open and the schism persists, fueled by competing anecdotes.

The microfinance movement encompasses diverse programs, all of which focus on providing financial services to poor households. Some programs have made financial sustainability the chief goal, and others have centered on economic and social impacts. While there is much common ground, there are also critical differences. There appears to be ample room, however, for a diversity of programs, with competing methods and financial arrangements.

Addressing the schism opens up the chance to address misconceptions. It is not profit maximization that makes a program efficient. Instead, what matters is having a hard budget constraint, something possible even with subsidies. Nor does subsidization necessarily lead to mistargeting. Fear of mistargeting may limit the size of the optimal subsidy, but it does not necessarily make it zero. Moreover, savings mobilization is not necessarily held down by charging interest rates on loans that are below levels needed to break even. And finally, as Conning (1999) has argued, the need to preserve management incentives means that even financially sustainable, socially minded programs will likely have ongoing difficulties raising substantial amounts of capital on the open market.

While these arguments run counter to hard line positions on financial sustainability, opening up the discussion may also help foster continued efforts to develop new financial products that ultimately are financially sustainable. Addressing the schism may also mitigate the emerging backlash against the microfinance movement. The insistence on the win-win proposition has alienated many potential supporters. Those willing to trade off costs for benefits have become frustrated as microfinance institutions stretch accounting data in order to claim profitability while simultaneously eschewing social evaluations. Perhaps more problematically, those interested in replicating the well known success stories have only had partial and unreliable evaluations on which to base their plans.

The arguments above stand in opposition to 'lessons' of failed programs of the past. And the arguments suggest that there is much yet to learn.

As Hulme and Mosley (1996, p.135) conclude:

> Ironically, it is the success of the 'first wave' finance for the poor schemes, and particularly the Grameen Bank, that is the greatest obstacle to future experimentation. Most designers and sponsors of new initiatives have abandoned innovation, and 'replication' is leading to a growing uniformity in financial interventions.

This paper has mapped avenues to pursue in rethinking microfinance to date and in constructing foundations for a next wave of microfinance innovation.

Notes

1 The paper was initially prompted by a meeting with representatives of the Consultative Group to Assist the Poorest (CGAP), the US Agency for International Development, ACCION International, and the Harvard Institute for International Development, convened in Cambridge in Spring 1997. My views have evolved through conversations with Abhijit Banerjee, Gregory Chen, Monique Cohen, Peter Fidler, Mike Goldberg, Claudio Gonzalez-Vega, Albert Park, Marguerite Robinson, Richard Rosenberg, Jay Rosengard, J. D. von Pischke, Jacob Yaron, and participants at lively seminars at Ohio State and the World Bank. I have particularly benefited from input from practitioners in Bangladesh, Indonesia, and China, and from Christopher Dunford and his colleagues at Freedom From Hunger. Throughout, Mark Schreiner has provided particularly comprehensive and thoughtful criticisms. The paper was completed during a year as a National Fellow at the Hoover Institution, Stanford University. The views expressed here are mine solely.

Reprinted from *World Development*, 28 (2), pp. 617–29, 2000.

2 See, for example, Brugger and Rajapatirana, 1995; Hulme and Mosley, 1996; Otero and Rhyne, 1994; and Morduch, 1999 for broader discussions of microfinance programs.

3 The relevant groups are those whose clients maintain average loan balances under US$150 or loans as a percentage of GNP per capita under 20 percent; they include, for example, village banks such as the Foundation for International Community Assistance's (FINCA) programs and exclude programs like BancoSol and the Bank Rakyat Indonesia's (BRI) Unit Desa (UD) system. The figures are after adjustments to account for subsidies on capital costs, the erosion of the value of equity due to inflation, and adequate provisioning for nonrecoverable loans. As best possible, the figures are comparable to data for standard commercial enterprises. The included programs all have a 'commitment' to achieving financial sustainability and voluntarily submitted the financial information, so they are already a self-selected group. Some of the programs are young and their financial performance will likely improve over time.

4 This speculation has been widely cited, and Richard Rosenberg reports that its origin is a microfinance panel discussion at Boulder, Colorado. The consensus among a group of (sustainability-minded) panelists was that 1 percent or fewer of programs were presently sustainable and that no more than 5 percent would ever be. These rough speculations concerned NGO programs only, excluding, for example, credit unions, the Indonesian Badan Kredit Desas (BKDs), or private banks that are serving poor clients. Even if

experience shows the correct number to be 10 percent – or 15 percent or 25 percent – there remains a fundamental 'disconnect' between rhetoric and action. In the end, the most important measure concerns the number of clients served, not the numbers of particular types of programs.

5 Information is from the unpublished notes of Don Johnston. His calculation shows average BKD loan sizes to be US$71 at the end of 1994, still well below the Grameen Bank level.

6 A growing list of examples demonstrates the ability to serve these richer households without ongoing subsidies, and their experiences hold important lessons for programs with poorer target clients. But, as documented in a recent study of BancoSol, typical clients are among the 'richest of the poor' and the nonpoor (where poverty is based on access to a set of basic needs like shelter and education; Navajas, Schreiner, Meyer, Gonzalez-Vega and Rodriguez-Meza, 1998). Average loan balances for BancoSol and BRI are around US$500, while they are around just US$100 for well known poverty-focused programs in Bangladesh like the Grameen Bank, Bangladesh Rural Advancement Committee (BRAC), and the Association for Social Advancement (ASA).

7 Apart from the Indonesian BKDs (caveats aside), no programs that I know have achieved demonstrably outstanding outreach while achieving clear financial sustainability, but some like ASA appear to be doing remarkably well on both fronts (Rutherford, 1995). Mexico's Compartamos and El Salvador's Financiera Calpia also deliver impressive financial performance while serving poor (but not close to the poorest) rural clients. In urban Bolivia, both BancoSol and Caja los Andes serve a broad range of clients, including a minority that are among the 'core' poor (Navajas *et al.*, 1998). Indonesia's BRI provides savings facilities to many relatively poor clients, although they are excluded from borrowing for lack of collateral.

8 At present SafeSave is covering operating costs but is not fully financially sustainable. It has only been operating since August 1996 and trends appear promising (SafeSave, 1998).

9 The idea is related to Hulme and Mosley's (1996) idea to charge 'tapered' interest rates that fall with loan size – although the proposition would appear to conflict with their evidence that poorer households do not in general receive higher returns than richer households.

10 Hulme and Mosley (1996) suggest that impacts may be greater for less poor households. This provides additional support for sustainable programs in the calculation.

11 While Grameen no longer receives concessional loans from the Bangladesh Bank, they do receive guarantees from the government for the bonds that they now rely upon for the majority of their funding.

12 A related series of questions has been raised by van de Walle (1997), and Morduch (1999) provides a more comprehensive discussion of the empirical research agenda and cost-benefit studies.

13 See also MkNelly's and Dunford's (1998) work in Ghana. The argument about whether financially sustainable or subsidized programs have the greatest impact on poverty comes down to a question about the elasticity of demand for financial services with respect to their costs. This elasticity (and social impacts more broadly) can only be estimated with information on both participants and nonparticipants.

References

Adams, D., Graham, D. and von Pisckhe, J. D. (1984). *Undermining rural development with cheap credit*. Boulder, CO: Westview Press.

Banerjee, A., and Newman, A. (1994). Poverty, incentives and development. American Economic Review (AEA Papers and Proceedings). 84 (2), pp. 211–15.

Brugger, E., and Rajapatirana, S. (1995). *New perspectives on financing small business in developing countries*. San Francisco: ICS Press.

Christen, R., Rhyne, E., Vogel, R., and McKean, C. (1995). *Maximizing the outreach of microenterprise finance: an analysis of successful programs, program and operations*. Assessment Report No. 10. Washington DC: United States Agency for International Development.

Conning, Jonathan (1999). Outreach, sustainability and leverage in microlending: a contract design approach. *Journal of Development Economics*. 60 (1), October.

Consultative Group for Assistance to the Poorest (CGAP) (1995). The missing links: financial systems that work for the majority. CGAP Focus, No.3, October.

Consultative Group for Assistance to the Poorest (CGAP) (1996). Microcredit interest rates. CGAP Occasional Paper, No.1, August.

Foster, J., Greer, J., and Thorbecke, E. (1984). A class of decomposable poverty measures. *Econometrica*. 52 (3), pp. 761–6.

Gonzalez-Vega, C. (1998). Do financial institutions have a role in assisting the poor? In M. Kimenyi, R. Wieland, and J. D. von Pischke (Eds), *Strategic Issues in Microfinance*. Aldershot, UK: Ashgate Publishing.

Hatch, J., and Frederick, L. (1998). *Poverty assessment by microfinance institutions: a review of current practice*. Microenterprise Best Practices Report. Washington DC: Development Alternatives, Inc.

Hulme, D., and Mosley, P. (1996). *Finance against poverty*. London: Routledge.

MkNelly, B., and Dunford, C. (1996). Are credit services effective against hunger and malnutrition? – A literature review and analysis. Freedom From Hunger Research Paper No. 1, Davis, CA.

MkNelly, B., and Dunford, C. (1998). Impact of credit with education on mothers and their young children's nutrition: Lower Pra Rural bank credit with education program in Ghana. Freedom From Hunger Research Paper No. 4, Davis, CA.

Morduch, J. (1998). Poverty, growth, and average exit time. *Economics Letters*, 59, pp. 385–90.

Morduch, J. (1999). The microfinance promise. *Journal of Economic Literature*, 37 (4).

Morduch, J., Park, A., and Wang, S. (1997). Microfinance in China. *Poverty and Development.* Beijing.

Navajas, S., Schreiner, M., Meyer, R., Gonzalez-Vega, C., and Rodriguez-Meza, J. (1998). *Microcredit and the poorest of the poor: theory and evidence from Bolivia*. Columbus, OH: Department of Agricultural, Environmental, and Development Economics, Ohio State University.

New York Times (1997). In Gulf casinos' wake, a pawnshop boom. December 13, A1, A13.

Otero, M. and Rhyne, E. (1994). *The new world of microenterprise finance*. West Hartford, CT: Kumarian Press.

Rhyne, E. (1998). The yin and yang of microfinance: reaching the poor and sustainability. *MicroBanking Bulletin*.

Robinson, M. (1995). Indonesia: The role of savings in developing sustainable commercial financing of small and micro enterprises. In E. Brugger, and S. Rajapatirana (Eds), *New perspectives on financing small business in developing countries*. San Francisco: ICS Press.

Robert, C., and Jennifer, M.D. (1998). *MicroBanking Bulletin*. Boulder CO: Economics Institute.

Rutherford, S. (1995). *ASA: the biography of an NGO*. Dhaka: Association for Social Advancement.

Rutherford, S. (1997). Informal financial services in Dhaka's slums. In G. Wood, and I. Sharif (Eds), *Who needs credit? Poverty and finance in Bangladesh*. Dhaka: University Press.

SafeSave (1998). 30 September 1998 Update, Dhaka

van de Walle, D. (1997). Comment on rural finance in Africa: institutional developments and access for the poor by Ernest Aryeetey. In *Annual World Bank Conference on Development Economics 1996* (pp. 52–6). Washington, DC: World Bank.

Woller, G., Dunford, C., and Woodworth, W. (1999). Where to microfinance? *International Journal of Economic Development*.

Wright, G., Hossain, M., and Rutherford, S. (1997). Savings: Flexible financial services for the poor. In G. Wood, and I. Sharif (Eds), *Who needs credit? Poverty and finance in Bangladesh*. Dhaka: University Press.

4

THE NEED TO SAVE

Stuart Rutherford[1]

4.1 INTRODUCTION

Although their incomes may be tiny or irregular, there are many times when poor people need sums of money that are bigger than what they have in hand. The need for these 'usefully large lump sums' arises from life-cycle events such as birth, education, marriage, and death, from emergency situations, and from the discovery of opportunities to make investments in assets or businesses. The only reliable and sustainable way that they can obtain these sums is to build them, somehow or other, from their savings. So poor people have to save, and financial services for the poor are there to help them find ways to do so.

4.2 THE POOR AS SAVERS

The poor want to save, and do save … but it is not easy.

A popular and useful definition of a poor person is someone who does not have much money. Among academics, and in the aid industry, this definition has gone out of fashion. But it suits my present purposes well, so I shall stick to it. In this [chapter], when I talk about 'the poor', I mean people who, compared to their fellow citizens, don't have much money.

If you do not have much money it is especially important that you manage well what money you have. Poor people are at a disadvantage here, because the banks and insurance companies and other financial institutions that serve the better-off rarely cater to the poor. Nevertheless, poor people do seek and find a wide variety of ways of managing their money, as examples in this essay will show. The essay argues that we can learn a lot from the more successful money-managing efforts of the poor, and use that learning to design new and better ways of bringing banking services to the slums and villages of the developing world.

Choosing to save …

Managing money well begins with hanging on to what you have. This means avoiding unnecessary expenditure and then finding a safe place to store whatever money is left over. Making that choice – *the choice to save rather than to consume* – is the foundation of money management.

… but finding it hard to do so

Poor people run into problems with money management at this very first hurdle. If you live in an urban slum or in a straw hut in a village, finding a safe place to store savings is not easy. Bank notes tucked into rafters, buried in the earth, rolled inside hollowed-out bamboo, or thrust into clay piggy banks, can be lost or stolen or blown away or may just rot. Certainly their value will decline, because of inflation.

But the physical risks may be the least of the problem. Much tougher is keeping the cash safe from the many claims on it – claims by relatives who have fallen on hard times, by importunate neighbours, by hungry or sick children or alcoholic husbands, by your mother-in-law (who knows you have that secret hoard somewhere)[2] and by landlords, creditors and beggars. Finally, even when you do have a little cash left over at the day's end, if you do not have somewhere safe to put it you will most probably spend it in some trivial way or other. I have lost count of the number of women who have told me how hard it is to save at home, and how much they would value a safe, simple way to save.

Nevertheless, the poor *can* save, *do* save, and *want* to save money. Only those so poor that they have left the cash economy altogether – elderly disabled widows and widowers for example, who live by begging food from neighbours – cannot save money. This essay is not about them.

Can the poor really save?

The fact that the poor want to save and have some capacity to save is not self-evident. If you do not know much about how the poor actually organize their lives you may assume that the poor 'are too poor to save'. The poor spend all their income and still do not get enough to eat, so how can they save? The poor may need loans, but the last thing they need, you may think, is a savings service.

Ins and outs

By the time you have finished this [chapter] you will see that this is a misconception. But for the time being, notice that people and (and not just the poor) may save money whilst most of it goes out (like keeping a few coins back from the housekeeping money) as well as when it comes in (deducting savings at source from your wage or other income). Even the poorest have to spend money to buy basic items like food and fuel, and each time they do so there is the opportunity to save something, however tiny. Many poor housewives try to in this way, even if their working husbands fail to save anything from their income.

That the poor do succeed in saving something is shown by their habit of lending each other small amounts of money (as well as small amounts of rice or kerosene or salt). In this 'reciprocal lending', I lend you a few cents today on the understanding that you'll do the same for me at some other time. This practice is so common that such loans form the bulk of financial transactions that poor people get involved in, even if the amounts involved add up to only a small proportion of the total value in circulation through financial services for the poor. The practice depends entirely on the poor's capacity and willingness to save.

This [chapter] is about saving *money*. People save in other ways, of course, and we shall take that into account, briefly, in the notes at the end of this chapter. But for the time being I want to pursue my basic message in the simplest way, and that means concentrating on money savings. The poor, I have claimed, can and do save. But why do they do so?

4.3 THE POOR AS BIG SPENDERS

The poor need, surprisingly often, to spend large sums of money.

You may not yet be fully convinced that the poor can and do (and want to) save. So we shall move on to the spending needs of the poor, which are less controversial.

The need to spend

Just because you are poor does not mean that all your expenditure will be in small sums. Much of if may be – you may buy only a little food or clothing at a time. But from time to time you need to spend large sums. How we classify these needs is a matter of choice: I like to list them under three main categories, 'life-cycle' events, emergency needs, and investment opportunities.

'Life-cycle' needs

In Bangladesh and India, the dowry system makes marrying daughters an expensive business. In parts of Africa, burying deceased parents can be very costly. These are just two examples of 'life-cycle' events for which the poor need to amass large lump sums. Other such events include childbirth, education, home-building, widowhood and old-age generally, and the desire to bequeath lump sums to their heirs. Then there are the recurrent festivals like Eid, Christmas, or Diwali. In each case the poor need to be able to get their hands on sums of money which are much bigger than the amounts of cash which are normally found in the household. Many of these needs can be anticipated, even if their exact date is unknown. The awareness that such outlays are looming on the horizon is a source of great anxiety for many poor people.

Emergency needs

Emergencies that create a sudden and unanticipated need for a large sum of money come in two forms – personal and impersonal. Personal emergencies include sickness or injury, the death of a bread-winner or the loss of employment, and theft or harassment. Impersonal ones include events such as war, floods, fires, cyclones, and – for slum dwellers – the bulldozing of their homes by the authorities. You will be able to think of other examples. Each creates a sudden need for more cash than can normally be found at home. Finding a way to insure themselves against such troubles would help millions of poor people.

Investment opportunities

Besides innumerable needs for spending large sums of cash, there are opportunities to do so. There may be opportunities to invest in an existing or new business, or to buy land or other productive assets. The lives of some poor people can be transformed if they can afford to pay a bribe to get a permanent job (often in government service). The poor, like all of us, also like to invest in costly items that make life more comfortable – better roofing, better furniture, a water-pump, a fan, a television. One of these investment opportunities – setting up a new business or expanding an existing one – has recently attracted a lot attention from industry and from the new generation of banks that work with the poor. But business investment is in fact just one of many needs and opportunities that require the poor to become occasional 'big spenders'.

4.4 FINANCIAL SERVICES FOR POOR PEOPLE

In this essay, I shall be concentrating on how the poor obtain the large lump sums they need from time to time. I shall be reviewing the financial services – formal and informal – that have evolved to serve this need. These are services that are urgently and frequently needed for the vast majority of poor people, for the reasons set out in the previous section. They are the ones discussed in this essay.

Of course, there are other services used by the poor that are 'financial' in the wider sense, such as those that ease the transmission or conversion of currency. Examples are sending money home from town or abroad. Apart from this brief mention, these services (important though they are to many poor people) are not dealt with in this essay.

So, to return to my main question: how are the poor to get hold of the large lump sums they so often need? They might be lucky and have cash gifted to them, or be in some other way the beneficiary of charity – but this can hardly be relied on. It is not a sustainable way of getting access to large sums.

Three common ways of raising large sums are:

- selling assets they already hold (or expect to hold)
- mortgaging (or 'pawning') those assets
- finding a way of turning their many small savings into large lump sums.

Stocks and flows

The first method listed above – the sale of assets – is usually a straightforward matter that doesn't ordinarily require any 'financial' services. However, poor people sometimes sell, in advance, assets that they don't hold now but expect to hold in the future. The most common rural example is the advance sale of crops. These 'advances' are a form of financing, since the buyer provides, in effect, a loan that will be repaid from the yet-to-be harvested crop. The advance may be spent on financing the farming costs required to produce that crop. But they may just as likely be used on any of the other needs and opportunities we reviewed in the previous section, or simply on surviving until harvest time.

The second method – mortgage and pawn – enables poor people to convert assets into cash and back again. It is the chance (not always realized) to regain the asset that distinguishes this second method from the first. As in the straightforward sale of assets, such services require the user to have a stock of wealth in the form of an asset of some sort. They allow the user to exploit their ownership of this stock of wealth by transforming it temporarily into cash. The most common examples are the pawning in shops in towns and the mortgaging of land in the countryside.

These first two methods require the users to have assets, and poor people, almost by definition, have very few assets. This fact severely limits the effectiveness of these two methods. It makes them neither reliable nor sustainable. Only the third method is free of this limitation.

The third method enables poor people to convert their small savings into lump sums. This requires the users to have a flow of savings, however small or irregular. It allows them to exploit their capacity to make savings by offering a variety of mechanisms by which these savings can be transformed into lump sums.

These three methods are at the heart of all financial services for the poor, whether they are informal or formal, large or small.

A set of simple diagrams will make this clearer, I hope, so I proceed to introduce the basic system of diagrams that I use throughout this essay. In these diagrams, time is represented by the horizontal axis, and value (of money) by the vertical axis.

Saving up

'Saving up' is the most obvious way to convert savings into lump sums. It allows a lump sum to be enjoyed in future in exchange for a series of savings made now. Many poor people prefer this mechanism because it produces an 'unencumbered' lump sum – it is yours to do what you like with once you've built it up. But as we have seen, the poor find it hard to find a safe place to keep their savings.

In Figure 4.1, savings made by the user are shown as negative values (below the

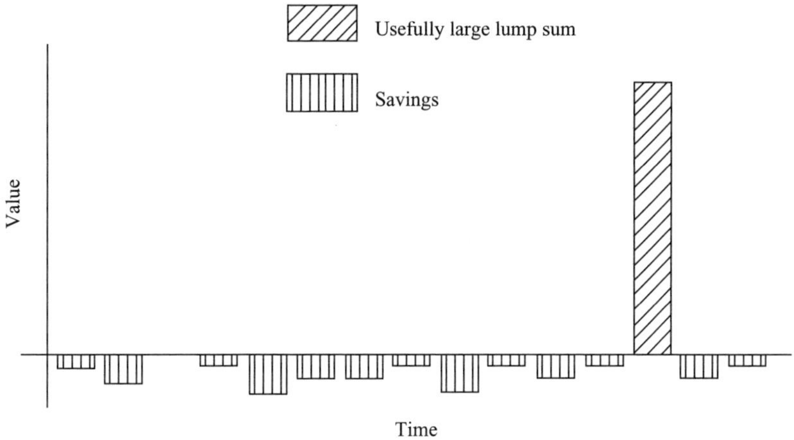

Figure 4.1 Saving up.

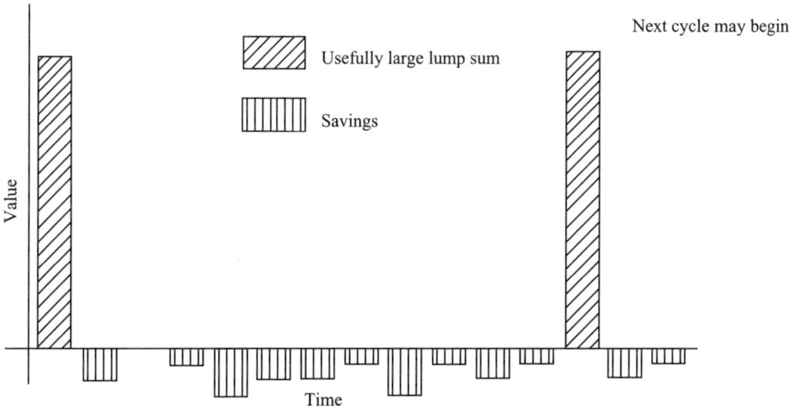

Figure 4.2 Saving down.

horizontal line) since they are saved (deducted) from the user's expenditure, and the saved-up sum is shown as a positive value when it is 'withdrawn' and becomes available to be spent. Note that as soon as a sum is 'withdrawn' most savers like to start saving all over again: the diagram shows this as two further saved sums on the right hand side of the withdrawal.

Saving down

Another way to turn exactly the same series of savings into a lump sum is to get someone to give you the lump sum *first*, as a loan, and then use the savings to repay the loan over time. Such loans can be thought of as 'advances against future savings'. This is what I call 'saving down' (Figure 4.2) – since it is the exact opposite of saving up. But just as the poor find it hard to find a safe place to save up, many of them also find it very hard to find someone to help them 'save down'. Indeed, the most common complaint about moneylenders in developing countries is not that they charge extortionate rates of interest (though some do, of course), but that they are simply not available. As an Indian proverb has it, 'a good village is one with a good well and a good moneylender'.

Saving through

Finally we come to 'saving through', as shown in Figure 4.3, in which the saver goes on making a more or less continuous stream of savings that get converted to a lump sum at some intermediate point in time. Insurance policies do this – when

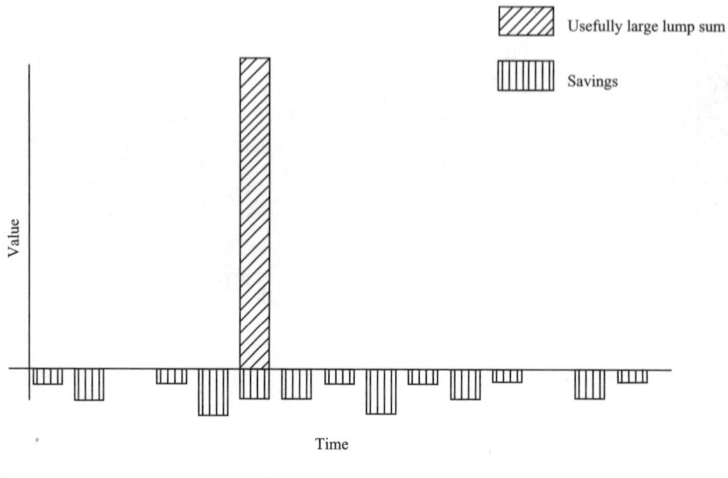

Figure 4.3 Saving through.

you insure your car you make a series of savings (monthly premiums or whatever) and take lump sums back each time you crash into the gatepost and need to repair the body work. Not many poor people are insured – though many would dearly like to be – but other 'saving through' mechanisms are popular among them. They usually take the form of savings clubs of one sort or another.

No choice but to save ... in whatever available way

Whichever way the poor find to turn their savings into lump sums – savings up, down or through – they *have* to save. The great irony of being poor is that you are 'too poor to save, but too poor not to save' – you may not be able to save much, but if you do not save at all you have no way of getting hold of those 'usefully large lump sums' that you so often need. When the poor are not saving, it is rarely the case that they do not want or need to. More often it is due to the lack of a safe opportunity to save – no reliable place to save up, no friendly moneylender to help you save down, or no saving club to help you to save through.

Which of these three methods the poor most often use will depend to a large extent on where they happen to live. For example, if you live in South Asia you are much more likely to use a moneylender than if you live in East Africa, where there are not many moneylenders serving the poor. East Africa doesn't have many deposit collectors, either, whereas in many countries of West Africa they are very common. All these regions have many savings clubs which allow the poor to 'save through', but the East African poor have to rely on them more than the poor of South Asia and West Africa. The fact that South Asians will probably be 'saving down', whereas West Africans are more likely to be 'saving up' and East Africans 'saving through' is another fact that has led me to believe that moneylending, deposit collecting and savings clubs are devices that may look very different but are in fact all essentially doing the same job – the job of helping poor people turn their savings into usefully large lump sums.

Basic personal financial intermediation

The set of mechanisms I call saving up, down and through need a name that is less clumsy than 'services which enable poor people to convert their small savings into usefully large lump sums'. I suggest the term 'basic personal financial intermediation'. I admit this is still a mouthful, but it does describe the process at work.

The process is one of 'financial intermediation' of the kind that a regular banker would recognize,[3] because many small savings are 'intermediated' ('carried across') into lump sums. But the process is 'personal' because we are talking about how one poor person can turn her savings into a lump sum for her own use (whereas bankers normally talk about intermediating the savings of many into loans for a few – who may be entirely different people). Finally, I call the process 'basic' because it is a basic requirement of everyday life for most poor people.

Notes

1 The text in this chapter is extracted from Chapter 1 of Stuart Rutherford (2000), *The Poor and Their Money*, New Delhi: Oxford University Press.

2 In several languages there are special words for that small hidden sum of cash that a woman will try to keep secret from her men-folk. For example, in the slums of Dhaka women use the Bengali word 'jula'.

3 *The Economist* defines a financial intermediary as 'any individual or institution that mediates between savers (that is sources of funds) and borrowers (that is users of funds)'. *Pocket Finance*, Economist Books: London, 1994, p. 94.

5

SUPPLY AND DEMAND IN MICROFINANCE

The case for a financial systems approach[1]

Marguerite S. Robinson

5.1 INTRODUCTION

This chapter explores the reasons for the 'absurd gap' between supply and demand in microfinance. Among the economically active poor of the developing world, there is strong demand for small scale commercial financial services – for both credit and savings. Where available, these and other financial services help low income people improve household and enterprise management, increase productivity, smooth income flows and consumption costs, enlarge and diversify their microbusiness, and increase their incomes. But the demand for commercial microfinance is rarely met by the formal financial sector. One reason is that the demand is generally not perceived. Another is that many actors in the formal sector believe, wrongly, that microfinance cannot be profitable for banking institutions.

What matters to microfinance clients is the access and cost of financial services. Many poor people are served by informal moneylenders, who generally provide easy access to credit but at a high cost, charging poor borrowers nominal monthly effective interest rates that typically range from about 10 per cent to more than 100 per cent – many times the monthly effective rates of sustainable financial institutions, which are usually 2–5 per cent. Even when real (inflation adjusted) interest rates are used and borrowers' transaction costs are included, it is normally far less expensive to borrow money from a commercial microfinance institution than from a local moneylender. Commercial microfinance institutions can also offer much in demand savings services that provide savers with security, liquidity, and returns, a combination not generally available in the informal sector.

Some poor people are served by government or donor financed nonbank financial institutions such as nongovernmental organisations (NGOs) and village banks. But most of these organisations are capital constrained and can meet only a tiny fraction of the demand for credit. While such institutions provide credit at relatively low cost, access to credit by borrowers is limited. Access to voluntary savings facilities is poor or nonexistent at many of these institutions.

Other households are served by state owned formal financial institutions that provide government and donor financed subsidised credit. But the below market subsidies are often siphoned off by local elites and so may not reach the poor. In addition, many such institutions have high arrears and large losses. Access by the poor tends to be low; despite the subsidies, the costs of borrowing maybe high because of widespread inefficiency and corruption.

Microfinance in the 1990s was marked by a major debate between two leading views on how to fill the absurd gap in microfinance: the *financial systems* approach and the *poverty lending* approach. Both approaches share the goal of making financial services available to poor people throughout the world. But the poverty lending approach focuses on reducing poverty through credit and other services provided by institutions that are funded by donor and government subsidies and other concessional funds. A primary goal is to reach the poor, especially the poorest of the poor, with credit. Except for mandatory savings required for receiving a loan, savings is not normally a significant part of the poverty lending approach to microfinance. Often the poor cannot save in such an institution unless they also borrow from it. As indicated by the term poverty lending, the emphasis is on microcredit, not microfinance.

Many institutions using the poverty lending approach provide microcredit to poor borrowers at low cost. But these institutions are typically not sustainable, primarily because their interest rates on loans are too low for cost recovery. In addition, they do not meet the demand among the poor for voluntary savings services.

In contrast, the financial systems approach focuses on commercial financial intermediation among poor borrowers and savers; its emphasis is on institutional self sufficiency. With worldwide unmet demand for microcredit estimated in the hundreds of millions of people and characterised by requests from creditworthy borrowers for continuing access to loans of gradually increasing size, government and donor funds cannot possibly finance microcredit on global scale. But within the past several decades, fully sustainable commercial microfinance intermediaries have emerged. These intermediaries provide loans and voluntary savings services to the economically active poor, and they offer easy access at reasonable cost. Their loan portfolios are financed by savings, commercial debt, and for-profit investment in varying combinations.

Commercial microfinance is not appropriate, however, for extremely poor people who are badly malnourished, ill, and without skills or employment opportunities. Starving borrowers will use their loans to buy food for themselves or their children. Such people do not need debt. They need food, shelter, medicines, skill training, and employment – for which government and donor subsidies and charitable contributions are appropriate. For these people, microfinance is the next step – after they are able to work.

Bank Rakyat Indonesia's microbanking system and Bolivia's Banco-Sol are introduced here as leading examples of profitable microfinance institutions. Their records show that commercial financial institutions can attain nationwide outreach among the economically active poor, thus providing microfinance extensively and profitably. In this context the relationship between institutional self sufficiency and the scale of outreach to low income borrowers and savers is examined; over time the breadth of outreach is shown to depend on the self sufficiency of the institution [...]

The *microfinance revolution* is emerging in many countries around the world. As it is used here, this term refers to the large scale, profitable provision of microfinance services – small savings and loans – to economically active poor people by sustainable financial institutions. These services are provided by competing institutions at the local level – near the homes and workplaces of their clients – in both rural and urban areas. Financial services delivered at the local level refer to those provided to people living in low income neighbourhoods in semi urban or urban areas. *Large scale* as used here means coverage by multiple institutions of millions of clients; or, for small countries or middle and high income countries with low demand, outreach to a significant proportion of the microfinance market. *Profitability* means covering all costs and risks without subsidy and returning a profit to the institution.

In aggregate, commercial microfinance institutions can provide outreach to a significant segment of their country's poor households. In a few countries this has already occurred; in others it is at various stages of progress.

5.2 ESTIMATING THE DEMAND FOR MICROFINANCE

The microfinance revolution is best understood in the context of the population and income levels of developing countries, and of estimates of unmet global demand for formal sector commercial financial services [...]

The following are crude but conservative assumptions:

- Some 80 per cent of the world's 4.5 billion people living in low and lower middle income economies do not have access to formal sector financial services. (It is probably accurate to say 90 per cent, but these are conservative estimates.)
- Among these 3.6 billion people, the average household size is five people (720 million households).
- Half of these households (360 million) account for the unmet demand for commercial savings or credit services from financial institutions.

The average productivity of these households could be increased substantially with access to appropriate institutional savings and credit services delivered locally. Because the benefits of financial services would also extend to the dependants of microfinance clients, the economic activities and the quality of life of more than 1.8 billion people could be improved by providing them with local access to formal commercial enterprise.

This is not a scale that can be reached by government or donor funded institutions. Microfinance demand can be met on a global scale only through the provision of financial services by self sufficient institutions.

Most of the demand for microfinance comes from households and enterprises operating in the unregulated, informal sector of the economy [...] [A] number of features generally associated in aggregate with informal enterprises tends to be absent from formal enterprises. These include scarcity of capital, family ownership, small scale operations, nonlegal status, lack of security of business location, operation in unregulated markets, relatively easy entry into markets, labour intensive production modes, nonformal education and low skill levels, irregular work hours, small inventories, use of indigenous resources, and domestic sales of products, often to end users. But the informal sector is far from homogenous. It includes people who collect and recycle cigarette butts and people who subcontract for large industrial contracts – and many others in between (such as petty traders, carpenters, brickmakers, recyclers of paper and metal, shoemakers, and tailors).

The formal financial sector has generally been self deterred from financing informal enterprises by characteristics typically associated with such business, including the nonlegal status of enterprises, the frequent lack of an authorised business location, the unavailability of standard forms of collateral, the small size of transactions (and associated high cost per transaction), and the perceived riskiness of such business.

The full magnitude of the demand for microfinance has begun to be understood only recently. During the second half of the twentieth century credit for agriculture has generally been accorded high priority, if usually in misguided ways. But the high demand for finance from self employed microentrepreneurs has typically been ignored by the formal financial sector. Until the 1980s the presence of informal microenterprises – street vendors, home workshops, market stalls, providers of informal transportation services – was generally perceived by policymakers and economists to be a result of economic dysfunction [...]

Given this perspective, the typical response on the part of governments was to focus on improving the management of the formal economy [...] The result was that the huge informal sector in many countries remained essentially invisible – in government plans and budgets, in economists' models, in bankers' portfolios, and in national policies [...] Yet microenterprises provide an income stream for poor entrepreneurs. They create employment. They recycle and repair goods that would otherwise become waste. And they provide cheap food, clothing, and transportation to poor people – including those at the lower levels of the formal sector – who would not otherwise be able to live on their salaries. Microentrepreneurs accomplish all of this despite several obstacles, since they generally lack capital, skills, legal status, and business security. But they generally have strong survival skills: shrewd business sense, long experience of hard work, knowledge of their markets, extensive informal support and communication networks, and a fundamental understanding of flexibility as the key to microenterprise survival [...]

The growing interest in commercial microfinance is related to the recent recognition on the part of some policymakers that the informal sector is very large, it is here for the foreseeable future, it provides employment and contributes to the economy, and its performance can be improved with the removal of legal and financial obstacles. Thus increasing microenterprise access to financial services – both credit and savings – has become a priority for many governments and donors. With this has come awareness that the demand for commercial microfinance is far larger than was previously understood.

5.3 INFORMAL COMMERCIAL MONEYLENDERS AND THEIR INTEREST RATES

Financial institutions that provide commercial microfinance help poor people manage enterprise growth and diversification and raise their household incomes. Yet informal commercial lenders – local traders, employers and landlords, commodity wholesalers, pawnbrokers, and moneylenders of various types – provide loans to the poor in many developing countries. Why, then, are formal commercial loans so crucial for social and economic development? Why fix a system that seems to work?

Many bankers, economists, and government officials assume that the informal commercial credit market works efficiently, satisfies demand, and helps the poor. A common view is that 'widespread use of informal finance suggests that it is well suited to most rural conditions' (Von Pischke, Adams and Donald, 1983: 8). 'Most informal lenders provide valuable financial services at a reasonable cost to borrowers' (Gonzales-Vega, 1993: 23) [...] From a development perspective, therefore, there has been no broadly recognised, compelling reason to afford high priority to establishing self sufficient microfinance institutions [...]

While it is true that informal commercial moneylenders provide important financial services to the poor, they typically charge very high interest rates to low income borrowers in developing countries. The reasons for the high interest rates have been hotly debated, but the evidence for the high rates is unmistakeable. While the transaction costs of obtaining a loan are normally higher for a borrower who obtains credit from a commercial finance institution than from an informal moneylender, the difference in interest rates is often so large that the total cost to the borrower is much lower at the institution. [For example] four Bank Rakyat Indonesia (BRI) *unit desa* [rural branch] borrowers reported paying previously to informal commercial moneylenders [...] These interest rates ranged widely, but all were much higher than the *unit desas*' monthly effective rate, which for most loans was 2.8 per cent for prompt payers. Three of the four borrowers paid enormously higher interest rates to the moneylenders: JR and TR [...] paid 47 times the BRI rate, AC [...] paid from 119–588 times the BRI rate, and RM [...] paid 693 times the BRI rate.

In addition to the high interest rates, the moneylenders' loan terms were not suitable for the borrowers' needs. RM and JR and TR wanted 12–18 month working capital loans, but RM could only obtain a one-week loan, and JR and TR only a one month loan, from their moneylenders. NP [...] wanted to borrow several hundred dollars, but the moneylender would only loan her US$45.

[This] range of interest rates [...] is common elsewhere as well. Each moneylender tends to have a range of interest rates that he or she charges to different customers. Poor borrowers are usually charged the higher rates for two main reasons: because poor borrowers have fewer other options and low bargaining power, and because for lenders the transaction costs for making small loans are essentially the same as for large loans. If the interest rates were the same, small loans would be less profitable. In some cases there is also a third reason: moneylenders may consider poor borrowers risky, and so add a premium to cover the extra risk. In my experience, however, this factor is generally considered less important than the other two. Outside of risks that borrowers may face because of collective shock in the region – drought, hyperinflation, war – moneylenders normally do not lend to poor borrowers who pose high risks.

Informal credit from moneylenders is often provided in the context of interlinked transactions; the borrower is also the lender's commodity supplier, employee, tenant, or sharecropper, for example. In such situations the lenders have good information about the borrowers and a variety of methods for ensuring loan repayment.

Moneylenders typically calculate interest rates on a flat rate basis – that is, on the original loan balance. This is in contrast to most standard banks, where the effective interest rate is used, calculated on the (declining) outstanding loan balance. Converting moneylenders' stated rates to effective monthly interest rates enables comparison with the rates of commercial microfinance institutions. In general, moneylenders' rates tend to be much higher than those of commercial microfinance institutions. In many parts of the developing world informal commercial lenders typically charge nominal effective interest rates of 10 per cent to more than 100 per cent a month, while sustainable microfinance institutions usually charge nominal effective rates between 2 and 5 per cent a month. Moreover, some moneylenders charge even higher rates to poor borrowers [...]

In assessing the cost of credit to borrowers, transaction costs must also be considered. These are the costs that borrowers incur in obtaining loans, such as paying for transportation, producing certified records, absorbing the opportunity cost of time spent travelling and waiting, paying fees and bribes, and the like. Low income borrowers often report that their transaction costs in borrowing from informal moneylenders are quite low. So too, profitable institutions providing commercial microfinance keep procedures simple and quick, locations convenient, and staff trained and motivated to be efficient and helpful to clients. In such institutions borrowers' transaction costs are moderate – if still typically higher than their transaction costs in borrowing from moneylenders.

Because of the large difference in interest rates, however, low income clients of commercial microfinance institutions typically have a much lower total cost of credit than those who borrow from moneylenders. The crucial point here is that the poor pay unnecessarily high interest rates for credit because commercial microfinance institutions do not yet exist in most areas of the developing world.

5.4 THE ECONOMICALLY ACTIVE POOR AND THE EXTREMELY POOR

Poverty comes in many forms and causes multiple harms. The poor suffer from lack of food and water, unemployment or underemployment, disease, abuse, homelessness, degradation, and disenfranchisement. The results among those affected often include physical, mental, and emotional disability, limited skills and education, low self esteem and lack of self confidence, and fear, resentment, aggression, and truncated vision. Some individuals break out of poverty. Some societies have social safety nets that prevent the poor from reaching destitution. Impoverished refugees face special problems. These effects of poverty combine in different ways and in varying degrees, affecting the poor differently depending on the society and the individual.

While all such people are poor by the standards of the wider society, there are substantial differences among them. Those who are severely food deficit, bonded labourers whose full time work pays only the interest on their loans, and displaced refugees are different from poor people who have some land, employment, or a microbusiness – except that in many cases the latter were once the former. Sometimes it works the other way around. At any level of poverty, however, women and some minorities tend to be the poorest, with girls typically the most deprived [...]

Though there are multiple degrees and kinds of poverty, here we distinguish only between the extremely poor and the economically active poor [...] People living in extreme poverty exist below the minimum subsistence level; they include those who are unemployed or severely underemployed, as well as those whose work is so poorly remunerated that their purchasing power does not permit the minimum caloric intake required to overcome malnutrition. Also included are people who live in regions severely deprived of resources; those who are too young, too old, or too disabled to work; those who for reasons of environment, ethnic identity, politics, gender and the like have little or no employment opportunities – and who have no earning assets or household members to support them; and those who are escaping from natural and manmade catastrophes.

The term *economically active poor* is used in a general sense to refer to those among the poor who have some form of employment and who are not severely food deficit or destitute [...] The distinction between the extremely poor and the economically active poor is not precise. Households move from one category to the other over time. People with skills may not find employment. The issue may be further complicated by gender, because women may not be permitted to learn marketable skills or to leave their homes. Even within a single household, women may be poorer and more malnourished than men [...]

Poverty contains many anomalies. Imprecise as they are, however, the two general categories of the economically active poor and the extreme poor can be usefully distinguished in the planning and implementation of effective strategies for overcoming poverty. The delineation of an official poverty line, defined by the consumption of a basket of goods, can be a useful tool for governments and donors in making policy decisions and in planning long-term development strategies. But the poverty line concept is not directly relevant for microfinance. Savers are commonly found on both sides of the official line, and many borrowers below the line are creditworthy, while many above the line are not.

In commercial microfinance the critical distinctions among the poor are those that differentiate the economically active poor from the extremely poor, and the poor who participate in a cash economy from those who do not (some pastoralists, subsistence agriculturalists, and hunters and gatherers). There is also a crucial distinction between creditworthy and noncreditworthy borrowers.

On the savings side, people with incomes that provide for their most minimal needs often save in small amounts in whatever forms are appropriate for their purposes and conveniently available. The demand among even the lowest levels of the economically active poor for secure, convenient, and appropriately designed financial savings services is well documented from many parts of the world. Such facilities are often more in demand among the poor than are credit services.

While the extremely poor may not be directly affected by commercial microfinance, they can benefit indirectly from its development. Thus microfinance helps to create employment; some of the extremely poor may find jobs if kin and neighbours among the economically active poor have access to commercial financial services. And if commercial microfinance is made locally available, the very poor who become employed will eventually be able to make use of its services.

5.5 A POVERTY ALLEVIATION TOOLBOX

Alleviating poverty requires many tools, including food, shelter, employment, health and family planning services, financial services, education, infrastructure, markets, and communication. The key to reducing poverty is knowing how to use these tools.

Credit is a powerful tool that is used effectively when it is made available to the creditworthy among the economically active poor participating in at least a partial cash economy. But other tools are required for the very poor who have prior needs, such as food, shelter, medicine, skills, training, and employment.

It is sometimes forgotten – although generally not by borrowers – that another word for credit is debt [...] Placing in debt those who are too poor to use credit effectively helps neither borrowers nor lenders. Food deficit borrowers without opportunities to use credit or to market their output may have no choice but to eat their loans. This can, in turn, lead to humiliation and the diminishing of an already low level of self confidence. Lenders to the extremely poor also face difficulty because low repayment rates caused by borrowers who cannot repay prevent the development of sustainable financial institutions.

The poorest of the poor should not be the responsibility of the financial sector.

The food, employment, and other basic requirements needed to overcome desperate poverty are appropriately financed by government and donor subsidies and grants. These tools are properly the responsibility of ministries of health, labour, social welfare, and others, as well as donor agencies and private charities.

But credit subsidies to the economically active poor – who could make good use of commercial credit – prevent them from having widespread access to available loans because subsidised loans are usually rationed. In addition, this approach uses scarce donor and government funds that would be better spent on other forms of poverty alleviation. The use of tools in this way – providing credit to the extremely poor and credit subsidies to the economically active poor – is like trying to build a house by using a saw to hammer the nails and a screwdriver to cut the boards.

A schematic diagram of a poverty alleviation toolbox, with an emphasis on its financial component, is shown in Figure 5.1. The first column in the figure shows three income levels: lower middle income, the economically active poor, and the extremely poor. No attempt is made to define these income categories because both the absolute scale and the relative proportions of the three categories vary considerably by country and region. In general, the extremely poor are those living on less than 75 cents a day, while the economically active poor have sufficient employment and income to meet basic nutrition, housing, and health needs [...], the economically active poor category is broad, ranging from households just barely above extreme poverty to those about to enter the lower middle income group. The lower middle income category is also a broad one. Although there is wide variation, such households typically have a relatively reliable income; higher standards of health, nutrition, housing, and education; a selection of consumer durables; and some forms of investment. Both economically active poor and lower middle income households tend to have some savings, and, where possible, to emphasise nutrition, health, housing, and children's education. The amounts and degree generally depend on their income levels and the availability of these services.

The second column in Figure 5.1 shows the financial services that are typically suitable for the different income levels. Commercial microcredit is appropriate both for many lower middle income households and for most of the economically active poor, including some below the official poverty line. Microsavings services reach even the lowest levels of the economically active poor, some well below the poverty line.

The third column in Figure 5.1 shows non financial poverty alleviation tools that are appropriate for those below the poverty line and essential for the extremely poor. The tools shown in the third column are funded by direct subsidies and grants; their purpose is to provide the very poor with immediate necessities. In addition, broader tools such as education, health, and family planning (as well as the development of infrastructure, wastelands, markets, industries, communications, and the like) benefit the larger population – often, though not always, including the poor.

Some households start extremely poor and gain employment. They may then

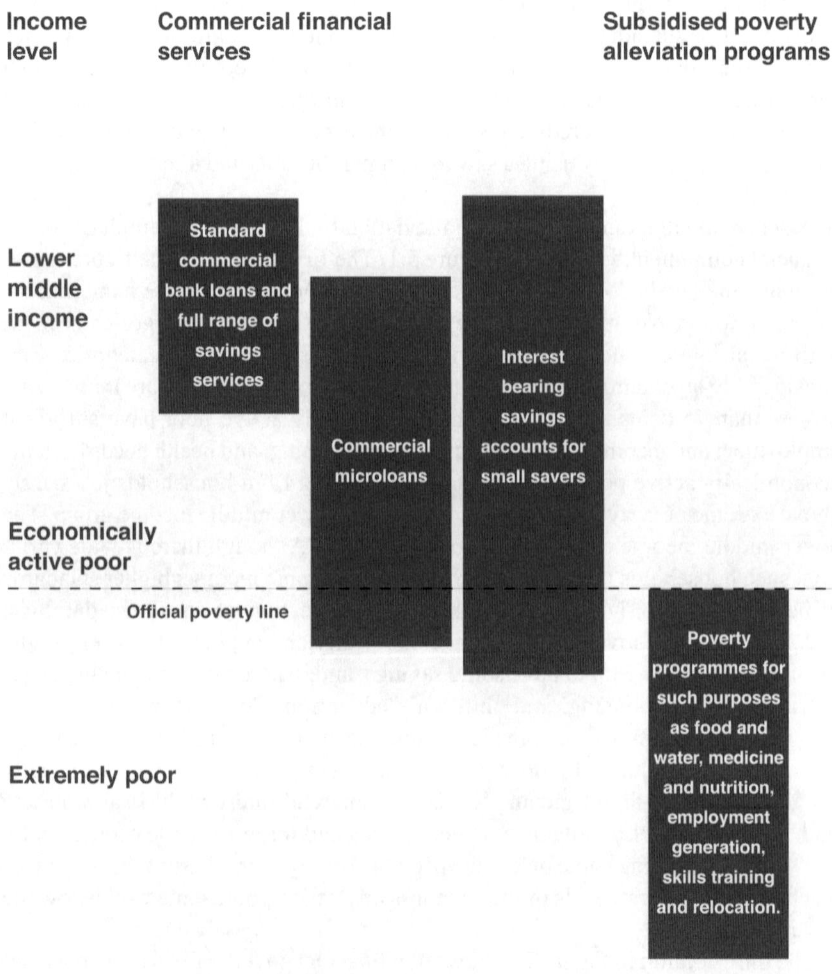

Figure 5.1 Financial services in the poverty alleviation toolbox.

open small savings accounts. Some households with savings accounts then add small loans. Some start with loans and add voluntary savings accounts when these become available. Some clients are able to expand and diversify their enterprises and to qualify for larger loans. When permitted by the institution, many microbanking clients save continuously and borrow only occasionally. Over time, some qualify to become clients of standard commercial banks. The people represented in Figure 5.1 whose demand is suitable for commercial microfinance inhabit most of the households of the developing world.

5.6 THE FINANCIAL SYSTEMS APPROACH AND THE POVERTY LENDING APPROACH

A fork in the road

Microfinance in the 1990s was marked by a major debate between two leading views: the financial systems approach and the poverty lending approach. The financial systems approach emphasises large scale outreach to the economically active poor – both to borrowers who can repay microloans from household and enterprise income streams, and to savers. The financial systems approach focuses on institutional self sufficiently because, given the scale of the demand for microfinance world wide, this is the only possible means to meet widespread client demand for convenient, appropriate financial services.

The poverty lending approach concentrates on reducing poverty through credit, often provided together with complementary services such as skills training and the teaching of literacy and numeracy, health, nutrition, family planning, and the like. Under this approach donor and government funded credit is provided to poor borrowers, typically at below market interest rates. The goal is to reach the poor, especially the extremely poor – the poorest of the poor – with credit to help overcome poverty and gain empowerment. Except for mandatory savings required as a condition of receiving a loan, the mobilisation of local savings is normally not a significant part of the poverty lending approach to microfinance.

Bangladesh's Grameen Bank and some of its replicators in other countries represent leading examples of the poverty lending approach [editors' note: the Grameen Bank shifted to a financial systems approach in 2001, as Hulme describes in this volume]. The microbanking division of Bank Rakyat Indonesia (BRI), BancoSol in Bolivia, and the Association for Social Advancement (ASA) in Bangladesh are at the forefront of the financial systems approach.

In a discussion about the debate between the two views, Elisabeth Rhyne (1998: 6) points out, '*everyone involved in microfinance shares a basic goal: to provide credit and savings services to thousands or millions of poor people in a sustainable way*. Everyone wants to reach the poor, and everyone believes sustainability is important'. Rhyne is right that the debate is about the means, not the goals. But the means can limit the goals that can be achieved. Thousands of clients can be served through either method. But serving millions of clients on a long-term basis in multiple, competing institutions requires a financial systems approach.

Rhyne goes on to say that 'it became clear that the poverty/sustainability debate is ultimately about whether to subsidise interest rates' (ibid: 7). She comments further that '*there is in fact only one objective – outreach. [Institutional] sustainability is but the means to achieve it*' (ibid: 7).

Substantial contributions to the development of institutional microfinance have been made through both approaches. Some institutions using the poverty lending approach to microcredit have successfully reached poor people with donor and government subsidised credit services. These institutions have helped their borrowers develop their enterprises and increase their incomes, and they have had high repayment rates. But the literature on microfinance and rural finance is filled with examples showing that most institutions that provide subsidised credit fail. And even successful institutions following the poverty lending approach, in aggregate, can meet only a small portion of the demand for microfinance.

In contrast, formal sector commercial microfinance has proven itself able to make financial services – both credit and savings – available to low income clients on a large scale, and to do so profitably. Institutions such as BRI and BancoSol have demonstrated that broad outreach to economically active poor clients can be achieved without ongoing subsidies.

As a global solution to meeting microfinance demand, the two views on microfinance – and the means they advocate – are not equal. Governments and donors cannot finance the hundreds of millions of people who constitute present unmet demand for microcredit services. In addition, the poverty lending approach, as indicated by its name, does not attempt to meet the vast demand among the poor for voluntary savings services.

Let me specify where and why I disagree with advocates of poverty lending. I agree with many of their views on poverty, both its causes and its solutions. I share their goal of providing financial services to poor people through sustainable institutions. I admire their commitment to eradicating poverty. And I recognise their important contributions to the development of methodologies for microcredit. But the tools of the poverty lending approach are poorly suited for building microfinance on a global scale. Resources for developing microfinance are limited, and donors and governments must choose among options if microfinance services are to be made available to all who can use them. In these choices are very large stakes.

Michael Chu, a former Wall Street financial specialist in the use of capital markets for company acquisitions, became a leader of the financial system approach to microfinance. While president of ACCION International, Chu described his view of the future of microfinance:

> Microfinance today stands as the threshold of its next major stage, the connection with the capital markets [...]. The reason why the connection with capital markets is a watershed lies in the fact that, if accomplished,

> it will make the outreach of microfinance to date [...] a mere prologue for what will come. The millions reached today will increase a hundredfold. This is nothing short of changing *the very nature of banking*, from servicing the top 25 or 30 per cent (at the most) of the population of the developing world to meeting the demand of the rest. It is the reclaiming of finance for society at large – the true democratisation of capital.
>
> (Chu, 1998: 2)

In contrast, a microcredit summit held in Washington, DC, in 1997 developed a charter stating that 'credit is more than business. Just like food, credit is a human right'. A commitment was made 'to ensure that 100 million of the world's poorest families, especially the women of those families, receive credit for self employment and other financial and business services by the year 2005' (Muhammad Yunus, in a speech to the Microcredit Summit, February 1997). This aim is to be met through a campaign that seeks to raise US$21.6 billion.

A second Microcredit Summit was held in New York in 1998. But these were microcredit summits, not microfinance summits; the distinction is crucial. The goal, the billions of dollars earmarked for microcredit loan portfolios could be spent much more effectively. Five issues can be highlighted:

- Food is a universal need; credit is not. Not all poor people want or need debt [...]
- If credit were a human right, the poverty lending approach would not enable the right to be widely exercised. The first reason is that [...] the scale is well beyond the reach of donor and government funding. The second is that a one time microloan carries little development impact. Low income people throughout the developing world need continued access to credit and savings services, with the option of gradually increasing the size of their loans as borrowers become qualified through repayment records and enterprise performance [...]
- From the point of view of poverty alleviation, the funds collected for financing microcredit portfolios in developing countries could be better used in other ways [...] it would be more effective to use donated funds to provide the extremely poor with food, water, medicines, training, and employment rather than to put them in debt before they are financially able.
- For many of the world's poorest people, appropriately designed voluntary savings services are a more important and appropriate development instrument than credit [...]
- Where are the institutions qualified to handle the microcredit summit's projected massive increase in the volume of lending – from the summit's estimated 8 million borrowers in 1997 to 100 million borrowers in 2005? [...]

Overall, the poverty lending approach poses a deep dilemma for governments, microfinance institutions, donors, and others. This is because microfinance has reached a fork in the road [...] The poverty lending approach uses subsidies primarily to fund loan portfolios. The financial systems approach uses subsidies primarily to disseminate lessons from the best practices of fully sustainable microfinance systems and to finance the development of financially self sufficient microfinance institutions. These institutions then finance their microloan portfolios commercially, enabling them to multiply outreach by leveraging additional capital. One road leads toward donor dependent microcredit institutions that cannot meet the demand for credit and do not meet the demand for savings services. The other leads to self sufficient financial intermediaries and large scale microfinance outreach.

5.7 FINANCIALLY SELF-SUFFICIENT MICROFINANCE INSTITUTIONS

Sustainable microfinance is carried out by commercial institutions that deliver financial services to the economically active poor at interest rates that enable the institutions to cover all costs (including the commercial cost of funds) and risks, and to generate a profit. Such institutions include banks and, in some countries, savings and credit cooperatives, credit unions, and other nonbank financial organisations.

The term *commercial microfinance institution* refers here both to institutions that provide microfinance to the public (such as banks) and those that serve only their members (such as credit unions). It refers to institutions that finance their loan portfolios from locally mobilised savings, those that access commercial debt and for profit investment, and those that use retained earning to finance their lending. The term also includes institutions that provide only microfinance, as well as those that offer microfinance as part of a wider set of financial services.

Commercial microfinance institutions are differentiated from informal commercial lenders who lend money for profit (often as part of interlinked transactions with borrowers), from subsidised formal microcredit (in which a regulated institution such as a state owned bank channels government or donor funds to borrowers at subsidised interest rates), and from unregulated institutions such as NGOs (which onlend subsidised donor or government funds to their borrowers).

Commercial microcredit provided by financial institutions is not new. It was common in parts of Europe in the nineteenth century and was sometimes exported to countries under colonial rule. Thus Indonesia's oldest institutions providing commercial microcredit profitably – the Badan Kredit Desas (BKDs) […] were begun by the Dutch in the late 1890s. While not developed specifically as microfinance institutions, the BKDs provide microcredit and voluntary savings to large numbers of poor clients.

Financial institutions that mobilise the savings of the poor are also not new. In Colombia, for example, the Banco Caja Social began mobilising savings from poor households in 1911 […]

The microfinance revolution is a commercial revolution, based on new financial technology and greatly accelerated by the information revolution that developed concurrently. It began in the 1970s, developed in the 1980s and took off in the 1990s. The profitable provision of small loans was made possible by the lending methodologies, pricing, products, and services that were designed specifically for microcredit clients during the 1970s and 1980s. In Indonesia the new lending methods were joined with the widespread mobilisation of voluntary microsavings in the 1980s; in Bolivia they were combined with access to commercial debt and investment in the 1990s. These combinations enabled institutional profitability and long-term viability, making possible large scale for profit sector financial outreach to low income segments of the population.

Information on these breakthroughs spread widely through rapidly expanding forms of communication, and institutions in a variety of countries began experimenting with commercial microfinance during the 1990s. Other advances followed. It became possible to deepen outreach by reducing the denomination of financial services and serving even poorer clients, while maintaining institutional profitability and self sufficiency. ASA in Bangladesh and Compartamos in Mexico, provide good illustrations of this process. By the late 1990s in a few countries, the result was – for the first time in history – competition among commercial microfinance institutions for the business of low income clients.

From the point of view of borrowers, the crucial words in microcredit are access and cost. Subsidised loan programs typically have limited capital and do not provide low income households with wide access to credit. Informal commercial moneylenders, in aggregate, provide wide access to credit, but generally at very high cost to borrowers.

From the perspective of savers, the key words are security, convenience, liquidity, confidentiality, access to credit, good service, and returns. Indigenous forms of saving – in gold, animals, raw materials, cash held in the home, grain or other agricultural commodities, rotating savings and credit associations (ROSCAs), savings collectors, and the like – normally do not provide this combination of characteristics.

In contrast to informal commercial moneylenders and informal savings methods, formal institutions providing commercial microfinance can make financial services – both credit and savings – widely available at a cost that enables both the profitability of the financial institutions and the growth and diversification of their clients' enterprises.

5.8 PROVIDING CREDIT AND SAVING SERVICES PROFITABLY

Microcredit methods designed for individuals and those designed for groups have both proven effective; these can also be combined in the same institution. For both kinds of microloans, however, commercial microfinance institutions must charge interest rates that are significantly higher than the normal lending rates of the country's standard commercial banks. Operating costs are typically several times those of the banking industry standard in the same country. There are a number of reasons. Microfinance institutions are necessarily labour intensive. They must maintain and staff many small, widely dispersed outlets that are conveniently located for clients. Infrastructure and communications in the areas serviced are often rudimentary. And it is more costly to process many small loans and savings accounts than a smaller number of larger ones.

In the microfinance arena, discussion of 'market rates' and 'subsidised rates' tends to be confused. The term 'market rate' should mean a rate that arises from the interplay of supply and demand *in some defined range of transactions* [...] Market rate is used to refer to the rate at which commercial banks and their conventional customers conduct deposit and loan transactions. Loan interest rates are called 'subsidised' or 'unsubsidised' depending on whether they cover the full cost of providing the loan. Costs of providing microloans are higher, as a percentage of loan amount, than costs of conventional bank loans. Thus a market rate (as defined here) is likely to be a 'subsidised rate' if it is applied to microloans.

Delivering microfinance services at many small, scattered locations is considerably more expensive than providing clients with services for larger loans and deposits in centrally located urban banks. Still, the interest rates on microloans charged by profitable financial institutions – even though they are higher than standard bank rates – are highly attractive to low income borrowers in many developing countries because they represent a small fraction of the rates normally charged to such borrowers in the informal commercial market.

Politicians, journalists, social workers, and the general public often have a difficult time understanding why interest rates on microloans need to be higher than those on larger loans. This is, after all, somewhat counterintuitive. Often mistakenly perceived as discrimination against the poor, the issue of commercial microcredit interest rates can be highly controversial. Institutions and governments that want to introduce commercial microfinance into the formal financial sector must be well informed about the reasons that interest rates permitting full cost recovery are important for the clients, the institutions, and the economy – and must hone their political skills.

Microsavings, on the other hand, [are] inclusive. More of the economically active poor generally want to save than want to borrow at a given time. Such savers will take advantage of savings facilities in secure, conveniently located formal institutions if the kinds of products and services that meet their demand are made available to them. And with careful pricing, commercial financial institutions can accommodate nearly all microsavers. In addition, a commercial microfinance institution that serves the public mobilises deposits from anyone – rich or poor – who lives or works nearby and wants to save in the institution's local branch. This approach makes it possible to serve poor savers cost effectively while making available increased funds for microlending.

There are many types of successful microcredit and microsavings programs. But only financially self sufficient, commercial microfinance institutions can meet the demand for microfinance on a global scale.

5.9 REACHING SCALE

The defining characteristic of the microfinance revolution is its large scale outreach in the provision of financial services to low income clients – a scale that is made possible by regulated, self sufficient financial intermediaries. This does not mean that other types of microfinance programs are not valuable or that other kinds of institutions have not contributed to the development of the microfinance revolution; they are and they have. But the future of most microfinance is in profitable financial intermediaries operating within their countries' formal financial sectors. Still few in number, such institutions nevertheless serve large numbers of clients and represent the frontier of the microfinance industry.

Components of the microfinance revolution emerged, slowly and sporadically in many countries, with each institution in relative isolation from the others. Generated by a mix of public and private sector involvement, the revolution gained momentum in the 1980s and 1990s, galvanised in part by the large scale successes beginning in Indonesia in the 1980s and in Bolivia in the 1990s.

Indonesia has played a special role in the microfinance revolution because it was the first country where the following pieces of the puzzle were put together on a national scale:

- A loan methodology and savings services suitable for microfinance clients.
- Staff training and incentives that encourage in-depth knowledge of the microfinance market.
- High loan repayment rates.
- Pricing based on full cost recovery and returning a profit to the institution.
- Management and organisational systems with capacity to deliver financial services efficiently to low income people throughout a large country.
- Continuing institutional profitability without subsidy.
- Widespread outreach among the economically active poor.

At the microbanking division of BRI, a large state owned commercial bank, local savings are mobilised and lent out profitably in small loans in both rural and urban areas throughout the country. BRI's microbanking division, which began its commercial approach to microfinance in 1984, reaches millions of clients. It has been profitable each year since 1986 and independent of subsidy since 1987. In December 1999 the division had US$802 million in 2.5 million outstanding loans, US$2.3 billion in 24.1 million savings accounts and a long-term repayment rate of 98 per cent. The 1999 record of BRI's microbanking division was achieved in a year when Indonesia was just beginning to emerge from the most serious economic downturn of any country in recent history. There are also smaller financial institutions in Indonesia with a similar orientation; in that country, the world's fourth most populous, a substantial part of the large demand for microfinance, for both credit and savings, is met by profitable institutions that do not require ongoing subsidies from donors or from the government. These institutions have proven extremely stable, even in time of severe national crisis.

In Bolivia the microfinance revolution emerged in the 1990s. Large scale commercial microcredit is provided there by BancoSol, a privately owned bank for microentrepreneurs, and by a number of competitors following hotly on BancoSol's heels (and profits). By 1997 BancoSol, financed by a combination of domestic and international commercial debt and investment and locally mobilised voluntary savings, provided loans profitably to more than one quarter of Bolivia's bank clients. Overall, the 1990s saw massive efforts to spread best practices in microfinance, to develop standards for the infant industry, and to bring to the attention of policymakers the potential contributions that formal commercial microfinance institutions could make to their countries and their economies. More than a hundred institutions in many parts of the world are developing sustainable microfinance programs, and the number is steadily increasing.

The revolution is still emerging, however, and commercial institutions providing microfinance remain relatively rare. Instead, in many countries funds provided for microcredit by governments and donors continue to be misdirected into large subsidised credit programs. This leaves most of the economically active poor without access to credit for working capital or investment, except at high cost from informal moneylenders. It also leaves them without access to savings services that provide security, liquidity, and returns.

In many parts of the developing world, microfinance continues to be perceived by the financial sector as unimportant for the economy, unprofitable for financial institutions, and unnecessary for the poor [...] all these views are wrong: that institutional commercial microfinance is of major importance for the economy, that it can be profitable for the financial institution, and that it is a necessary component of large scale poverty reduction.

5.10 WHY HAS THE DEMAND FOR INSTITUTIONAL COMMERCIAL MICROFINANCE NOT BEEN MET?

The lack of reliable information is the main reason for most of the unmet demand for formal sector commercial microfinance today. The formal financial sector has been poorly advised from many quarters, including people who:

- Advise that formal institutions cannot provide microfinance profitably because of the high transaction costs the institution would have to bear.
- Warn of high institutional risk because of asymmetric information, moral hazard, and the adverse selection of borrowers.
- Assert the institutions cannot compete successfully with the informal commercial credit market.
- Believe that institutional commercial microfinance is not a development priority because informal commercial lenders meet the credit demand of low income households and are generally beneficial to the poor.

- Think that low income people are uneducated and backward, and so unable to participate in the formal financial sector.
- Assume that low income people cannot afford commercial loans and so require government or donor funded credit subsidies (thereby insuring that demand remains unmet).
- Believe that most rural economies in developing countries do not generate a sufficient volume of business to be attractive to formal financial institutions.

All this advice, has served for decades to slow the learning curve of the formal financial sector about the profitability of microfinance. The conventional wisdom – that microfinance is not suited to the commercial formal financial sector – is still widely believed within many governments, banks, and donor agencies. This, in turn, leads to the kinds of government supervision and regulation that, when enforced, do not permit the development of sustainable microfinance institutions. It also contributes to the dearth of high-level, skilled managers willing to commit themselves to the development of commercial microfinance [...]

The 1990s will likely be seen as a watershed period in the development of commercial microfinance. The decade has been marked by expanding international and regional communication about aspects of commercial microfinance; growing attention to crucial issues of regulation, supervision, and governance; increasing visits of policymakers and microfinance practitioners to leading microfinance institutions; the founding of microfinance training programs and practitioner networks; the introduction of internet discussion groups and websites; the early development of industry standards and the birth of rating agencies; and a shift in focus by some donors from direct financing of microloan portfolios to allocation of their scarce resources to institution building for selected commercial microfinance institutions and to dissemination of information about best practices in sustainable microfinance.

5.11 WHY DOES MEETING THE DEMAND FOR INSTITUTIONAL COMMERCIAL MICROFINANCE MATTER?

[...] Microfinance matters because it increases the options and the self confidence of poor households by helping them to expand their enterprises and add others, to decrease risks, to smooth consumption, to obtain higher returns on investment, to improve management and increase their productivity and incomes, to store their excess liquidity safely and obtain returns on their savings, to escape or decrease exploitation by the locally powerful, and to conduct their business with dignity. The quality of their lives improves. Children are sent to school, and child labour decreases. And housing and health improve. In addition, the economically active poor who are able to expand their economic activities often create jobs for others; among those who gain employment in this way are some of the extremely poor.

Commercial microfinance institutions can become profitable and viable over the long term. Governments benefit because they do not need to provide credit subsidies or cover the losses of subsidised credit programs – and because the resulting savings can be used as needed for direct poverty alleviation programs for the extremely poor. Economies benefit from the increased production, from the new resources made available for investment, and from improvement in equity. Further, large scale sustainable microfinance helps create an enabling environment for the growth of political participation and of democracy.

Note

1 The text in this chapter is extracted from Chapter 1 of Marguerite S. Robinson (2001), The Microfinance Revolution: Sustainable Finance for the Poor, Washington, DC: World Bank.

References

Chu, Michael (1998), 'Key Issues of Development Finance', Somervilla, Mass: ACCION International.

Gonzalez-Vega, Claudio (1993), 'From Policies to Technologies, to Organisations: The Evolution of the Ohio State University Vision of Rural Financial Markets', *Economics and Sociology Occasional Paper 2062*, Columbus: Ohio State University, Rural Finance Program.

Rhyne, Elizabeth (1998), 'The Yin and Yang of Microfinance: Reaching the Poor and Sustainability', *Micro Banking Bulletin*, 2: 6–8.

Von Pischke, J. D., Dale W. Adams, and Gordon Donald (eds) (1983), *Rural Financial Markets in Developing Countries: Their Use and Abuse*, Baltimore, Md.: The Johns Hopkins University Press.

6

MICROENTERPRISE FINANCE

Is there a conflict between growth and poverty alleviation?

Paul Mosley and David Hulme[1]

6.1 INTRODUCTION

The idea of attempting to reduce poverty in developing countries through the provision of loans by specialized financial institutions to microenterprises,[1] urban and rural, has in recent years generated enthusiasm bordering on hysteria (Rogaly, 1996). Politically, it appeals to the left as being redistributive and a direct approach to alleviating poverty, and to the right as facilitating the emergence of an independent, self-sustaining 'penny capitalism.' Financially, institutions such as the Grameen Bank of Bangladesh, the BKKs (Badan Kredit Kecamatan) of Indonesia and BancoSol of Bolivia have often achieved higher loan recovery rates than those achieved by commercial banks in the same country in spite of lending to poor, uncollateralized individuals, making it appear that a reliable organizational technology for lending to the poor of developing countries now exits (Remenyi, 1991; Yaron, 1991; Christen *et al.*, 1994; Otero and Rhyne, 1994; Robinson, 1996). Elements in such a technology are the freedom to charge interest rates which cover costs, the provision of savings facilities and the adaptation of financial services to local demand through 'mobile banking.' Various institutional initiatives, including the World Bank-based Consultative Group to Assist the Poorest (CGAP), the Microcredit Summit held in Washington, DC in February 1997, the Dhaka-based Grameen Trust and Asia's CASHPOR network, have been taken to diffuse that technology, on the premise that so doing will make a large contribution to reducing the level of world poverty.[2]

The implicit assumption behind such initiatives is, of course, that the existing technology reduces poverty; but this assumption, with the exception of studies of the Grameen Bank (Hossain, 1984, 1988; Khandker, Khalily and Khan, 1993; Pitt and Khandker, 1996) has rarely been tested. The major comparative studies of microfinance, including the five listed in the opening paragraph, avoid calculations of poverty impact, often treating the fact that small loans are being repaid as proof that incomes have increased. As a consequence we remain rather ignorant about the poverty impact of existing microfinance schemes, and *a fortiori* about the possibilities for extending the 'standard technology' outside the experimental target groups so far reached and into the banking sector more generally. This paper reports on research designed to address this question. Having presented general evidence on impact (Section 6.2), it then offers evidence supporting the idea that there is a systematic positive relationship between impact and household income (Section 6.3) the position of which, however, appears to vary according to the design of the scheme. The implications of these findings for anti-poverty strategies are discussed in the concluding Section 6.4.

6.2 SCOPE, METHOD AND AGGREGATE FINDINGS ON IMPACT

Over 1991–93 we attempted to measure the financial performance and income impact of 13 microfinance institutions in seven countries, all poverty-reducing in intention (although, as shown by column 9, aimed at very diverse segments of the income distribution) and all, as depicted by Table 6.1, using slightly different combinations of design features to achieve this objective. Financial performance is measured by means of two alternative indicators: the proportion of loans more than six months in arrears (depicted in column 4) and the Subsidy Dependence Index,[3] which measures the extent to which interest rates would have to be raised to break even in an environment free of all subsidy (depicted in column 5). The two measures are highly correlated (Table 6.1): the cases with the lowest indices of subsidy dependence have the lowest arrears rates, and vice versa. Both of these measures may be taken as measures of financial (un)sustainability; the higher they are, the harder it is for the lender to continue in business without subsidy. If we divide the sample into the 'less financially sustainable' institutions with arrears rates above 20 percent and the 'more sustainable' institutions with arrears rates below 20 percent, it appears, as shown in columns 7 and 8 of the table, that financial sustainability correlates not only with the charging of market interest rates and the availability of savings facilities (as the 'Washington microfinance consensus' view cited above would predict) but also with frequency of loan collection and the existence or otherwise of material incentives to borrowers and staff of the lending agency to maximize the rate of repayment. It does not correlate with the tendency to lend to groups; we find both group and individual schemes in both the successful and the unsuccessful categories. All of these attributes are significantly greater for the 'high sustainability' group than for the 'low sustainability' group. Correlation, of course, does not imply causation, and it does not follow from the above that any of the design features mentioned can be proved to be a necessary condition for good financial performance.

We now turn to a preliminary consideration of impact. We calculated this by comparing the change in household income and other target variables in a random stratified sample of 100 borrowers with the change in that target variable in control group of 50 non-borrowers selected so as to have similar initial income, asset holdings and access to infrastructure to the borrower group.[4] As shown by the penultimate column of the table, all schemes had positive measured effects on income, dramatically so in the case of Indonesia BRI unit desas and Bolivia BancoSol. Average impact for 'more financially sustainable' schemes is higher than for 'less financially sustainable' schemes with higher arrears rates and levels of subsidy dependence, but this difference is not statistically significant. In addition, as will be noted from the last column of the table, average income impact for borrowers *below the poverty line* only is invariably modest, much lower than for borrowers as a whole. If this finding turns out to be robust it clearly has important implications for the ability of the microfinance instrument to reduce poverty. To gain a clearer picture of how poverty impact varies with income, let us now examine that relationship across schemes and between schemes.

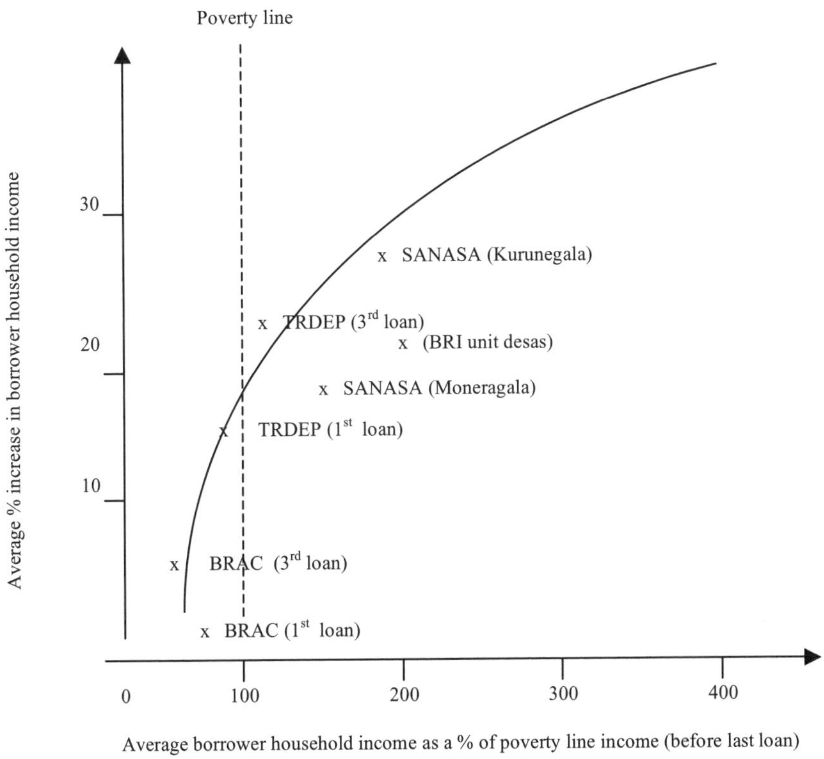

Figure 6.1 The relationship of the average income to average increase in household income since last loan: Comparison between schemes.
Source: Hulme and Mosley (1996, Vol. 1, p. 113).

Table 6.1 Overview of 13 microfinance institutions

	Number of borrowers (1992)	Real interest rates (%) (1992)	Subsidy Dependence Index (1988–92 average)	6-month arrears rate (1992)	Savings[b]	Frequency of loan collection[c]	Incentives to repay	Proportion of borrowers below poverty line (%)	Average increase in borrower income as % of control group: Whole sample	Individuals below poverty line only
Group A										
Bolivia BancoSol	51,000	45	135	0.6	V and C	M	1	29	270	101
Indonesia BRI unit desas	1,800,000	6	9	3.0	V	W	2	7	544	112
Indonesia BKK	499,000	60	32	2.1	V	W	2	38	216	110
Indonesia KURK	158,000	60	35	13.7	V	W	2	29		
Bangladesh Grameen Bank[e]	1,050,000	15	142	4.5	C	W	1	95+	131	126
Bangladesh BRAC	598,000	11	199	3.0	C	W	1	95+	143	134
Bangladesh TRDEP	25,000		199	0.0	No	W	1	90+	138	133
Sri Lanka PTCCs	702,000	11	226	4.0	V and C	M	1	52	157	123
Kenya KREP Juhudi	2,400	9	217	8.9	V and C	W	1	–	133	103
Average Group A	542,777	27.1	144.9	4.4					216.3	117.8

(*continued*)

Table 6.1 Overview of 13 microfinance institutions (*continued*)

	Number of borrowers (1992)	*Real interest rates (%) (1992)*	*Subsidy Dependence Index (1988–92 average)*	*6-month arrears rate (1992)*	*Savings*[b]	*Frequency of loan collection*[c]	*Incentives to repay*	*Proportion of borrowers below poverty line (%)*	*Average increase in borrower income as % of control group:*	
									Whole sample	*Individuals below poverty line only*
Group B										
India RRBs	12,000,000	3	133	42.0	V and C	A	0	44	202	133
Kenya KIE-ISP	1,700	–1	267	20.2	No	M	0	0	125	
Malawi Mudzi Fund	223	8	1,884	43.4	No	W	1	Vast majority	117	101
Malawi SACA	400,062	7	398	27.8	No	A	0	7	175	103
Average Group B	3,100,000	4.3	670.5	33.4					154.7	112.3

Notes

a t-statistic for difference 4.98** 2.83** 3.67** 2.14* 4.32** between sample means.

b Savings: V = voluntary savings, C = compulsory savings.

c Repayment intervals: M= monthly, W = weekly, A = annually.

d Incentives to repay: 0 = none, 1 = larger repeat loans only available if repayment performance satisfactory, 2 = as 1, plus staff pay and borrower interest rates related to repayment performance.

e The Grameen Bank was not studied by survey but the large literature on it was used extensively in our study.

*Significant at the 5% level; ** significant at the 1% level.

6.3 THE 'IMPACT CURVE'

Figure 6.1 and Figure 6.2 represent the measured relationship between borrower household income and loan impact on household income for two different populations. Figure 6.1 shows the relationship between average income level (measured as a percentage of the national poverty line) and average loan impact *across* institutions. In Figure 6.2 the relationship between income level and loan impact across borrowers *within* institutions is shown. In both cases the estimated relationship is a curve (henceforward referred to as the 'impact curve') sloping upward at a decreasing rate: formally, it is positive in income but negative in the square of income, as depicted by the regression equations of Table 6.2.[5] The regression coefficients on these terms are significant, except in the case of Malawi Mudzi Fund. In other words, higher-income households experience on average higher program impact than households below the poverty line, as already suggested by Table 6.1. For households *a long way* below the poverty line average loan impact is negative, although there are outliers from this trend, some of them depicted in Figure 6.1 and Figure 6.2 and discussed below. In addition, the slope coefficients for the different institutions differ: generally, as a consequence, the curves for the 'more financially sustainable' institutions (Bolivia BancoSol and Indonesia BKK/KURK) lie above the curves for the 'less financially sustainable' institutions (Kenya K-REP, Malawi SACA and Malawi Mudzi Fund),

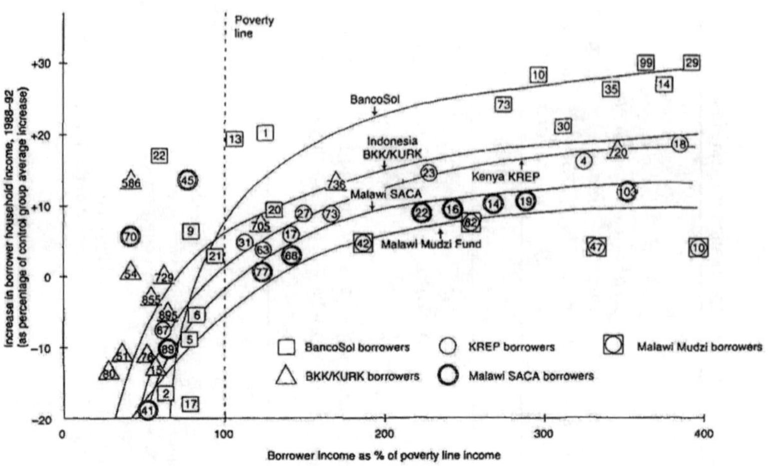

Figure 6.2 Loan impact in relation to borrower income: within-scheme data.

Source: Hulme and Mosley (1996, Vol. 1, p. 113).

Note: Only a few specimen data points, together with the regression line for each organization, are indicated. Full data arrays are available from the authors on request.

suggesting a higher average loan impact in the financially sustainable institutions. Again, this is consistent with the picture emerging from the penultimate column of Table 6.1.

Plausible reasons for the patterns revealed by Figure 6.1 and Figure 6.2 are not difficult to find. We believe that the upward slope of the impact curve reflects a tendency for the willingness to take risks and to invest in new technology to increase with income. The poor are probably more risk-averse.[6] Very poor borrowers, given the choice, tend to take out small, subsistence-protecting loans; these are seldom invested in new technology, fixed capital or even the hiring of labour but rather in working capital or, in a majority of cases, in protecting consumption standards.[7] As a consequence, loans to the very poor are not normally able to produce dramatic changes in borrower income: at these lower levels of income, there is also a greater risk that unlucky or improvident borrowers may be forced by their greater exposure to debt into selling assets which will permanently lower their income possibilities. By contrast, loans to higher income groups are more often used for 'promotional' activities (following the terminology of Dreze and Sen, 1990) such as the purchase of fixed capital and the hiring of labor from outside the borrower family. In addition, higher income households can commonly access larger loans because of their greater savings capacity and their ability to offer collateral and this widens the choice of investment opportunities to include 'lumpy' investments.

Likewise, there are good reasons why more financially sustainable financial institutions may have higher impact. As shown by Table 6.1, such institutions tend to charge relatively high rates of interest, which act as a screen to deter borrowers whose projects have relatively low rates of return; they tend to operate savings schemes, which provide a limited degree of insurance to protect repayments if projects fail to yield expected rates of return and serve to screen out prospective borrowers who lack financial discipline. They also tend to collect loan installments frequently on or close to the borrower's premises, which tends to deter borrowers with projects yielding low returns.

The impact curve represents only an underlying relationship for each institution, and a substantial part of the variation in loan use between borrowers cannot be explained by income; in other words there are significant outliers to all the impact curves represented on Figure 6.2. Particularly interesting among these outliers are those lying above the left-hand end of the impact curves, i.e. very poor households who, against the general pattern, achieved substantial increases in income from their loans. A preliminary analysis of these outliers suggests that they typically fell into the rather specialized category of *capital investments entailing a low increase in risk*, for example, minor irrigation (Malawi SACA # 70), high-yielding seeds in rain sufficient areas (Indonesia BKK # 586) and replacement of existing handicrafts-making equipment (Bolivia BancoSol # 22) The existence of such investment opportunities is dependent on personal circumstances and on the specific economic environment in which an institution is operating.

Table 6.2 Microenterprise finance institutions: Determinations of impact

Institution (size of borrower sample in brackets)	*Financial performance data for institution:*		*Impact data for borrower sample:*				
			a) Mean loan impact per borrower[c]	*b) Regression coefficients on impact*[d] *of:*			
	SDI[3]	*Arrears rate*[b]		*Constant*	*Borrower income*	*Borrower income squared*	r^2
Bolivia: BancoSol (48)	135	1	270	–15.12* (2.80)	0.20** (2.80)	–0.00027 (1.63)	0.44
Indonesia: BKK/KURK (280)	32	2	216	–30.24** (5.47)	0.55** (5.42)	–0.0018** (4.57)	0.52
Kenya: Rural Enterprise Programme (145)	217	9	133	–37.6** (5.01)	0.58** (4.68)	–0.0019** (4.17)	0.38
Malawi: Small holder Agricultural Credit Administration (140)	398	27	175	–39.5** (3.46)	0.53** (4.01)	–0.0015** (2.79)	0.67
Malawi: Mudzi Fund (135)	1,884	43	125	–69.8* (2.11)	1.29 (1.46)	–0.006 (0.80)	0.21

Notes

a The Subsidy Dependence Index (see Yaron (1991) and endnote 3) is a measure of the percentage by which the lending institution's interest rate would have to be raised to cover its costs.

b Percentage of borrowers more than six months in arrears on final day of year specified.

c Change in income of borrower household as percentage of change in income of a control group of non-borrowers living in same area and having similar income, assets, and access to infrastructure as the sampled borrower group. (See note d for fuller details.)

d Ordinary least-squares analysis; the number of observations is as specified in first column. Dependent variable if impact of lending on borrower's income as specified in note c. Figures in brackets below coefficients are Student's t-statistics.

e Initial income (as measured before loan intervention).

* Significant at the 5% level; ** significant at the 1% level

Source: Hulme and Mosley (1996, Table 8.1, p. 181), and field survey data described therein.

6.4 IMPLICATIONS FOR POLICY AND INSTITUTIONAL DESIGN

The findings reported above, consistent though they appear to be with intuition, urgently need to be complemented by research for institutions and periods other than those we have surveyed before it is possible to claim that what we have described as the 'impact curve' represents a general tendency. Nonetheless, we believe that there is sufficient material in the findings themselves to motivate both encouragement and a warning. Because the impact curves for financially sustainable institutions lie above those for non-sustainable institutions, it may be that the adoption by micro-finance institutions of those design features which Table 6.1 suggests are significantly associated with good financial performance (market interest rates, savings and insurance facilities, intensive collection of loan installments and incentives to repay) will increase poverty impact as well as financial sustainability. 'May be' are the operative words: the adoption of the package described has indeed worked well in the reform of some of the institutions discussed here, in particular the Bank Rakyat Indonesia unit desa (village unit) schemes (see Pattern and Rosengard, 1991). But it has also failed to work in other cases, such as the Malawi Mudzi Fund's attempt to introduce Grameen Bank principles into a land-scarce, labor-rich area of Africa (Hulme and Mosley, 1996, ch. 16). Nonetheless, it is encouraging that the impact curve, which in the short term appears as a tradeoff between poverty impact and overall loan impact, can in some cases be shifted. As our Bolivian, Indonesian, Bangladeshi and Sri Lankan institutions (Hulme and Mosley, 1996, ch. 16) demonstrate, microfinance institutions do learn from their field experience how to operate more effectively. Other design features tried as yet only on an experimental basis, such as flexible repayment patterns on consumption loans and interest rates inversely related to loan size, may also increase the average rate of return on loans to the very poor and thereby move the tradeoff upward.

The patterns revealed by Figure 6.1 and Figure 6.2 also contain their own warning. If it is indeed the case that average loan impacts diminish with income and approach, if they do not fall below zero at very low levels of income, it follows that attempts to scale up credit-based solutions to rural poverty of the type described at the beginning of this article are likely, at the present state of knowledge, to hit rapidly diminishing returns. Several of the more thoughtful recent contributions to the microcredit literature, in particular Montgomery (1996) and Rutherford (1996) emphasize that a different model of lending to the poorest may be required from that implied by Table 6.1, focused on the provision of savings facilities, simple insurance facilities (e.g., against drought) and small consumption loans with flexible repayment periods. Although this model would almost certainly achieve a financial product better matched to the needs of the poorest in most areas,[8] it would not necessarily increase *short-term impact*, in terms of the productivity of the asset which the loan finances. It may be best to think in terms of a sequence in which the very poor, by borrowing for consumption, are able to reduce gradually their income-vulnerability and thereby get themselves into a position where they can contemplate riskier investments in working capital, the hiring of extra-family labor, and ultimately fixed capital. Such sequences might permit the poorest to overcome successively the barriers of self-exclusion, social exclusion and institutional exclusion that currently block their access to microenterprise loans (Hulme and Mosley, 1996, ch. 5). But such sequences take time to work successfully, and involve a lengthy process of learning from experience and from error. The process is not readily compatible with targetry such as 'reaching 100 million of the world's poorest families … with microcredit for self-employment by 2005.'

Notes

1 Our main focus in this paper is the impact of loans for microenterprise. Issues relating to more broadly based microfinancial service approaches (voluntary savings, insurance, consumption and production loans) are discussed in Hulme and Mosley (1996, chaps. 5 and 9).

2 The draft declaration for the Microcredit Summit (November 2 1996) states that:
The time has come to convene the people and organizations necessary to launch a global movement to reach 100 million of the world's poorest families, especially the women of those families, with microcredit for self-employment by 2005.
More radically still, Joanne Salop, the World Bank's Chief Economist for South Asia, at a World Bank-sponsored conference in Dhaka, according to a report in the Dhaka *Financial Express* for March 20 1995, appreciated credit programs for the poor being run by a Grameen Bank and some NGOs. She reasoned as follows: if the average cost for the Grameen Bank to bring one person up above the poverty line is only the equivalent of US$10 (as may be inferred from Khandker, Khalily and Khan, 1993) would it not be possible to eradicate world poverty altogether by applying the same Grameen Bank approach to the billion people currently below the poverty line?

3 The formula for the Subsidy Dependence Index (SDI) of a financial institution, as originally devised by Yaron (1991) is:

$$SDI = \frac{A(m-c)+(Em-P)+K}{Ln}$$

Where
A = value of institution borrowed funds outstanding
m = interest rate the institution would be assumed to pay for borrowed funds on the open market, i.e. if all access to concessional funds were eliminated
c = rate of interest paid by the institution on its average borrowed funds outstanding
E = average annual equity
P = reported annual profit (adjusted for loan loss provision)
K = value of non-interest subsidies received by the institution
L = value of institution's outstanding loan portfolio
n = institution's average on-lending interest rate.

4 Data on net household income and other target variables were obtained from a pre-coded questionnaire and from semi-structured interviews with borrowers, lenders and key informants. Questions on income and other dimensions of the impact were repeated over 1991–93, so that the income impact data for 1988–92 presented in Table 6.2 and Figure 6.2 contain some dependence on memory recall (for 1988–90 only); but it was often possible to cross-check the data for this period through recourse to baseline surveys conducted by the sampled organizations. The questionnaires were administered by trained enumerators in the language most appropriate for each country or region. An English language 'ideal type' of the questionnaire is reproduced in Hulme and Mosley (1996, Vol.2, pp. 409–31). For each institution we targeted 100 microenterprise borrowers for questionnaire completion: 50 borrowers who had recently completed their first microenterprise loan and 50 borrowers who had recently completed their third loan. For these two subsamples borrowers were selected randomly in one region in which the economic environment was judged to be above the national average (50 percent of sample) and a different region judged to have an economic environment below the national average (50 percent of sample). The impacts measured by this method were compared against the changes in a control group of 50 non-borrowers selected so as to have similar initial income, asset holdings, and access to infrastructure to the borrower

group; the control sample was also selected to have similar gender and educational structure to the control group. Wherever possible we selected the control group, at random, from households that had been approved for a loan from the institution under study but who had not yet received the loan. For full details of each sample see the case study chapters in Hulme and Mosley (1996, Vol.2).

5 Splitting of the samples into borrower groups specialized by sector (traders, manufacturers, other services, etc.) did not in general produce significant intersectoral differences in average impact or in the slope coefficients (columns 6 and 7 of Table 6.2). There is one exception. In the one case where an institution had significant numbers of both agricultural and non-agricultural borrowers (Indonesia BKK/KURK) both the intercept term and the slope coefficient are lower for the sample of agricultural than for the sample of non-agricultural borrowers. The estimated subsample equations are shown in the Appendix in Table 6.A.1. The difference between the subsample regression coefficients on borrower income is significant at the 5 percent level.

6 For convincing expositions of this hypothesis see Lipton (1968) and Weeks (1971), but see also Binswanger and Sillers (1983) for the contrary view.

7 Mahajan and Ramola, 1996 (p. 216) find that across a range of Indian financial institutions providing credit to the poor 'consumption credit needs are in the range of two-thirds of total credit needs'.

8 It is to be emphasized that those institutions which offer consumption loans to the very poor – Sri Lanka SANASA, Indonesia KURK and Kenya K-Rep Juhudi – have repayment rates on those consumption loans not inferior to (in fact slightly higher than) repayment rates on the loan portfolio as a whole. See Mosley (1996).

References

Binswanger, H. and Sillers, D. (1983) Risk aversion and credit constraints in farmers' decision making: a reinterpretation. *Journal of Development Studies* 20, 5–21.

Christen, R., Rhyne, E. and Vogel, R. (1994) *Maximizing the Outreach of Microenterprise Finance: The Emerging Lessons of Successful Programs.* USAID, Washington, DC.

Dreze, J. and Sen, A. K. (1990) *Hunger and Public Action*, Oxford University Press, Oxford.

Hossain, M. (1984) Credit for the rural poor: The experience of the Grameen Bank of Bangladesh. Bangladesh Institute of Development Studies, Dhaka.

———— (1988) Credit for alleviation of rural poverty: The Grameen Bank of Bangladesh, International Food Policy Research Institute Research Report 65, Washington, DC. February.

Hulme, D. and Mosley, P. (1996) *Finance Against Poverty: Effective Institutions for Lending to Small Farmers and Microenterprises in Developing Countries*, 2 Vols, Routledge, London.

Khandker, S., Khalily, B. and Khan, Z. (1993) Grameen Bank: what do we know? Unpublished paper.

Lipton, M. (1968) The theory of the optimizing peasant. *Journal of Development Studies* 4, 327–51.

Mahajan, V. and Ramola, B. G. (1996) Financial services for the rural poor and women in India: access and sustainability. *Journal of International Development* 8, (March–April), 211–16.

Montgometry, R. (1996) Disciplining or protecting the poor? Avoiding the social costs of peer pressure in micro-credit schemes. *Journal of International Development* 8. (March–April), 289–305.

Mosley, P. (1996) Financial sustainability, targeting the poorest, and income impact:

are there trade-offs for micro-finance institutions? *World Bank Focus Note*, No.5 (December).

Otero, M. and Rhyne, E. (1994) *The New World of Microenterprise Finance.* Intermediate Technology Publications, London.

Pattern, R. H. and Rosengard, J. (1991) *Progress with Profits: The Development of Rural Banking in Indonesia.* The International Centre for Economic Growth, San Francisco.

Pitt, M. and Khandker, S. (1996) *Household and Intrahousehold Impact of the Grameen Bank and Similar Targeted Programs in Bangladesh*, World Bank Discussion Paper 320. World Bank, Washington, DC.

Remenyi, J. (1991) *Where Credit is Due: Income-generating Programmes for the Poor in Developing Countries*, Intermediate Technology Publications, London.

Robinson, M. (1996) Some key questions on finance and poverty. *Journal of International Development* 8, (March–April), 153–61.

Roglay, B. (1996) Micro-finance evangelism, 'destitute women' and the hard selling of a new anti-poverty formula. *Development in Practice* 6, (May), 100–2.

Rutherford, S. (1996) Learning from the urban informal sector. Paper presented at an international workshop on Poverty and Finance in Bangladesh. IDPAA and Proshika, Dhaka.

Weeks, J. (1971) Uncertainty, risk and wealth and income distribution in peasant agriculture. *Journal of Development Studies* 8, 28–36.

Yaron, J. (1991) *Successful Rural Finance Institutions.* Agricultural Policies Department, World Bank, Washington, DC.

APPENDIX 6.A

Table 6.A.1 Subsample regression coefficients

Regression coefficients on impact of:				r^2
Constant	*Borrower income*	*Borrower income squared*		
Non-agricultural borrowers	−16.2	0.59**	−0.0017	0.56
Agricultural borrowers	−32.5	0.40*	−0.0019	0.44

Reprinted from World Development, 26 (5), pp. 783–90, 1998.

7

PROGRAMS FOR THE POOREST

Learning from the IGVGD program in Bangladesh

Imran Matin and David Hulme[1]

7.1 INTRODUCTION

Programs and policies to assist poor people and overcome deprivation are underpinned, either implicitly or explicitly, by ideas about 'who' is poor and 'why' they are poor. Such ideas have deep historical roots but they are also shaped by the dominant discourses of their time and by the emerging knowledge base about the causes of poverty and how these can be tackled.

In recent years there have been three significant advances in the ideas that inform poverty reduction policies and programs. First, is the recognition that the poor are not a homogeneous group, such as small farmers or landless people, but have many different characteristics and thus will need different forms of assistance. This recognition was initially associated with regard to the poverty that women experience but has also led to attempts to identify and assist the poorest (Lipton, 1988; Sen & Begum, 1998) and the chronically poor (Hulme *et al.*, 2001). Second, the 'promotion approaches are best' versus the 'protection approaches are best' argument is increasingly recognized as sterile. It is now clear that effective poverty reduction requires both a promotional component (that increases the incomes, productivity or employment prospects of poor people) and a protectional component (that reduces the vulnerability of the poor). The third significant advance is the understanding that the agency of poor people has to be seen as central to the goal of poverty reduction: policies and programs that seek to decree exactly what poor people are to do are likely to fail because they are infeasible to implement and show a fundamental misconception of what poverty reduction is about.

In this paper we explore these issues through an analysis of an innovative program that has sought to reach the country's poorest people – the Bangladesh Rural Advancement Committee's (BRAC) Income Generation for Vulnerable Group Development (IGVGD) Program. This program seeks to extend the outreach of poverty reduction initiatives beyond what are referred to in Bangladesh as the 'moderate poor' to the 'hardcore poor': those who experience the deepest deprivations and are the least likely to be able to overcome their poverty and/or give their children childhoods that will allow them to escape from poverty. This paper uses information from a range of previous studies and from a primary study of three BRAC village organizations (VOs) that involved a survey of all 97 active members, extended focus group discussions and detailed interviews with key informants.[2] Section 7.2 presents the analytical framework for the case study. The following section describes the history of the IGVGD Program and its performance. In Section 7.4 we explore the IGVGD in practice looking at 'how' IGVGD targeting works, 'why' it diverges from what was planned and 'who' among the poorest cannot access the IGVGD. The final sections examine the ways in which BRAC is attempting to apply the lessons of IGVGD to design its latest program and present a set of conclusions.

7.2 ANALYTICAL FRAMEWORK

The key elements of the analytical framework used in this paper concern the identification and disaggregation of the poor, the relative roles of protection and promotion in poverty reduction and the concept of the implementation gap between policies and practices.

(a) Poverty, chronic poverty and poverty dynamics

Theories about poverty have become increasingly sophisticated over the last 20 years. At their heart is the notion that poverty occurs when people experience some form of severe deprivation. The nature of those deprivations remains, however, a keenly debated topic. The narrow materialist conceptualizations of poverty as an inability to meet minimum income requirements or basic needs (food, shelter, water and clothing), which have dominated empirical studies and program design, have been challenged recently by more holistic views. Many of these multidimensional approaches have been stimulated by the idea of human capabilities, and argue that materialist conceptualizations conflate the means of wellbeing with the ends (Sen, 1999). There is now a set of competing 'lists' of human development (Alkire, 2002) identifying the differing dimensions of the good life and deprivation. In the last few years, even these multidimensional approaches have come under attack and it has been argued that subjective appreciations of poverty are required in which the poor themselves identify the forms of deprivation that they believe to be poverty. Despite these conceptual advances, most past practice of poverty reduction has been, and much contemporary practice is, based on the narrow materialist conceptualization. The task of poverty reduction is seen as ensuring that a household meets its minimum material or physiological needs. From this materialist perspective a household's inability to meet such needs is viewed as being due to either:

i having a stable income that is below the appropriate income, consumption or expenditure poverty line, or
ii a sudden shock that causes a household's income, consumption or expenditure to drop below the poverty line.

In the former case, the policy prescription has often been for a single intervention that raises the productivity or earnings of the household so that the household 'escapes' from poverty. This is the story that has been commonly associated with microcredit with the claim that once a poor woman has access to a loan for micro-enterprise her income will increase, because of the high returns on her investment, and her household will become nonpoor.[3] Poverty reduction, according to this idea, may be visualized as a 'one-step' process that is irreversible (Figure 7.1). In the latter case, an unexpected shock, the practice has been to view the household as suffering a temporary decline in income or access to food. At the simplest level of analysis, this is overcome by a grant to the household (usually of food but sometimes in cash) so that the temporary shortfall is overcome and the household returns to its previous level of income and material wellbeing (Figure 7.2). Such ideas make program design relatively simple and lie behind many poverty reduction initiatives. Unfortunately, they often fail to meet the needs of poor people.

The multidimensional approaches encourage more complex program designs (multisectoral and interorganizational partnerships), that seek to help poor people not only meet minimum material needs but also access health, education and other services. Subjective approaches take this even further and posit that program design, management and assessment should be placed as much as possible in the hands of poor people so that they not only get the goods and services that they need but are also empowered in social and political terms.

More elaborate understandings of poverty have not only expanded the number of dimensions that may be considered but have also pointed out that poverty needs to be seen in dynamic terms. These have challenged the assumptions that poor people have steady incomes that are low and/or occasionally exposed to shocks. Empirical work in many parts of the world has pointed out that the incomes of the poor fluctuate all of the time in ways that are only partly predictable. Many people, perhaps most in some areas, experience transient poverty as their incomes and expenditure rise and fall depending on a host of factors – the climate, seasonality, crop prices, relationships with landlords, access to work in urban areas or remittances, health status, paying for funerals and weddings and other factors. Such an understanding makes poverty reduction more complex as different forms of support may be needed for different households. At the very least it suggests that assisting households to smooth their incomes, and thus reduce the severity of deprivation that is associated with deep troughs in income, should be pursued. This applies to the occasionally poor and churning poor (see Hulme & Shepherd, 2003)

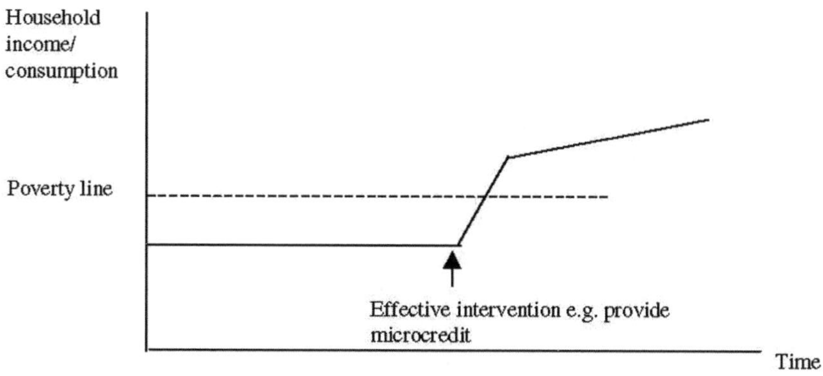

Figure 7.1 Poverty reduction as a 'one-step' increase in household income.

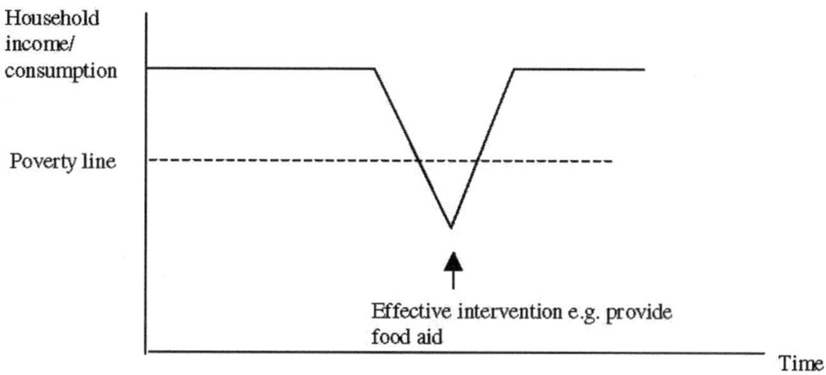

Figure 7.2 Poverty reduction as a 'one-off' grant returning household income to previous levels.

to stop their income from dipping under the poverty line, and to the chronic poor to reduce the level that their income falls below the poverty line. It also makes it important for program designers to try to understand the poverty dynamics of those they seek to help.

Another way in which the practice of poverty reduction has developed in recent years has been through attempts to identify and assist those who experience the greatest deprivations. These have been variously described as the poorest, the poorest of the poor, the ultra poor, the hardcore poor, the destitute, the extreme poor, the highly dependent poor and, in this volume, the chronic poor. While 'common sense' might suggest that these are all describing the same group of people a number of different criteria are used to identify these groups – the severity of poverty, the duration of poverty and the number of dimensions of poverty that are experienced (for a full discussion see Hulme *et al.*, 2001). Commonly it is assumed that those who experience the severest poverty are also the long-term poor, but this is not necessarily the case. Some who are deeply income poor at a moment in time have experienced a severe shock but they can rapidly recover from this because of the human and social capital that they possess. Conversely, some who are only a little below the income poverty line may stay there throughout their lives as they are adversely incorporated, suffer other forms of deprivation intensely, and lack an asset base that would permit them to escape poverty.

In Bangladesh, the main focus has been on dividing the poor into the moderate and hardcore poor through their consumption levels (see later). It is commonly assumed that the hardcore poor are also chronically poor. In this paper, we make this assumption. This is based on qualitative work that we have conducted over the years and on materials in Section 7.3. While such an assumption may be reasonable for Bangladesh and India (Mehta & Shah, 2001, 2003) it would be inappropriate in other contexts.

(b) Livelihood protection and livelihood promotion

Dreze and Sen (1989, pp. 60–1) distinguish two different, but related, goals and means for poverty reduction – protection which seeks to prevent a decline in living standards (and especially hunger and starvation), and promotion which aims to eliminate deprivation (commonly by raising low incomes). Devereux (2001) has extended these into the concepts of livelihood protection and livelihood promotion. Protection and promotion are closely interlinked. Effective livelihood protection makes livelihood promotion more likely, as a household will have the confidence to take on more risky, higher return economic activities so that income can be raised. Successful promotion raises the earnings and assets of a household so that there are more resources available for protection.

Throughout the 1980s and 1990s there was a global shift away from protectional approaches to poverty reduction and toward promotional approaches and 'workfare' (Peck, 2001). This is associated with the ascendancy of neoliberal ideas which emphasize the need for higher levels of aggregate economic production and the capping of public expenditure, and warn of the moral hazard of welfare dependency. This shift has particular relevance to understanding public action in Bangladesh where the large nongovernmental organization (NGO) sector has moved from its early operational focus on welfare and social protection to an emphasis on microenterprise development, self-employment and income generation.

(c) Program plans and program practice: the implementation gap

Studies of program plans and practice around the world have shown that commonly there are large differences between what is planned and what happens in the field. These 'implementation gaps' are often very great in developing countries (Grindle, 1980; Turner & Hulme, 1997). They arise for many reasons – a lack of administrative capacity, manipulation by more powerful individuals and social groups to capture benefits, local cultural contexts and the pursuit of organizational needs over program goals. In the IGVGD program, as in most programs in Bangladesh (Wood, 1994), what happens during implementation is often very different from what is described in the official 'operations manual.' While this implementation gap often has negative consequences in terms of outcomes, and is associated with the 'elite capture' of resources for poverty reduction, it can also have a positive side. It may occur because an inappropriate plan is modified to reflect local conditions or because the program managers have gained new knowledge during implementation and have refined operations. It can even occur because of the personal agency of the poor, acquiring resources from whatever programs they can and then fitting these resources into their livelihood portfolios. Poor people can convert microenterprise loans into urgently needed food or school fees (Hulme & Mosley, 1996) or, conversely, they can substitute old age pensions for agricultural loans (Lund, 2002). Poor households are engaged in complex sets of economic and social activities to meet their present needs and the futures to which they aspire. Even the poorest have agency!

7.3 POVERTY, POVERTY DYNAMICS AND TARGETING POVERTY REDUCTION PROGRAMS IN BANGLADESH

(a) Poverty in Bangladesh

Bangladesh is a country with high levels of deprivation, but things have been improving. Income poverty has declined from an estimated 58 percent of the population in 1983–84 to just under 50 percent in 2000 (World Bank, 2001). However, this remains a high figure as it means that 65 million people fall under the official upper poverty line. Around 34 percent of the population fall below the lower poverty line. Commonly in Bangladesh those falling between the upper and lower poverty lines are termed the 'moderate poor,' while those below the lower poverty line are termed the 'hardcore poor.' The conceptualization behind the hardcore poor is that they experience extreme poverty and that, because of their lack of opportunities for upward mobility, their poverty lasts a long time or throughout their entire life. It is the chronic poor that are the focus of this paper.

The considerable progress in human development during the 1990s (primary school enrollment, reduction of gender gaps, reductions in infant and maternal mortality) has not been matched by an equivalent decline in income poverty (Sen, 2001). While the incidence of poverty in rural areas remains higher than in urban areas there has been a qualitative change in the economic environment of the rural poor. A majority of villages are now linked to urban centers by all-weather infrastructure allowing a higher degree of mobility and a greater ability to make commuting to work or migration a component of a household's livelihood strategy.

Social attitudes toward women's economic roles have changed in the direction of acceptance of women working. Nevertheless, the burden of poverty still remains disproportionately high on women in terms of nutritional intake, access to gainful employment, wage rate, and access to maternal health care. Female headed households experience a higher incidence of poverty relative to male headed households. In addition, households dependent on female earners are poorer than households who are dependent on male earners (Rahman & Razzaque, 1998).

(b) Poverty dynamics

Quantitative research on poverty dynamics is relatively rare in Bangladesh compared to the wealth of cross-sectional studies and comparisons of poverty trends.[4] There is evidence however, that despite the modest decline in income poverty, there have been some positive shifts in the dynamics of poverty. There has been a significant decline in certain manifestations of extreme poverty: the intensity of seasonal deprivations has reduced considerably; the percentage of the population going without three meals a day has lowered substantially; access to basic clothing has become almost universal; and, the proportion of the population living in houses vulnerable to adverse weather conditions has gone down (Rahman & Razzaque, 1998). Improvements have not been spread uniformly across the poor and, in particular, those living in the flood prone areas beside major rivers have benefited little from poverty reduction. Persistent extreme poverty in these areas has been found to be the result of geographical factors rather than household characteristics. The functionally landless also remain poor (World Bank, 1998). Rahman and Razzaque (1998) have argued that the net result of the emerging poverty dynamics on the poor has been the shift from being vulnerable to income erosions to being more resilient to income shocks. The first half of the 1990s pointed to fluctuating incomes faced by the poor resulting in their movements in and out and within the poverty line. The experience in the latter half of the decade indicated improvements in the coping capacities of the poor, highlighted by the rapid recovery from the debilitating effects of the 1998 floods. The main survey that has attempted to examine poverty dynamics at the household level is that of Hossain *et al.* (2000). This was based upon the subjective assessment of poverty by a carefully selected sample of 1,245 rural households. In 1990 these households assessed their economic position for the previous year (as extremely poor, moderate poor, self-reliant or solvent). They were resurveyed in 1995, when 1,166 were traced, and asked to assess their status in the previous year (Table 7.1). Table 7.2 provides a transition matrix revealing the patterns of mobility reported by this sample. The results confirm the significant reduction in levels of poverty that was reported in the official poverty estimates, although they place the 1989 level at the high rate of 73.1 percent. The poverty figure reported for 1994, 50.1 percent, is very close to that produced by the objective estimates.

Table 7.1 Mobility of households by self-categorization of household's economic position, 1989 and 1994

	Self-categorization (1995 survey)					
Self-categorization (1990 survey)	*Extremely poor*	*Moderately poor*	*Self-reliant*	*Solvent*	*Total*	*Percent*
Extremely poor	146	76	38	13	273	23.4
Moderately poor	69	254	202	55	580	49.7
Self-reliant	1	28	111	60	200	17.2
Solvent	1	9	9	94	119	10.2
Total	217	367	360	222	1166	100
Percentage	18.6	31.5	30.9	19.0	100	

Source: Hossain et al. (2000).

Table 7.2 Downward mobility by self-categorization of households, 1989–94

Self-categorization (1989)	*Percentage of group in extreme poverty in 1994*	*Percentage of group in extreme or moderate poverty in 1994*
Extremely poor	53.5	81.3
Moderately poor	11.9	55.7
Self-reliant	0.5	14.5
Solvent	0.8	8.4

Source: Computed from Hossain et al. (2000).

A number of interesting points emerge from this matrix. First, the number of households that were poor in both 1989 and 1994 (these are chronically poor households)[5] is high at 46.7 percent of the sample. Second, while the reduction in overall poverty levels indicates that in aggregate upward mobility has exceeded downward mobility there are considerable differences in the mobility patterns of different groups. Most significant is the lower upward mobility of the extremely poor compared to the poor. By 1994 only 18.7 percent of those reported as extremely poor in 1989 had 'graduated' out of poverty: for the moderately poor in 1989 the comparative figure was 44.3 percent. This suggests that the probability of a poor household graduating out of poverty in the five year period was almost 2.5 times greater than an extremely poor household. For Bangladesh, it thus appears likely that the overlap between those experiencing extreme poverty at a moment in time and those who remain poor for extended periods of time is relatively high. Third, when patterns of downward mobility are examined (Table 7.2) then the relative propensity of those who are poor to remain poor becomes clear. Only a negligible percentage of the self-reliant and the solvent dropped into extreme poverty while the proportion of them sliding into moderate poverty averaged out at only 11.6 percent over the five years.

(c) Targeted poverty reduction programs in Bangladesh

There are numerous poverty reduction programs in Bangladesh and it is not feasible to review all of them here. What must be noted, however, is that there is a broad consensus that even well respected programs generally fail to reach the chronic poor. This was demonstrated in detail by Rahman and Hossain (1995) and has been a common finding about government and NGO activities throughout the 1990s. While government failure to reach the poorest should come as no surprise, given the problems that the state encounters in service delivery in Bangladesh (Landell Mills, 2002), the problems that NGOs have encountered, despite their commitment to assisting the poorest, have been greater than expected. The Dutch aid agency NOVIB reported in the mid-1990s that 'the NGOs have not yet taken a pro extreme poor approach to poverty alleviation' (NOVIB Report, 1996). A nationally representative survey found that 41 percent of eligible, poor households did not have any contact with the NGOs operating in their localities (Husain, 1998). While it is well documented that NGO microfinance programs do not reach the hardcore poor and may actively exclude them (Hashemi, 1997; Hulme & Mosley, 1996; Rahman & Razzaque, 1998), Rahman and Razzaque (2000) have found that almost three-quarters of the hardcore poor have never received social development services from NGOs. Indeed, they find that the percentage of households who do not receive the nonfinancial services provided by NGOs is almost the same between the hardcore poor and the nonpoor. They argue that the main reason for this lies in the fact that most NGOs offering social development services, such as essential health or basic education, do so through the structures which deliver microfinance. By design, these tend to exclude the hardcore poor.

Microfinance, the mainstay of most NGO programs in Bangladesh, though an effective poverty alleviating instrument, is not suitable for all categories of the poor. For those trapped in chronic food insecurity with no asset base to protect themselves from the myriad web of shocks, microfinance can be ineffective and sometimes counterproductive. But the idea of microcredit has dominated thinking on poverty reduction in the country. Much good has come of such a common rallying point. It has raised awareness of the role that poor people's own agency plays in development, has reduced dependence on donor funding and provided models for mass outreach to millions of poor people. The flip side of the coin however is that such a powerful idea has encouraged programs that treat the poor as a homogeneous group of self-employed microentrepreneurs who need to raise the profitability of their businesses.[6]

The dominant approach to poverty reduction targeted at the chronic poor has been food transfer which although vital only provides short-term food security. These programs are usually time bound and once over, the overall livelihood situation and prospects of those receiving them change little. Is it possible to package and sequence interventions so that those receiving food transfers can get to a more solid footing to take on the challenge of improving their lot? Can a process be initiated that will enable these people to gradually take on the challenge of using more market based instruments, such as microfinance?

7.4 THE IGVGD PROGRAM[7]

(a) Program evolution and description

In the wake of the 1974 famine in Bangladesh the United Nation's World Food Program (WFP) initiated the Vulnerable Group Feeding (VGF) Program. This sought to reduce the chronic food insecurity of millions of extremely poor households by providing them with 31.25 kg of wheat each month for a two-year period. It is a classic livelihood protection scheme. The WFP maps food insecurity at the upazilla level (this is an administrative unit that on average encompasses about 275,000 people) and allocates VGF cards to those upazillas where insecurity is highest. The VGF cards are then allocated to specific households by local government. They are intended to go to the most vulnerable – the poorest and female headed households.

In 1985 BRAC approached WFP to become a partner with the VGF Program. There was an appreciation, at least in some parts of this NGO, that its microfinance programs were unlikely to meet the needs of the extreme poor and it was seeking an 'entry point' to involve the poorest.[8] BRAC understood that the wheat donations provided a 'breathing space' for the poorest, and created a strong incentive for them to interact with development agencies, but it doubted the capacity of such handouts to remove chronic poverty. The organization sought to combine food relief with its skills training program, to create a basis for enhanced household income in the future. In addition, participating households were to make compulsory savings of 25 taka[9] per month during the period of their food relief to build up a lump sum for investment.

WFP and BRAC agreed to pilot this experimental program and to focus training on poultry and vegetable production for 750 female VGF cardholders. At the end of the 24-month program the women were encouraged to 'graduate' by joining BRAC's VOs[10] and becoming eligible for access to microcredit, health care, legal awareness and other BRAC services. In effect, it was developing a 'two-step' model of poverty reduction for the hardcore poor (Figure 7.3).

The results of this pilot program were impressive. A BRAC study found that the women's income increased significantly and that this additional income exceeded the value of the wheat donations. Around 80 percent of the women had entered BRAC's Rural Development Program (RDP) and were accessing microcredit and social development services. This compared more than favorably with assessments of the VGF which had found that many participants were no better off when they left the VGF than when they had joined. The experiment had shown that inputs aimed at livelihood protection could be used to initiate livelihood promotion. As a consequence, in 1987 the government and WFP transformed the VGF Program,

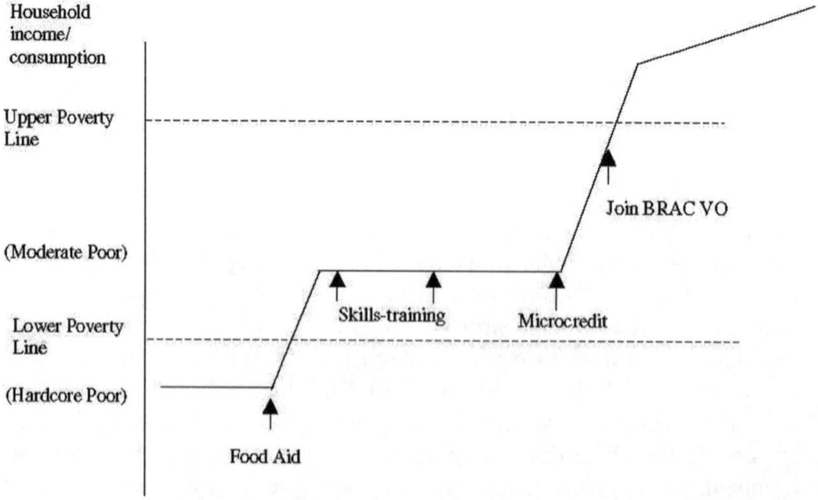

Figure 7.3 The IGVGD model: Poverty-reduction as a 'two-step' process of livelihood protection and livelihood promotion.

into the Vulnerable Group Development, VGD Program. They also reached an agreement with BRAC to expand the pilot scheme into the IGVGD Program and numbers have grown significantly since then. More than 1.2 million households had passed through the program by 2000 and around 200,000 VGD cardholders are active participants at any time.

This expansion had not led to complacency and the IGVGD has constantly evolved (see Matin, 2002). For example, in 1989, field staff pointed out that during their IGVGD membership period many women could only buy and raise a single chicken at a time because of a lack of capital. Why not provide loans to program recipients as soon as they had completed training? This led to the addition of a third element to the IGVGD – microcredit – with the aim of speeding up the processes of livelihood promotion and graduation to BRAC's programs for the moderate poor. Subsequently, in their first year IGVGD participants were provided with a loan of 1,000 taka and a loan of 2,000 taka was accessed in the second year.

This three-pronged approach (food grant, skills training and microcredit) has been the basis of IGVGD throughout the 1990s (Appendix 7.A summarizes the operational cycle of IGVGD for 1999–2000). The composition of the package has changed, however. The livelihood promotion component has been increased, and by the late 1990s IGVGD participants could get loans of 2,500 taka in year one and 5,000 taka in year two. By contrast, the social protection component has been reduced with WFP reducing the monthly ration from 31.25 kg to 30.00 kg and the period of entitlement from 24 to 18 months. This is a reduction of 30 percent per household, but it has meant that the IGVGD can be offered to more households in each cycle.

The selection of VGD cardholders is done by locally elected representatives and subsequently vetted by an upazilla level committee.[11] Recipients should meet three criteria: be widowed or abandoned female heads of household; households owning less than 0.5 acres of land; and, earnings of less than 300 taka (US$6 in 2000) per month.

In 1999–2000 a further change was made and the IGVGD program (for the hardcore poor) was merged with the RDP (for all the poor but, as discussed earlier mainly the moderate poor). Separate accounts are kept for the IGVGD and RDP but both sets of participants sit at the same weekly VO meeting with BRAC field officers. BRAC took this step to 'integrate' VGD women with RDP women to reduce the social isolation of the poorest, stop them from being branded as a separate category and to build their confidence and self-respect. It must also be noted that it offered administrative efficiencies for BRAC.

(b) IGVGD performance

Reviews of the IGVGD have been favorable and a study commissioned by the WFP[12] found evidence that the program reached the very poor, that the economic position of IGVGD recipient households improved and that access to NGO microfinance services was greatly enhanced. Hashemi's (2001) comparison of the 1994 WFP baseline survey with key poverty indicators for rural Bangladesh (Figure 7.4) found that IGVGD members had significantly higher levels of absolute landlessness, functional landlessness (owning less than half an acre of land), owning two sarees or less and lacking winter clothing than the 'hardcore poor' identified by Rahman and Hossain (1995). While 8 percent of rural households and around 10 percent of hardcore poor households were headed by widowed, divorced or abandoned women some 44 percent of households entering the IGVGD in 1994 were from this social category. This indicates that the program reaches a cohort of the population for whom poverty is likely to be persistent.

In terms of economic indicators the survey found that on average IGVGD client incomes rose significantly, material assets (ownership of homestead plots, land, beds and blankets) increased and the percentage of households engaged in begging dropped dramatically (Table 7.3). But the economic impacts of IGVGD varied over time and between households. Impact on income was greatest at the time of program completion, with average household income rising to 717 taka per month. Three years after completing IGVGD it had declined to 415 taka. Participatory appraisals in 1999 provided accounts of why this decline occurred. Virtually all households experienced a drop in income and consumption because of the withdrawal of the food subsidy. For some this was not too dramatic as the new microcredit funded activities they were pursuing kept their incomes well above pre-program levels. But around a quarter of households reported that 'they could never recover from the loss of the food grain. They sold off their chickens, used up the loan for consumption and worried about making repayments … they were as destitute as they were before [the program]' (Hashemi, 2001, p. 7). As is discussed

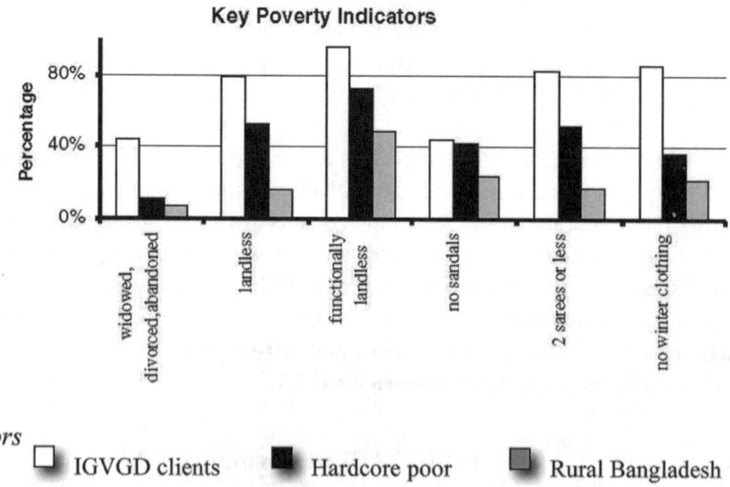

Figure 7.4 Key poverty indicators and differences between groups.

Table 7.3 Economic changes in IGVGD households, 1994–99

Variables	*Time* *1994 (pre-program)*	*1996 (end of program)*	*1999 (3 years after program)*
Monthly income (taka)	75	717	415
Percentage of households earning more than 300 taka per month	7	64	31
Percentage of households with homestead land	73	87	na
Percentage of functionally landless households	94	72	na
Percentage of households with beds	58	60	64
Percentage of households with blankets	14	na	25
Percentage of households begging	18	2	0

Source: Adapted from Hashemi et al. (2001, p. 9).

later (and is illustrated in detail in Matin, 2002), the IGVGD experience follows quite different trajectories for different households. But for this group it has clearly not worked. We return to the question of what *would* work in the conclusion.

Another performance indicator examines how successful the IGVGD program is at 'graduating' very poor households into regular microfinance programs. Again this provided evidence of improvement. Pre-program only 15 percent of the IGVGD entrants were microfinance institution (MFI) clients. By program end, in 1996, this increased to 28 percent and by 2000 it had reached 66 percent. While across Bangladesh access to microfinance was increasing over the late 1990s a 440 percent increase in MFI membership for such a very low income, very low asset cohort represents a massive improvement in access to financial services.

There are no comprehensive cost effectiveness or cost benefit analyses of the IGVGD available, but Hashemi (2001, p. 11) estimates that the subsidy element of the program was US$135 per household per cycle for the year 2000 and argues this is a reasonable cost for the improvements that have been recorded.

This evidence, and other reviews, have certainly convinced aid agencies that IGVGD can reduce poverty for sections of the population that few other programs can reach. Over the last few years they have been keen to build on the IGVGD experience and expand programs for 'those left behind.'

7.5 THE IGVGD IN PRACTICE

All policies and programs operate differently in the field than their plans and directives would suggest. The 'implementation gap' in development programs has been widely chronicled and the IGVGD proves no exception. In the sections that follow we examine 'how' targeting works in practice, 'why' it diverges from what was expected and 'who' among the poor cannot gain access to the IGVGD.

(a) IGVGD targeting in practice

The IGVGD conceptualizes poverty reduction as a linear process that permits extremely poor female headed households to escape poverty by taking 'two steps up' (Figure 7.3). A period of basic needs security permits the household to move into enhanced income generation and graduate[13] to BRAC's 'normal' programs for the moderate poor. There are three important assumptions in this model.

- i That VGD cards will be allocated to the hardcore poor who are unable to access BRAC's (and other agencies') conventional microfinance and self-employment schemes.
- ii That IGVGD recipients graduate into BRAC's RDP after a single period of access to food aid. (This means that future food aid can be targeted at new hardcore poor households so the program has a cumulative impact).
- iii That moderate poor (and nonpoor) households will not get VGD cards and be recruited to the IGVGD.

A survey of three BRAC VOs in Tangail District (see note 1) revealed the gap between IGVGD theory and practice and provided evidence of both 'errors' of exclusion and inclusion. All three organizations were functioning as typical BRAC VOs with members recruited directly, through the RDP, and by graduation from the IGVGD. But, during focus group discussions two significant divergences from official policy became clear. The first was that a number of moderate poor households who had joined the VO through the RDP had subsequently 'downshifted' and acquired VGD cards. In theory this cannot occur as these households are ineligible as they should already be well past the bottom rung of the ladder out of poverty. Second, a number of IGVGD clients, and at least one RDP client, had been repeat VGD cardholders having held cards on two or more occasions. The planned VO model recognizes seven categories of member and nonmember.

In practice, at least four other categories exist: IGVGD graduate repeaters, RDP downshifters, RDP repeat downshifters and the eligible excluded (Table 7.4). The dynamics of the IGVGD in practice are more complex than the IGVGD in theory[14] and cyclical movements need to be added to the linearity that the program assumes.

The survey of the 97 active members of the three VOs indicated that 16 percent of them had repeated the IGVGD program and that 37 percent of IGVGD entrants had repeated the program (Table 7.5). Seventeen percent (nine out of 54) of those who had entered the VO through the 'moderate poor' RDP had subsequently 'downshifted' and entered the IGVGD. Discussions with BRAC field officers confirmed that repeating and downshifting are common elements of the IGVGD in other districts. Indeed, the WFP survey (World Food Program, 1999,

Table 7.4 Categories of BRAC VO members and nonmembers

Categories identified in fieldwork	*Characteristics of this category*	*Does the program expect this group to exist?*
Eligible excluded	Eligible households unable to acquire a VGD card	No
VGD screen-outs	VGD cardholders who are not accepted for the IGVGD program	Yes
IGVGD non graduate dropouts	VGD cardholders accepted for IGVGD but who do not graduate to the RDP	Yes
IGVGD graduate dropouts	VGD cardholders who graduate from IGVGD to RDP but subsequently dropout	Yes
IGVGD graduates	VGD cardholders who graduate from IGVGD to RDP and are active RDP members at time of survey	Yes
IGVGD graduate repeaters	VGD cardholders who graduate from IGVGD to RDP, are active RDP members but who get a repeat VGD card(s)	No
RDP downshifters	RDP entrants who get access to a VGD card	No
RDP repeat down-shifters	RDP entrants who get access to a VGD card more than once	No
RDP members	RDP entrants who continue as RDP members ('normal RDP members')	Yes
RDP dropouts	RDP entrants who later dropout	Yes
Ineligible excluded	Villagers who are nonpoor and thus ineligible for RDP or IGVGD	Yes

Table XIX) of VGD cardholders in the 1998–99 cycle shows that almost 22 percent of them were BRAC VO members before they got VGD cards demonstrating that IGVGD repeats and RDP downshifters are a major component of the programs across the country.

(b) Unpacking VGD card eligibility: Sympathy, social networks, BRAC's organizational needs and personal agency

Why are the patterns of access to VGD cards and the IGVGD program markedly different to the planned process and, in particular, why do 'downshifting' and repeat IGVGD enrolment occur? To pursue these questions lengthy focus group discussions were conducted with members of the three VOs and key informant interviews with BRAC field officers and local government office bearers. These revealed that the knee jerk answers that are often reported – 'elite capture,' 'corruption' and 'nepotism' – fail to appreciate the complexity of the processes and the moral economy that partly influences these decisions.

Villagers identified three main categories of household which are allocated VGD cards.

i Widows and abandoned wives who have young children.
ii Households which have recently experienced a major shock, such as a severe illness, accident or death, particularly if this involves a male head of household.[15] This applied to poor households but also to nonpoor households.
iii Chronically poor households that at times have to go without food and that sometimes may need to beg for food.

These three categories are highly interrelated: abandoned wives and widows with

Table 7.5 Membership status of participants in three BRAC VOs, Tangail, 2001

	VO1	*VO2*	*VO3*	*Total (%)*[a]
IGVGD graduates	5	12	9	25(28)
IGVGD graduate repeaters	7	3	7	17(16)
RDP downshifters	4	2	1	7(8)
RDP repeat downshifters	2	0	0	2(1)
RDP members	7	14	24	45(46)
Total active members	25	31	41	97(99)
Dropouts (all types)	4	6	6	16
Total members (active and dropouts)	29	37	47	113

Source: Survey – for more details see Matin (2002).

Note
a Percentages relate to active members only.

young children are likely to be among the long term poor and are very vulnerable to shocks; a deep shock or repeated shocks can reduce a moderately poor, or even a nonpoor, household to chronic poverty. The importance VO members attached to trying to manage shocks, particularly relating to ill health and health expenses, so that their effects on household status do not become irreversible, came out very strongly in discussions.

In addition, villagers recognized that the number of VGD cards available at any one time was small compared to the numbers of potentially eligible households in a village. Some criteria for rationing had to operate and at the local level the most legitimate was 'sympathy' for a household because of sudden downward mobility pressures that were not its fault. Sympathy, along with social networks, BRAC's organizational needs and personal agency, were the four factors that emerged in discussions as explaining 'how' VGD cards, and subsequently IGVGD membership, were acquired.

(i) Sympathy

In general, chronic poverty does not raise the same level of 'sympathy' at the village level as does the sudden downward mobility of a household. Households that were running well (*shochol*[16]) but then hit a major problem are likely to receive great sympathy, and have a strong likelihood of accessing a VGD card and the IGVGD program. Irreversible shocks, such as terminal illness, death of main income earner or business collapse are commonly triggers for VGD card eligibility. Households experiencing a shock can use 'cultural signifiers' of distress to mobilize social resources that can help them to cope with their difficulties (McGregor, 1998).

There is particular sympathy for widows, and even more for abandoned wives with young children. This partly stems from local social values but also from the way in which VGD cards have been presented to the public. As the ward member for one of the case study villages told us, 'This card was earlier known as the Distressed Mother's Card (Dustho Mata Card).' The high eligibility of this category for cards is firmly established in villagers' perceptions. The argument behind this is that widows and deserted wives with small children have to return to their children. The operative concepts here are 'young' and 'mother:' both generate general sympathy in a society with deep patriarchal values.

In some cases extreme and persistent poverty is the reason for initial access to a VGD card and repeat cards are acquired because of later shocks (see cases 5 and 6 in Matin, 2002). But, as a general principle it is downward mobility, rather than chronic poverty, that makes a household VGD eligible. Indeed, there was some evidence of a prejudice against the long term poor in the IGVGD (see later).

(ii) Social networks

As one would anticipate in a society where patron-client relationships are central to economic life, social networks and a household's position within wider social structures, are important factors in accessing public benefits. Favorable relationships with local elites who are connected to ward and union level elected representatives significantly increase the probability of acquiring a VGD card. Villagers identified that this commonly happens when: a woman is working as a house help for a better off family or, a man provides a member of the local elite with support during an election or, a man manages casual laborers for a landowner during the peak boro harvest season (see Annex A of Matin, 2002). Negotiating access to a VGD card for poorer, client households is a relatively low-cost means for patrons to maintain or secure control over clients. Interestingly, when discussing the issue of access to VGD and IGVGD, villagers did not feel that patronage led to benefits going to ineligible households. What concerned them was the unfairness of the process when ward members could allocate cards to their personal networks.

(iii) BRAC's influence and organizational needs

For the case study VOs BRAC field staff were not directly involved in the allocation of VGD 658 WORLD DEVELOPMENT cards.[17] Villagers believed however, that the linkage of VGD card allocation to the IGVGD program meant that BRAC field officers could influence the process. Indirectly, this linkage puts pressure on local government officials not to select households who are clearly ineligible for VGD benefits. The fact that BRAC field staff make an assessment of which VGD cardholders are eligible for the IGVGD program adds to the transparency of the entire VGD selection process. VO members were of the opinion that the incidence of bribing local government representatives to get a VGD card has decreased, although it still occurs (see case 15 in Annex A of Matin, 2002, for an example). There were also cases where BRAC staff played a direct role in acquiring VGD cards for members of VOs that they were managing (see cases 13 and 17 in Matin, 2002, for examples).

VO members emphasized that BRAC's need to develop a pool of prospective clients for their microfinance program, meant that field officers would encourage the allocation of VGD cards to women and households that have the potential to develop income generating activities. Households that are *ochol* (not going anywhere, the opposite of *shochol*) are not attractive to BRAC.

It is possible to test whether IGVGD members are more suited to 'promotional' programs than other VGD programs by analyzing data from the World Food Program (1999) survey. In Table 7.6 the characteristics of IGVGD members are compared with members of the Union Parishad Vulnerable Group Development (UVGD) program.[18] The UVGD is a quasi control as it provides only food aid to selected households and has no income generation, microcredit or 'graduation' components. For all of the poverty indicators listed, IGVGD members are relatively better off than UVGD members. In particular, IGVGD recipients are twice as likely to be 'living with a husband' than UVGD recipients, are less likely to work as day laborers and more likely to own land and purchase corrugated iron roofing. In addition, almost 37 percent of IGVGD members had an NGO affiliation prior to joining the IGVGD. For the UVGD the figure was only around 26 percent. These differences indicate that the IGVGD was not targeting the chronic poor effectively, but for good reason given that the aim of graduating clients meant selecting those with perceived potential.

(iv) Personal agency

Finally, the focus group discussions, interviews and case studies (Matin, 2002) constantly provided evidence of the personal agency of the poor in seeking ways of improving their livelihood and reducing their vulnerability. Most VGD cardholders in our fieldwork area were actively involved in acquiring their card and/or arranging for a 'repeat' card. This took many different forms ranging from letting neighbors know how deep a household's problems were, to maintaining relationships with patrons who were known to be able to negotiate access to grants, to directly asking BRAC field officers for assistance in acquiring a VGD card. The majority of VGD cardholders are not simply 'selected' by people with more social and economic power, they actively engage with local elites and NGO staff as part of broader and dynamic strategic portfolios to survive and, if possible, prosper. Those who are not able to exercise such personal agency – because of their infirmity, lack of mobility, disability or social exclusion – have a low probability of accessing

Table 7.6 Poverty indicators for IGVGD and UVGD members

Indicators	*IGVGD (%)*	*UVGD (%)*
I. Marital status of VGD women		
Married and living with husband	58	30
Deserted	0	6
Divorced	5	5
Widowed	32	58
II. Occupational background of VGD women		
Household work	63	48
Day labor	8	23
III. Asset base of VGD women		
Owning chowki / khat	60	47
Owning agricultural land	12	7
IV. Main income earner in VGD women's households		
VGD woman herself	37	54
Husband	39	21
Daughter	3	6
V. Expenditure in taka on nonfood items in the previous year		
Corrugated tin	138 taka	47 taka
Tree/bamboo	16 taka	4 taka
VI. NGO affiliation of VGD women (Yes)	36	25

Source: World Food Program (1999).

VGD and, if they do get a card, a high probability of being 'screened out' of the IGVGD program (see cases 14 and 15 in Annex 2 of Matin, 2002).

(c) Those left out: errors of exclusion

Earlier sections of this paper have provided evidence that IGVGD is able to 'reach down' to client groups who have low access to support from conventional NGO programs or the government. During fieldwork in Tangail however, it was clear that there were many desperately poor and vulnerable households who were not being reached. These 'errors' of exclusion relate to both the scale of the IGVGD program and the nature of the clients that it recruits.

(i) Program scale

The number of IGVGD 'places,' 200,000–250,000 per 18 month cycle, is small compared to the demand for such a program. At a rough estimate only 4–5 percent[19] of eligible households are currently active participants. While there are other programs that seek to provide benefits to the country's ultra poor[20] – the IGVGD's 'sister' programs (UVGD, JC and IFADEP), food for work, food/cash for education, emergency relief, gratuitous relief – there is still a case to be made that if the scale of IGVGD activity could be increased then a large number of very poor households with the potential to become more economically active could derive substantial benefits. To double the scale of the program, at a subsidy requirement of US$135 per household per 18 month cycle (Hashemi, 2001, p. 11), would require an additional US$18 million per annum. While such a sum is a significant amount of money it represents a small amount in terms of aid donor budgets and Government of Bangladesh expenditure, particularly when the benefits accrue to very poor people to whom it is difficult to deliver services.

(ii) The clients: *ochol* versus *shochol*

While the IGVGD goes 'deeper' than many other poverty reduction programs the design of the program does not make it accessible to all types of very poor households. Eligible households may miss out because of not getting a VGD card; may be screened out when BRAC field officers decide which cardholders can join the IGVGD;[21] and, may fail to use the full IGVGD package and not 'graduate' to the RDP. A recent WFP study found that women who were fully participating in the IGVGD 'were already more confident, with above average social and human capital, holding major assets prior to joining the cycle, having a more diversified income … they were more likely … to be married to an able bodied, income earning husband acting as intermediaries between the woman participant and male NGO/UP staff' (Webb *et al.*, 2001, p. iv). During fieldwork it became clear that eligible households that were perceived to have little or no prospect of becoming economically active were excluded from the IGVGD – as one would expect in an income generation program. In all three villages however, there were households that were *ochol* (not going anywhere) – households of the elderly (single widows, aged couples), with disabled or mentally impaired household heads or simply households that were socially categorized as 'hopeless.'[22] There is thus a whole subsection of poor households, often chronically poor, which the IGVGD does not reach. More worryingly, the mixing of livelihood protection and livelihood promotion strategies, may actually divert VGD food relief away from *ochol* households to *shochol* households i.e., some of the neediest may lose out on food aid because of the IGVGD. While it would be foolish to argue that the IGVGD should attempt to service households that have little likelihood of moving into higher levels of income generation, this finding does point to the need to monitor the impacts of ultra poor programs on non participants and of the need for separate programs that focus purely on livelihood protection. Such 'welfare' programs may be unpopular in a workfare age but, they are needed if many of the chronically poor are to avoid persistent deprivation.

7.6 LEARNING FROM THE IGVGD: BRAC'S CHALLENGING THE FRONTIERS OF POVERTY REDUCTION PROGRAM

BRAC, along with its partners, has systematically reviewed the IGVGD experience and is using this knowledge in the design of a new program. Challenging the Frontiers of Poverty Reduction (CFPR) seeks to be better targeted on households that experience deep poverty over long periods and to be more demand focused.

It recognizes that the poorest need more than one 'additional step' on the stairway of poverty reduction. Asset transfer, health care and social development training have been added to the package. It appreciates that the poorest will improve their living standards at different speeds and that reversals will occur, so emergency or shock loans and repeated stages will be necessary. The main lessons learned from IGVGD, and the ways in which the CFPR seeks to improve on IGVGD are briefly summarized in Table 7.7. For more details on CFPR see Matin (2002).

7.7 CONCLUSION

Earlier studies of poverty reduction programs in Bangladesh have demonstrated that programs that adopt a livelihood promotion approach, such as microcredit and skills training, can benefit poor households but do not directly benefit the hardcore poor (Hashemi, 1997, 2001; Montgomery *et al.*, 1996; Rahman & Hossain, 1995; Zaman, 1997). Such programs have the advantage of being relatively cost effective[23] but they come with a 'price' excluding the chronically poor. By combining livelihood protection and livelihood promotion approaches, as has been successfully done in the IGVGD, it is possible to deepen the reach of poverty

Table 7.7 Lessons learned from the IGVGD and ways in which the CFPR responds to those lessons

Topic	*Lessons learned from IGVGD*	*CFPR design features*
Targeting	Access to IGVGD is not seen as 'fair' by villagers and local government officials can use VGD cards for patronage.	BRAC staff will play an active role in client selection and geographical targeting.
Program components	The provision of food aid, skills training, savings schemes and microcredit is not sufficient to assist some/many very poor households to improve their situation.	Commence the program with social development training. Include asset transfer, basic health services and shock/emergency fund to the 'package' for clients.
Role of BRAC staff	Having BRAC's RDP staff take on training and microfinance services for IGVGD did not provide clients with the intensive and customized support they needed.	A separate cadre of staff to be developed for CFPR work only. More intensive interaction with clients, follow up and participatory impact monitoring.
Income generation activities	Providing training (and loans) only in sectors that BRAC had pre-existing course modules is too narrow a range of activities.	Extend the range of sectors and assets/enterprise types that are supported. Include wage employment as an activity and allow different regions to vary their range of activities.
Assimilation and graduation	Not all IGVGD clients can be rapidly assimilated into VOs according to a rigid timetable. Some clients will 'fall behind' and need additional support.	Customized assimilation and graduation timings to client needs and client progress. Clients do not have to take on microcredit and support for 'failing' clients is a program component.

reduction schemes so that the hardcore poor can derive direct benefits and some of them can 'escape' absolute poverty. This study of the IGVGD has identified a number of findings of which two are of particular importance in the search for ways to assist the chronic poor.

First, although it is both logical and practical to initially design programs that combine livelihood protection and livelihood promotion to be as simple as possible, as was done in the IGVGD (Figure 7.3), such schemes need to be continuously adapted so that they can deal with the complex of factors that keep poor people poor. The IGVGD experience reveals that:

- poverty reduction for the hardcore is not a linear process – reversals can be expected so that a range of livelihood protectional mechanisms (grants, emergency loans, basic health care) need to be available throughout the program cycle;
- poverty reduction will occur at different speeds for different households and so programs must be flexible enough to deal with this and not simply convert those who make slow progress into 'dropouts';

- to deepen the reach of programs for the hardcore poor then a range of asset transfers may be needed to create a platform from which a household can self-generate an improving livelihood. Limited transfers to raise human capital (food aid and skills training) may work for some households but others will need material and/or financial transfers to create their developmental platform.

To encourage the evolution of effective programs organizational directors (in the public or NGO sectors), and those who provide financial support (governments and aid donors) will need to ask program managers 'How have you improved program design this year?' as often as they ask 'What has the program achieved this year?'

The second major finding is that even programs that effectively combine livelihood protection and promotion components together will find it hard to provide assistance to some of the chronic poor. The IGVGD experience indicates that the program could assist the *shochol* (households that were 'on the move' and could seize economic opportunities) but had difficulties with the *ochol* (households that were unable to become upwardly mobile). The CFPR program is designed to reach the *ochol* and activate their economic potential by providing additional inputs – social development/social mobilization training, asset transfers, basic health care, emergency loans – and recognizing that progress will occur at different rates. But, even with these additional features the CFPR is unlikely to be able to assist those that cannot raise their levels of economic activity – elderly households (lone widows and aged couples), destitute without homes, households with heads that are in poor health, severely physically or mentally impaired or suffering from mental health problems, and families and individuals that, for whatever reasons, are socially outcast. Thus, there will remain a need[24] to continue, and in most countries to further develop, programs that are based solely on providing livelihood protection for those who cannot benefit from poverty reduction initiatives that require a capacity to be economically active. If one were to search for a criticism of the IGVGD it would be that it diverted food aid from deep and chronically poor *ochol* households to poor *shochol* households. The next generation of ultra poor programs may reach many of these *ochol* households but not all of them.

To conclude, the IGVGD experience confirms that programs combining elements of livelihood protection and livelihood promotion can reach deeper than purely promotional schemes and can benefit the chronic poor. Their relative success should not however, lead us to think that they can totally replace programs of pure social protection – a small proportion of the population will always need more traditional 'social welfare' support to avoid persistent deprivation.

Notes

1 Our thanks to colleagues at BRAC and BIDS and Allister McGregor, Karen Moore and Stuart Rutherford for comments. The research for this paper was supported by a Social Science Research grant (R7847) from the UK government's Department for

International Development. Reprinted from *World Development*, 31 (3), pp. 647–5, 2003.

2 For details of the methods used and case study area see Matin (2002).

3 For elaborations on this perspective visit the Microcredit Summit website at www.microcreditsummit.org.

4 See Sen (2003) for the most recent analysis. We have not been able to make reference to this study in the present paper.

5 The reader should note, however, that we do not know what happened to the household's poverty status between these two points in time.

6 This is ironic as Muhamad Yunus, the global leader of the microcredit movement, based his initial experiments on pointing out the diversity of the poor in terms of gender and land ownership.

7 The history and description of the various components of the IGVGD programs is based on Hashemi (2001).

8 Though BRAC now has one of the largest microfinance programs in Bangladesh, its coming to microfinance in a major way is relatively recent and a careful reading of this move reveals a contested organizational process and conflict among competing values (Kabeer, 2002). But, BRAC has always been a complex organization and the microfinance dominance could not totally overshadow questions such as its unsuitability for the extreme poor.

9 In the late 1980s US$1 was approximately 30 taka. By the late 1990s the exchange rate has slid to US$1 = 50 taka.

10 VOs, or village organizations, are a group of 40–5 members from a village who are supposed to own less than half an acre of land and sell their manual labor for at least 100 days per year. The VO is the focus of outreach by RDP. Through it, BRAC provides villagers with savings and loans, in addition to health, skills training and education.

11 In 2001 BRAC Area Managers became members of VGD card selection committees.

12 This survey is reported in Hashemi (2001). It involved a three-stage random sampling design that selected 400 respondents across the country. The longitudinal study interviewed 400 women in 1994 who were about to enter the IGVGD, 398 of these women in 1996 as they completed the program and 345 in 1999, three years after program completion.

13 'Graduates' are those VGD card holders who take out RDP loans after their VGD card has expired.

14 See Figure 7 in Matin (2002) for a diagram that charts the varying trajectories of IGVGD and RDP participants. See Annex A in Matin (2002) for details of the specific experiences of individual households.

15 It was also reported that households experiencing a shock due to a large expense, such as a daughter's marriage could be included in this category because of their increased vulnerability.

16 According to the Samsad Bengali-English Dictionary, the word shochol means, capable of moving, mobile. In local usage this word is used to describe something that is 'running,' 'working' this 'thing' can range from automobiles to factories to human beings. This term captures a combined sense of both basic physical fitness to work and using it to get the wheel of the family going.

17 Changes to the program in 2001 have meant that NGO field staff, and thus BRAC officers, are now members of the committees that allocate VGD cards.

18 There are four programs within VGD. The IGVGD, the UVGD, the Jagarani Chakra (JC) and the Integrated Food Assisted Development Project (IFADEP).

19 With around 13 million poor households in the country, perhaps 6.5 million fall into the 'vulnerable' or 'ultra poor' category. Roughly 1.5 million of these may lack the potential to pursue income generation opportunities. So, there are around five million eligible households which could utilize the IGVGD.

20 It should also be noted that a PKSF-BIDS study has found that smaller MFIs in Bangladesh are seeking out local market niches for their operations that are not serviced by the larger MFIs. Often, this means they are moving 'downmarket' to poorer clients (Zohir *et al.*, 2001).
21 During fieldwork one BRAC officer reported that he thought around 35 percent of VGD cardholders were 'untrainable' (i.e., lacked the ability to learn a skill and manage a loan) and should be screened out of IGVGD entry.
22 There are other factors that lead to exclusion. In a separate study, one of the authors came across a household comprised of a deaf widow and her physically disabled son. The widow had been allocated a VGD card by a UP member, but her wealthier relatives stopped her from using it because the UP member was from a different political party than them and they were suspicious of his intentions (Hulme, 2003).
23 Indeed, some of their proponents argue that they can become sustainable and require no public subsidies.
24 Assuming that governments, NGOs, aid donors and individuals are genuinely committed to poverty reduction and eventually the elimination of absolute poverty.

References

Alkire, S. (2002). Dimensions of human development. *World Development*, 30(2), 181–206.

Devereux, S. (2001). Social protection for the poor? *IDS Working Paper 142*, IDS, Brighton, UK.

Dreze, J., & Sen, A. (1989). *Hunger and public action*. Oxford: Oxford University Press.

Grindle, M. S. (Ed.). (1980). *Politics and policy implementation in the Third World*. Princeton: Princeton University Press.

Hashemi, S. (1997). Those left behind: a note on targeting the hardcore poor. In G. Wood, & T. Sharif (Eds), *Who needs credit? Poverty and finance in development*. Dhaka: UPL.

Hashemi, S. M. (2001). Including the poorest: linking microfinance and safety net programs. CGAP Occasional Paper 20, Consultative Group to Assist the Poorest (CGAP), Washington, DC.

Hossain, M., Sen, B., & Rahman, H. Z. (2000). Growth and distribution of rural income in Bangladesh: analysis based on panel survey data. *Economic and Political Weekly*, *30* (December).

Hulme, D. (2003). *Why does poverty endure? Mayamana and Mofizul's story*. Chronic Poverty Research Centre Working Paper 22, IDPM, University of Manchester. www.chronicpoverty.org.

Hulme, D., Moore, K., & Shepherd, A. (2001). Chronic poverty: meanings and analytical frameworks. Chronic Poverty Research Centre Working Paper 2, IDPM, University of Manchester. www.chronicpoverty.org.

Hulme, D., & Mosley, P. (1996). *Finance against poverty*. 2 vols. London: Routledge.

Hulme, D., & Shepherd, A. (2003). Conceptualizing chronic poverty. *World Development*, 31(3), 403–23.

Husain, A. M. M. (Ed.) (1998). *Poverty alleviation and empowerment: the second impact assessment study of BRAC's rural development program*. Dhaka: Bangladesh Rural Advancement Committee.

Kabeer, N. (2002). Safety nets and opportunity ladders: addressing vulnerability and addressing productivity in South Asia. *Institute of Development Studies*, draft.

Landell Mills, P. (2002). *Taming leviathan: reforming government in Bangladesh.* Washington, DC: World Bank.

Lipton, M. (1988). The poor and the poorest: some interim findings. World Bank Discussion Paper No. 25, Washington, DC: World Bank.

Lund, F. (2002). Crowding in care, security and microenterprise formation: revisiting the role of the state in poverty reduction and development. *Journal of International Development*, 14.

Matin, I. (2002). Targeted development programs for the extreme poor: experiences from BRAC experiments. Chronic Poverty Research Centre Working Paper 20, IDPM, University of Manchester. www.chronicpoverty.org.

McGregor, J. A. (1998). A poverty of agency: resource management amongst poor people in Bangladesh. *Paper presented at European Network of Bangladesh Studies*, University of Bath, April.

Mehta, A. K., & Shah, A. (2001). Chronic poverty in India: an overview study. Chronic Poverty Research Centre Working Paper 7, IDPM, University of Manchester. www.chronicpoverty.org.

Mehta, A., & Shah, A. (2003). Chronic poverty in India: incidence, causes and policies. *World Development*, 31(3), 491–511.

Montgomery, R., Bhattacharya, D., & Hulme, D. (1996). Credit for the poor in Bangladesh. In D. Hulme, & P. Mosley (Eds), *Finance against poverty* (vol. 2, pp. 94–176). London: Routledge.

NOVIB Report (1996). *Bangladesh country policy document: summary proceedings of the mid term review workshop*. Dhaka: NOVIB.

Peck, J. (2001). *Workfare states*. NewYork: Guildford Press.

Rahman, H. Z., & Hossain, M. (Eds). (1995). *Rethinking rural poverty: Bangladesh as a case study*. Dhaka: University Press Ltd.

Rahman, A., & Razzaque, A. (1998). *On reaching the hard core poor: redefining the NGO strategy*. Bangladesh Institute of Development Studies.

Rahman, A., & Razzaque, A. (2000). On reaching the hard core poor: some evidence on social exclusion in NGO programs. *The Bangladesh Development Studies*, XXVI(1): 1–36. Dhaka: BIDS.

Sen, A. (1999). *Development as freedom*. Oxford: Oxford University Press.

Sen, B. (2001). *Bangladesh: human development report*. Dhaka: ADB.

Sen, B., & Begum, S. (1998). Methodology for identifying the extreme poor at local level. Microeconomics, *Health and Development Series*, 27. Geneva: WHO.

Sen, B. (2003). Drivers of escape and descent: changing household fortunes in rural Bangladesh. *World Development*, 31(3), 513–33.

Turner, M., & Hulme, D. (1997). *Governance, administration and development: making the state work*. London: Palgrave.

Webb, P., Coates, J., Houser, R., Hassan, Z., & Zobair, M. (2001). Expectations of success and constraints to participation among IGVGD women: Report to WFP, Bangladesh.

Wood, G. (1994). *Bangladesh: whose ideas, whose interests?* Dhaka: UPL.

World Bank (1998). Bangladesh: from counting the poor to making the poor count. *Poverty Reduction and Economic Management Network*, South Asia Region.

World Bank (2001). Bangladesh poverty assessment: background paper on poverty trends. Dhaka, World Bank.

World Food Program, Bangladesh (1999). Round one impact evaluation report on women who participated in the 1998/99 cycle. *World Food Program*. Dhaka. IES-VGD-98/99/1/1999.

Zaman, H. (1997). Microcredit programs: who participates and to what extent. In G. Wood (Ed.), *Bangladesh: whose ideas, whose interests?* Dhaka: UPL.

Zohir, S., Mahmud, S., Sen, B., Asaduzzaman, M., Islam, J., & Al-Mamun, A. (2001). Monitoring and evaluation of microfinance institutions. *Bangladesh Institute of Development Studies*, Dhaka.

APPENDIX 7.A

The operational cycle of IGVGD, 1999–2000

Stage 1: Central government identifies the number of women in each thana (the lowest administrative unit) to receive free food grain under the VGD program. The allocation is based on a geographical targeting of food insecure areas. Thana-level committees of government officials, elected representatives and voluntary organizations determine the further distribution of the numbers of women for each local government unit under each thana (there are generally eight to 10 local government units or unions under each thana).

Stage 2: Elected representatives of local government submit the names of women to receive VGD cards and thus free food grain. Names are approved by thana committee.

Stage 3: BRAC field officers select IGVGD participants from the approved list of VGD cardholders. (Generally, about 90 percent of cardholders are selected for IGVGD.)

Stage 4: 18 month IGVGD cycle begins: 30 kg of food grain is distributed monthly to participants. IGVGD participants and BRAC choose a skills training subject and training commences.

Stage 5: Training is completed (in most cases) by Month 6 and the first of two loans is distributed to each woman. Participants attend weekly VO meetings and save 25 taka (US$0.50) per month. Loan repayments begin immediately.

Stage 6: Repayment of first loan is completed and second loan is disbursed to all IGVGD participants who have repaid on schedule.

Stage 7: At Month 16, participants may begin withdrawing their savings if they wish.

Stage 8: At Month 18, the cycle is completed and free grain distribution is halted. Loan repayments continue if the final loan is not repaid.

Stage 9: IGVGD graduates are encouraged to continue membership in BRAC as a regular member of the VO and to take loans from the RDP.

Source: Adapted from Maya Tudor, 'An Idea, Its Innovation and Evolution: BRAC's IGVGD Program,' mimeo, Dhaka, BRAC HQ.

APPENDIX 7.B

Abbreviations

BRAC Bangladesh Rural Advancement Committee
CFPR Challenging the Frontiers of Poverty Reduction (BRAC)
IFADEP Integrated Food Assisted Development Project
IGVGD Income Generation for Vulnerable Group Development
JC Jagarani Chakra
MFI Microfinance institution
NGO Nongovernment organization
RDP Rural Development Program (of BRAC)
UVGD Union Parshad Vulnerable Group Development
VGD Vulnerable Group Development
VGF Vulnerable Group Feeding
VO Village organization (of BRAC)
WFP World Food Program (of the UN)

8

CONFLICTS OVER CREDIT

Re-evaluating the empowerment potential of loans to women in rural Bangladesh

Naila Kabeer[1]

8.1 INTRODUCTION: CONFLICTING EVALUATIONS OF CREDIT

Microcredit programs for the poor have come to occupy a central place in poverty-oriented strategies in Bangladesh. Such programs have a number of features in common. They are largely targeted at women from the poorest sections of the population; they lend small sums of money to individuals as members of groups and rely on group liability to ensure loan repayment; they subsidize administrative costs rather than interest rates; and loans are repaid in weekly installments. Debates as to the actual effectiveness of these programs in reducing poverty continue. More recently, these debates have been extended to the possible implications of such programs for women's empowerment, with some evaluations claiming extremely positive results while others suggesting that microcredit leaves women worse off than before.

In this paper I want to focus on a number of attempts to evaluate the empowerment potential of loans to women in order to find out why such diametrically opposed claims can be made about the same, or very similar, programs. I will be exploring examples of both 'negative' and 'positive' evaluations, interrogating them for the methodologies they used, the questions they asked, the findings they reported and the interpretations they gave to their findings. In addition, I will be drawing on the findings of my own evaluation of a rather different credit program in Bangladesh in order to explore the question of empowerment when it is assessed on the basis of women loanees' own testimonies rather than deduced from selected aspects of their behavior.

(a) Does access to credit 'empower' women? The negative verdict

My first example of a negative evaluation is by Goetz and Sen Gupta (1994). They use a five-point index of 'managerial control' over loans as their indicator of empowerment. At one end of their index are women who are described as having 'no control' over their loans: these are women who either had no knowledge of how their loans were used or else had not provided any labor into the activities funded by the loan. At the other end are those who were considered to have exercised 'full' control, having participated in all stages of the activity funded by the loan, including the marketing of produce. The study found that the majority of women, particularly married women, exercised little or no control over their loans by these criteria. Interpreting this as evidence of widespread loss of control by women over their loans to men, Goetz and Sen Gupta go on to suggest three possible repayment scenarios, all with negative implications for women.

In the first, the male family member using the loan takes responsibility for its repayment, a satisfactory outcome from the woman's point of view but one which the authors believe negates the developmental objectives of lending to women. In the second, men are unable to supply the requisite repayment funds and women loanees have to substitute funds from other sources, drawing on their savings, cutting back on consumption, selling off utensils and other assets. They have responsibility without control. In the third, men are unwilling to repay the loans, leading to an intensification of tensions within the household, often spilling over into violence. In addition, violence against women was also exacerbated by the frustration of husbands at the wives' delay or failure in accessing credit. Facilities to enhance women's access to the market is put forward by the authors 'as the single most effective way of enhancing their control over loans, as well as their public presence and their self-confidence' (p. 59). The provision of transportation recommended to take women to the market place along with security measures to protect them against the possibility of male resistance to their presence in the market place are recommended as supportive measures.

In her study, Ackerly (1995) noted that underpinning most credit interventions in Bangladesh was an implicit model of the empowered woman:

> Empowered, the borrower wisely invests money in a successful enterprise, her husband stops beating her, she sends her children to school, she improves the health and nutrition of her family, and she participates in major family decisions.
>
> (ibid., p. 56)

Rather than seeking to measure these outcomes directly, she takes 'accounting knowledge' as her indicator of the likelihood of these and other transformative outcomes occurring. Women who were able to report on the input costs for loan-funded enterprise, its product yield and its profitability, were counted as empowered. She found that membership of some credit organizations was more likely than others to contribute to the likelihood of women's empowerment by this criterion. Women who provided labor to loan-assisted enterprise, sold their own products, or kept their own accounts were also likely to be empowered. She too concluded that women's access to the market was the primary route for their empowerment – 'knowledge and empowerment come through market access' (p. 64) – and warned against the likelihood of overwork, fatigue and malnutrition were loans used to promote women's labor involvement without also promoting their market access.

Our third example of a negative evaluation of the impact of credit for women's empowerment is by Montgomery *et al.* (1996). Although the evaluation of the empowerment impact occupies only a small section of their more general evaluation of credit programs for the poor, I have included it here because it exemplifies a particular understanding of households and gender relations within the literature on Bangladesh. According to their findings, only 9 percent of first-time female borrowers were primary managers of loan-funded activities while 87 percent described their role in terms of 'family partnerships.' By contrast, 33 percent of first-time male borrowers had sole authority over the loan-assisted activity while 56 percent described it as a family partnership. They also found that access to loans did little to change the management of cash within the household for either female or male loanees. Interpreting reports of 'joint' management as disguised male dominance in decision-making, the authors concluded that access to loans had done little to empower women. Its main effect had been to increase the social status of loan-receiving women vis-à-vis less well-off women rather than vis-à-vis men within their household or the wider community.

(b) Does access to credit 'empower' women? The positive verdict

In contrast to this set of evaluations are others which paint a far more positive picture of the impact of these same credit programs on women's lives. Rahman (1986) found that loanee households in general, regardless of the gender of the loanee, had higher income and consumption standards than equivalent non loanee households. Although loans to women were more likely to benefit male consumption standards than male loans were to benefit female consumption standards, women loanees nevertheless did benefit from their direct access to loans. Women who made active use of at least some of their loans had higher consumption standards and were more likely to have a role in household decision-making, either on their own or jointly with their husbands, than 'passive' female loanees, and both in turn had considerably higher consumption standards and were more likely to participate in household decision-making than women from male loanee households or from households who had not received any credit.

A study by Pitt and Khandker (1995) explored the impact of male and female membership of credit programs on a number of decision-making outcomes in order to establish the extent to which they were differentiated by the gender of the loanee. The outcomes included the value of women's non land assets, the total hours worked per month for cash income by men and women within the household, fertility levels, the education of children as well as total consumption expenditure. These authors also concluded that households receiving loans were largely better-off than those not receiving loans. In addition, the findings that the gender of the loanee did influence the pattern of household decision-making outcomes was interpreted as evidence that women's preferences carried greater weight in determining decision-making outcomes in households where they had received a loan compared to households where either men received the loans or in households where no loans had been received.

A third example of a 'positive' verdict is by Hashemi *et al.* (1996). They explored the impact of credit on a number of indicators of empowerment:

- i the reported magnitude of women's economic contribution;
- ii their mobility in the public domain;
- iii their ability to make large and small purchases;
- iv their ownership of productive assets, including house or homestead land and cash savings;
- v involvement in major decision-making, such as purchasing land, rickshaw or livestock for income earning purposes;
- vi freedom from family domination, including the ability to make choices concerning how their money was used, the ability to visit their natal home when desired and a say in decisions relating to the sale of their jewelry or land or to taking up outside work;
- vii political awareness such as knowledge of key national and political figures and the law on inheritance and participation in political action of various kinds; and finally,
- viii a composite of all these indicators.

They found that women's access to credit was a significant determinant of the magnitude of economic contributions reported by women; of the likelihood of an increase in asset holdings in their own names; of an increase in their exercise of purchasing power; of their political and legal awareness as well as of the value of the composite empowerment index. In addition, BRAC loanees tended to report significantly higher levels of mobility and higher levels of political participation while Grameen members reported higher involvement in 'major decision-making.' When women's economic contribution was used as an independent variable, the effect of access to credit on the empowerment indicators was reduced but remained significant, suggesting that one important route through which women's access to credit translated into 'empowerment' was via their enhanced contribution to family income.

The study also found that access to credit appeared to be associated with an overall reduction of the incidence of violence against women. Regression analysis suggested that older women, women who had sons and women with education were less likely to have been beaten in the past year (Schuler *et al.* 1996). These findings are consistent with the lower status of young wives who are relatively new in the husband's home, with the prevailing culture of son preference and with the greater agency attributed to women with education (see, for instance, Dreze and Sen, 1995). In addition, they found that membership of a credit program was associated with a statistically significant reduction in violence, but that the magnitude of women's economic contribution did not have any significant effect. They concluded that it was women's participation in the expanded set of social relationships embodied in membership of credit organizations rather than increases in their productivity per se which explained reductions in domestic violence.

(c) Explaining the conflicts: methods, questions, interpretations and models

These conflicting conclusions about the 'empowerment' potential of credit for women are both apparent and real. What appear to be contradictory findings concerning, for instance, the extent to which credit exacerbates or lessens violence against women, enables or fails to enable them to acquire independent assets, is associated with an increase or decrease in their living standards is partly a difference in methodology. It reflects the fact that some studies relied largely on statistical data and significance tests for their findings while others relied on more qualitative, sometimes anecdotal, evidence. Consequently, some of the differences in findings relate to differences in the incidence of empirical outcomes, some findings referring to 'average' and others to 'non average' outcomes. Thus Hashemi *et al.*'s finding that women's access to credit was associated with an overall reduction in the incidence of domestic violence is perfectly compatible with the finding that it exacerbated violence in a number of individual households reported both by them (see Schuler *et al.*, 1996) as well as by Goetz and Sen Gupta.

Conflicting conclusions about the impact of credit also reflect differences in the questions asked by different evaluations. By and large, the negative evaluations focused on processes of loan use while the positive ones focused on outcomes associated with, and attributed to, access to loans. The validity of both sets of measures depends on their conceptual clarity and on the validity of their underlying premises. There are, for instance, reasons to question whether some of the process-based measures do indeed measure what they are intended to measure. In conceptualizing the process by which women's access to resources translates into impact, Pahl (1989) had made an analytically important distinction between what she calls 'control,' the ability to make policy decisions concerning the allocation of resources, 'management' which relates to decisions to do with the implementation of policy and 'budgeting' which merely involves keeping track of income and expenditure. Ackerly's measure of empowerment is ambiguous because it does not distinguish between women who acquired their 'accounting knowledge' through an active involvement in the control and management of their loans, in the way that she appears to assume, or merely through a budget-keeping role of the kind pointed to by Pahl.

Goetz and Sen Gupta's index of managerial control is similarly ambiguous. It essentially conflates 'control' and 'management,' making no distinction between decisions about loan use and decisions related to implementation. But policy decisions about how loans are to be used are separate from, and indeed prior to, decisions relating to the management of the enterprise to which the loan is assigned. Since the authors offer no information on the decision-making processes by which the loans were allocated, we have no way of knowing the extent to which the observed allocations reflected a sound economic calculus on the part of women, the specific individual circumstances of their household or the blatant exercise of male power. Indeed, it is in principle possible (though in practice unlikely) that, with the exception of the unknown number of the 22 percent of women in their 'no control' category who did not even know how their loans were used, the remainder (at least 78 percent of their sample) participated fully in decisions about loan use.

There is also a need to be cautious about the causality implicit in process-based indicators. The possession of accounting knowledge or exercise of managerial control does not, on its own, suffice as evidence of empowerment. To be persuasive as such evidence, we would need to know more about their relationship to other valued achievements, perhaps of the kind outlined in Ackerly's description of the ideal-typical 'empowered woman.' Indeed, the assumption that managerial control over loan use is a necessary condition for women to be empowered by their access to loans is explicitly rejected by Hashemi *et al.* In their study, they classified all the women loanees in their sample according to the 'control' categories developed by Goetz and Sen Gupta and confirmed that large percentages of women loanees in their sample had indeed 'lost control' over their loans by these criteria. This did not, however, prevent a significant proportion of them from achieving a range of other valued impacts, although, as we noted, the likelihood of these positive impacts was strengthened if women used at least part of their loans to increase the value of their own economic contributions.

As far as outcome indicators are concerned, their validity depends on how well they capture changes in the structures of gender inequality within the household and community, not merely on how well they capture changes in household living standards or even in children's welfare. One of the strengths of the study by Hashemi *et al.* is that their indicators meet this criterion. They can all be seen as valued outcomes in their own right as well as being linked to the structures of constraint which give rise to gender inequality in Bangladesh. By contrast, the study by Pitt and Khandker is undermined by the absence of any obvious rationale for the particular decision-making outcomes selected for their study. Their findings are consequently not always easy to interpret. The only outcomes with relatively unambiguous theoretical links with women's empowerment are:

i women's ownership of non land assets, an increase in which could be interpreted as a strengthening of their fall back position; and
ii the gender gap in education, a reduction in which could be seen as addressing a longstanding gender inequality in the value given to children. Their own interpretations of some of their findings tend to be somewhat *ad hoc* and open to other equally plausible and very differing interpretations.

This takes us to yet another factor behind the conflicting conclusions we have been discussing which is the proclivity to 'read' empirical findings in the light of preconceived notions about loan impact so that the same findings are given extremely contradictory interpretations. Thus, Pitt and Khandker take their finding that loans to women led to an increase in their market-oriented work to indicate an empowerment effect. By contrast, all three negative evaluations warn against the intensification of women's workloads and fatigue. Pitt and Khandker interpret the higher level of household consumption expenditure associated with loans to women as evidence of the greater weight given to women's preferences in household decision-making; Montgomery *et al.* suggest that such findings demonstrate that loans to women are 'heavily compromised by the persisting responsibilities of women to cover the consumption needs of the family' (Montgomery *et al.*, 1996, p. 168). Similarly, the increase in women's welfare levels as a result of their access to credit is linked to their enhanced role in household decision-making by Rahman, but given a much more passive interpretation by Goetz and Sen Gupta who suggest that women give up their loans to men 'in exchange for the right to have greater expenditures on their own or their children's clothing and health.'

In short, there are differing judgments embodied in these evaluations as to what kinds of changes constitute evidence of empowerment, differences which in turn reflect the differing models of households, and the power relations within them, which these evaluations draw on. While both positive and negative evaluations accept the premise of gender inequality in intra household relations, they vary considerably in the significance and meaning attached to cooperation and conflict between men and women within the household and consequently to autonomy, dependence and interdependence within the household.

By and large, the negative evaluations tend to be negative because they stress gender antagonism within the household and discount the significance of co-operation. Thus, for Montgomery *et al.*, reports of 'jointness' in the management of household enterprise and income are merely examples of disguised male dominance; only the exercise of autonomous female authority is counted as evidence of empowerment. Goetz and Sen Gupta's discussion of the circumstances under which the investment of women's loans in the purchase of a rickshaw would, and would not, constitute exercise of 'control' also reveals this individualized notion of empowerment. Rickshaw-pulling in Bangladesh is a purely male activity so that the purchase of a rickshaw, an extremely common use of loans to poor women, represents investment in an activity to which women are unable to contribute any labor. While such women would automatically be classified in the 'little' or 'no' control category by Goetz and Sen Gupta's criteria, they suggest that a woman could still be classified as exercising 'significant control' if the rickshaw was licensed in her name and if she established a contractual rental relationship with the rickshaw puller. In the context of rural Bangladesh, however, this would constitute extremely anomalous behavior on the part of a woman who had an unemployed son or husband in the family who was able and willing to pull the rickshaw and to take responsibility for loan repayment.

The more positive evaluations, by contrast, are positive partly because they do not privilege individualized over joint forms of behavior. Pitt and Khandker attempt to capture possible increases in the weight given to women's preferences in a series of household decisions following their access to loans, but do not rule out joint decision-making. Both Hashemi *et al.*, as well as Rahman explicitly incorporate some 'jointness' on interests within the household into their indicators of empowerment. In the final analysis, the plausibility of one or other set of conclusions about the transformatory impact of credit for women will rest on the credence attached to the models of power which inform the analysis.

Despite their differences, however, both sets of evaluations share in common an absence of testimonies by women loanees themselves as to the impact of credit on their lives. Obviously, in the context of evaluation studies where valued resources are at stake, personal testimonies on impact have to be interpreted with caution, given that there may be a strong incentive among beneficiaries to present impact in a positive light. At the same time, participatory impact assessments can help to enrich academic theorizations of gender subordination by providing important insights into inequality as a 'lived experience.' In the rest of the paper, I want to report on the findings of my own evaluation of a rather different credit program in Bangladesh in which I sought out the testimonies of 50 female and 20 male loanees as to the impact of loans on their lives. In addition, I also carried a quantitative survey of 700 households to provide basic descriptive statistics on the loanees, their households, their patterns of loan utilization as well as on some of the impacts identified in the evaluation literature. I will be drawing on the loanees' testimonies as a different vantage point from which to contextualize and assess the findings of the various evaluations discussed here as well as to consider what the perspectives of women loanees themselves can add to our understanding of the transformatory potential of credit targeted at women. I will be concluding with some general conceptual and methodological comments on the evaluation of women's empowerment.

8.2 THE SMALL ENTERPRISE DEVELOPMENT PROJECT: LENDING TO THE NOT-SO-POOR

The Sustainable Energy Development Program (SEDP) was started in 1990 in Faridpur district in Bangladesh and extended in 1992 to Mymmensingh. It acts as an intermediary between eligible loanees and a special credit line which is funded by the Norwegian Agency for Development Co-operation, or NORAD, and managed by one of the country's nationalized banks. Its primary goal is the promotion of small-scale labor-intensive enterprises, including women's enterprises, in order to enhance income and expand employment. To be eligible, potential borrowers must have at least half an acre of land and some prior entrepreneurial competence. They are identified by project staff and attend a three-day training course in basic entrepreneurial skills and social development issues during which they are assessed for their entrepreneurial potential. Loans range from 5,000/- takas to 500,000/- takas. Interest rates are subsidized and vary between 10 percent and 14 percent according to loan size, while repayment is generally on a monthly basis. Repayment rates are high, at over 90 percent.

The household survey of male and female loanees found that while male loanees in both districts tended to be better off in terms of land owned and cultivated and education level of loanee, female loanees in Faridpur district were much better off than those in Mymmensingh. Female loanees in Mymmensingh came from the poorest households in the survey sample; they were also more likely to be female-headed than women loanees in Faridpur (14 percent compared to 7 percent). They were also given much smaller loans than those in Faridpur and reported correspondingly small rates of return to loan investments. There was nothing in the SEDP rule book to explain this pattern. It appeared to reflect differences in management orientation in the two districts.

The SEDP thus differed from the main poverty-oriented programs in a number of significant ways which are summarized in Table 8.1. While these programmatic differences mean that the findings from my study cannot not be directly compared to those discussed earlier, they nevertheless provide a useful basis for distinguishing between impacts which appeared to be associated with women's access to credit per se, regardless of delivery characteristics, and those impacts which were clearly associated with particular kinds of program delivery. In addition, a tentative degree of direct comparison was possible because of the pervasiveness of the poverty-oriented credit organizations and inevitable contact with their operations in the course of the field work. Where SEDP loanees in my qualitative sample or a member of their family had themselves borrowed from one of these organizations, interviews were extended to cover this experience.

Table 8.1 Differences in goals and organizational practice between SEDP and typical poverty-orientated lending in Bangledesh

Characteristics	*SEDP*	*Poverty-oriented lending*
Goal	Small enterprise development	Poverty alleviation
Role	Intermediary	Direct lending
Loan size (takas)	5000–500,000	1000–5000
Class eligibility	Own more than 50 decimals of land	Landless or less than 50 decimals of land
Other criteria	Prior entrepreneurial experience	No experience required
Gender	Men and women	Predominantly women
Interest rates	Subsidized (10–14% annually)	Nonsubsidized (18%)
Repayments	Monthly	Weekly
Emphasis on	Individual lending	Group-based lending

(a) Female mobility and social status: the contradictions of class and gender

In terms of impact, the central overall question framing the qualitative component of the evaluation was 'What difference did the loans make to the women's lives?' What changes did they bring about and how did women assess these changes? Let me start out by noting that, as in most of the evaluations discussed earlier, there was little evidence of any radical change in the gender division of labor as a result of women's access to loans. Access had increased their levels of economic activity, but not the range. The household survey showed that women remained confined to a small number of 'female' occupations, with livestock rearing predominating in Faridpur and paddy husking in Mymmensingh. Production of cane and bamboo goods was second in importance in both districts. In addition, a few women invested in poultry raising, home-based tailoring and itinerant hawking. Male occupations were more evenly distributed and over a wider range of activities: 'shops' of various kinds, engineering and other workshops of various kinds, seed nurseries, managing power tillers and rice mills as well as farming and livestock rearing.

This gender patterning of the occupational structure suggests that adherence to purdah norms continues to constrain women's public mobility, limiting their choice of enterprise and their ability to carry out transactions in the market place. Given that the resilience of purdah featured so centrally in some of the evaluations, it is worth analyzing what women loanees themselves had to say on this question. Two key insights emerged out of their testimonies. First of all, notions of purdah were closely interwoven with local understandings of class, social status and gender propriety so that behavior expressing gender norms was often simultaneously expressive of class hierarchy and social standing within the community. Conformity with purdah often featured in women's testimonies in terms of a voluntary adherence to status norms rather than as a direct manifestation of male control, as is evident from the following testimonies:

> I do all my work within the house, it is not a matter of fear, it is a matter of izzat [honour]. Women who can eat by staying within the home are given greater value. Everyone gives value to women who work within the home, people outside, as well as those in the family. Men work outside, and women inside. Otherwise why have men been made, you could have had only women. I will go without food, but I will not go without izzat.
>
> (F23)

> It is alright moving around within the neighborhood, but I have no time to go to the bazaar. Anyway, I am a woman, it is not possible for me to go to the bazaar. Some women go, those without husbands. But I have a husband and a son, I don't go. It is a matter of man-shonman (honour).

> People in the neighborhood will say, she has a husband, she has a son, how can she go to the bazaar?
>
> (F20)

The second point to come out of the women's testimonies was that the distinction between 'public' and 'private' space was not represented as a simple dichotomy but rather as a continuum of locations in the public domain, ranging from acceptable to unacceptable places for women to be seen. Many of the women in my sample moved around freely within their neighborhoods, were prepared to go into the district headquarters to attend the initial training and subsequently to the local SEDP office to deposit their monthly repayments. Rural markets, on the other hand, the weekly haat and the permanent bazaar, were located at the other, unacceptable end of the spectrum.

Because the need to adhere to purdah was not equally subscribed to by all women, or by all class groups, and because the decision to adhere to purdah did not impose the same costs, the relationship between women's presence in public activities and their empowerment was not a straightforward one. In this connection, we can distinguish between a number of different categories of women. There were those from better-off households for whom there was a convergence between the economic logic of earning a livelihood and the social logic of maintaining their honor. They owned homestead land and other facilitating assets so that returns to home-based work exceeded the returns to most forms of waged employment available to them. The majority of these women had never sought, or been forced to seek, outside employment. F23 cited above was one such woman.

It was a different story for women from poorer households who, nevertheless, had some social standing within the community. Purdah norms also constrained their mobility even if it carried a high economic cost. Prior to accessing loans, these women had either starved invisibly at home, or opted for badly paid and demeaning domestic labor within the shelter of other people's homes 'where nobody would see us.' Access to credit was a godsend for this group because it allowed them to feed themselves and their families without the humiliation associated with menial domestic labor in other people's homes.

The poorest women in the sample were least likely to have paid attention to notions of propriety. There were a number of them who had been working the public domain prior to accessing loans, some as agricultural wage laborers in the fields, others as petty traders in local markets or by the roadside. Even among this group, however, the prosperity which went with their loans often led to their withdrawal from public forms of activities. In some cases, the decision was on normative grounds. F25's testimony points to the role played by community opinion in her decision to withdraw from public transactions:

> So many people say to my husband, "Your wife goes outside the house, she goes to the field, she has gone bad". … I survive by my own effort, I do not borrow from my neighbors any more, nor do I lend … There is no

> dishonor in work. But I don't sell milk in the market anymore. My value has gone up from before, I feel ashamed, people say, she has improved so much, how can she still go and do this work?
>
> (F25)

More often, the decision to withdraw reflected the conditions which prevailed in the female segments of the labor market. For instance, F33's testimony illustrates why agricultural waged labor in the public domain was unlikely to be experienced as particularly empowering by most women:

> Before the loans, women used to work on other people's fields, cutting lentils, rice, wheat. They got 20/- to 30/- takas a day. That is happening less now because so many women are getting loans, they are raising cows, goats, they can work for themselves so why should they work for someone else? If you can work for yourself, well, look, I am sitting here with you, could I do that if I worked for someone else? They would pay me less. I would pull up lentils, they would give me 20/- a day, this was four years ago. Before women used to clear the irri blocks, they would stand in the water and get leeches on them. Now they don't. Now, with the loans, they have some peace.
>
> (F33)

By and large, women who remained in outside forms of employment were female household heads, who often had little choice in the matter, and a number of poorer women who had been itinerant traders before their access to loans.

In contrast to this general picture, however, it should be noted that there were a number of women in the sample who gave a positive value to their increased ability to move more freely in the public domain, associating it with the acquisition of 'courage' rather than as a source of shame. These women attributed their newly found self-confidence in dealing with local elites, with the police and with others who had previously intimidated them to their interactions with SEDP staff rather than to simply their access to credit per se. F29, who came from the poorer end of the economic spectrum, valued the fact that her access to loans had allowed her to move from selling a few vegetables under a tree outside the village bazaar to establishing her own permanent shop within it. She was the only woman in that bazaar, but was now such a familiar sight that she no longer aroused any comment. F50, who came from a poor, but status-conscious, household and had previously gone hungry at home rather than compromise her family's social standing, also valued her new mobility:

> By joining these samities [cooperatives], many women have got the courage of men. Women now have the same rights as men. If a man can go and cut earth, go to the haat-bazaar, to the towns, why can't women? I can go everywhere now, even to the haat. If my husband is not at home,

> if he has gone to the market, I will go to the laborers' house to fetch them. If I needed to go to the bazaar and my husband was not at home, I would go.
>
> (F50)

Our analysis thus highlights the ambiguities associated with the use of increased physical mobility, particularly in relation to the market place, as an indicator of empowerment in the context of rural Bangladesh. On one hand, as long as women adhere to norms of purdah and do not participate significantly in market transactions, they will remain dependent on male household members to undertake such activities on their behalf and to that extent their economic agency will be restricted. On the other hand, if empowerment entails the expanded capacity for making choices, for taking actions which express their own values and priorities, then it has to be recognized that these values and priorities are likely to be shaped by the values and priorities of the wider community (Kabeer, 1999). The paradox is that in many cases, this leads women to opt for some form of purdah if they can afford to, both to signal their social standing within the community and to differentiate themselves from those women who do not have this choice.

(b) Enhancing self-worth and perceived economic contribution

If there had been no radical change in the gender division of labor of the kind considered by many to be a necessary precondition to women's empowerment, what kinds of changes did occur as a result of women's access to loans? One important change that featured in many of the women's testimonies related to their sense of self-worth, of bringing something of value to their households. The significance of this has to be understood in the context of the increasing monetization of the Bangladesh economy and the gap that it has opened up between women and men in terms of accessing new opportunities. Men have been privileged by their gender, class and education in gaining such access while the resilience of purdah norms have kept women largely confined to the precincts of their homesteads, dependent on male members of their family for economic provision and social protection.

Most studies on gender relations in Bangladesh have pointed to women's status as dependants, but few have explored what such dependency might mean as a 'lived' experience. The testimonies of women loanees made it clear that many found the position of supplicant within the family galling and humiliating, particularly those who were forced to literally plead for money to meet their everyday needs. This was vividly illustrated in F15's comments:

> If I had not gone to that SEDP meeting, had not taken a loan, had not learnt the work, I would not get the value I have, I would have to continue to ask my husband for every taka I needed. Once I had a headache, I wanted

> one taka for a bandage to tie around my head, I wept for eight days, he still would not give me the money. Just one taka.
>
> (F15)

Testimonies such as this help us to appreciate the importance that women like F15 attached to their new identities as bearers of valued economic resources. Nor was it a case of purely passive access to such resources. According to the household survey, the majority of the women in the sample used at least part of their loans to enhance their own productivity. Those who had not been economically active previously were able to start up new activities. Others were able to put pre-existing enterprises on a more secure basis and yet others were able to move into their own home-based enterprises rather than working for others in forms of work they considered demeaning.

Consequently, while most women experienced an increase in their workloads, they did not give it the negative interpretations suggested by some of the evaluations discussed earlier. The distinction that they made between paid and unpaid work helps to explain why. It was not that these women were idle prior to their access to credit. Most were involved in domestic chores as well as in expenditure-saving work, but such activities, as we well know, were generally unremunerated and received little recognition within society or within the home. It was evident from the women's accounts that they too shared the low social value given to these activities. The new uses of their time made possible by their loans brought about an enhanced sense of self-worth as well as giving a new meaning to 'work.' As F43 put it: 'Ideas of the mind is everything. If you have money in your hand, you feel joy. If you have no money, you feel pain. My labor has increased, but I don't feel it because the money is also coming in. It doesn't feel like hard work.'

Nor was it only in relation to their own activities that women reported a sense of achievement. Their testimonies also highlighted the value they attached to the wellbeing and dignity of the work engaged in by other household members. There is little space allowed for such impacts, and their possible implications for gender relations, by models of the household which conceptualize it in confliction terms and fail to recognize the potential for solidarity between household members. Yet many of the women I interviewed pointed to the release of male household members from demeaning economic relationships as one of the valued achievements which they associated with their loans. F27 used her loan to mortgage in land for her husband to cultivate because, as she said, 'How long was he going to give labor on other people's land?'. For other women, their husband's dependence on moneylenders or wealthy landlords for credit, usually at extortionate rates, had been the most humiliating aspect of their pre-loan experience: 'My husband now works alongside me. He no longer has to hear harsh words if he does not pay his debt on time' (F43).

Greater social inclusion was another impact which was highlighted in the testimonies of poorer loanees, male as well as female. They spoke bitterly of how it had felt to be outside the orbit of community life, to be excluded from its social events and from everyday forms of hospitality. As a result of their loans-related prosperity, they had acquired a new respect in the eyes of those who had previously despised them and a position of strength from which to deal with them:

> Before I had to sit under a tree and sell my goods, people would make comments about me, I could say nothing. Now since the loan, they don't know what to say, they are nervous to say anything. After all, I haven't brought a loan just once, I have brought twice, thrice, four times. Now even if people want to say anything, they don't have the courage. Those who never acknowledged me now invite me, I have money, they might need to borrow. Before they looked down on me, never came to my house, I was poor, I could not feed them. And now even in houses where I do not expect to be invited, I am asked.
>
> (F29)

> Have things improved for us? Listen, when you have no money, there is nobody, but when you have money, you suddenly have so many friends and acquaintances. Money is all. All that time, when we had no food, nothing to eat, no one wanted to give us anything. And now, day and night, from house to house, it is "have a betel leaf, tobacco leaf, cigarettes, chair, chowki …."
>
> (F37)

While women's own sense of self-worth was enhanced by these various achievements, so apparently was their worth in the eyes of other family members. This was evident in the marked improvement in the quality of family relationships that many reported, particularly in the context of marriage. As primary, often sole, breadwinners for their families, men in poorer households experienced many difficulties in making ends meet. The women I interviewed were well aware of the stress and frustrations involved in this responsibility and the extent to which their own dependency contributed to it. Access to loans helped to reduce the burden for men since women were now able to share some of the responsibility of providing for the family. The result was a reduction in levels of tension and conflict and greater affection from their husbands:

> Before we had scarcity. Suppose we needed 5 seers of rice, and he brought home 4 seers, we would be short of food, the children's stomach would not be filled, they would cry and he would know why they were crying. I would keep it quiet, but the children would sometimes let it out. Now we sit down to eat together, those tears are gone. We eat properly, systematically now and there is no worry about food. He no longer has to worry about whether we have eaten or not. When he couldn't give the money, there would be words, I would say angry things to him, he would

> respond angrily: "I don't have it, how can I give it?" Now we don't have those words.
>
> (F24)

The effects of women's enhanced economic value were particularly marked in households where conflict between husband and wife had deteriorated into violence. The question of domestic violence cropped up sufficiently frequently in the interviews to suggest both that it had been a significant problem in the past and that at least those forms of violence which stemmed from scarcity-related frustrations had been reduced in the wake of women's access to SEDP loans. The link between credit and reduced violence was made directly by a number of women, including F25:

> My husband did not have clean clothes before, now he has, and they know it is because of me. My husband acknowledges this. He does not raise his hand to me any more. Before he used to hit me. What could one do if one's husband hits one …? In a house of scarcity, there is more kalankini. If he brought home four annas, and I could not buy enough rice, he abused me. The house where there is no scarcity, there is no abuse. Because of this scarcity, this poverty, the lives of the poor are so troubled.
>
> (F25)

(c) Gender, voice and decision-making

Another impact which featured widely in women's testimonies, and one which derived to some extent from the impacts discussed in the preceding section, related to their increased voice in household decision-making. The study provided both quantitative as well as qualitative evidence on this. The household survey had included separate questions on loanees' roles in decisions related to loan use and loan-funded activities, in order to capture the distinction between management and control noted earlier. As a result of the qualitative component of the field work in Mymmensingh, an additional question regarding to decisions relating to the allocation of loan-related profits was included in the Faridpur questionnaire. The results, reported in Table 8.2, make it clear that access to credit had not obliterated gender asymmetries in decision-making. Male loanees were much more likely to be primary decision-makers in relation to loan use and enterprise management as well as the allocation of profits than were female loanees who were more likely to report joint decision-making. On the other hand, women's access to credit does appear to have mitigated some of the gender asymmetries in decision-making. In male loanee households, the percentage of women having some sort of say in decision-making did not exceed 20 percent whereas in female loanee households, the figure varied between 40 percent, if we look at the exercise of primary decision-making role, and 90 percent, if we also include joint decision-making. The qualitative interviews with the women loanees suggested some of the reasons for their marginal, joint and primary decision-making roles.

The 10 percent of female loanees who played very little role in decision-making were made up of three subgroups. In some cases, their lack of voice reflected the straightforward appropriation of their loans by husbands. These women had not usually played a particularly active role in the decision to seek out loans and male appropriation was merely a further manifestation of a pre-existing marginalization within the household which the access to loans had done little to alter. Women who were either ill or had some disability also did not play much of a role in decision-making. Finally there were women who had conceded control over their loans to male household heads in recognition of their responsibility for the collective welfare of the household. As F2 pointed out,

> What need do I have to take decisions? Even if I die, my husband will continue to take responsibility for my children.... I keep the money, but it is his responsibility to spend it so it does not stay too long with me.
>
> (F2)

Around 40–50 percent of female loanees in the sample reported joint decision-making. In some cases, this reflected a taken-for-granted 'jointness' of household

Table 8.2 Decision-making in loan use, enterprise management and loan income by gender (precentages of loanees)

	Use of loan		*Running of business*		*Use of profit*	
	Male	*Female*	*Male*	*Female*	*Male*	*Female*
Faridpur: first loans						
Self	81	47	81	51	79	32
Others	11	8	11	12	11	5
Joint	8	45	8	37	10	63
Faridpur: second loans						
Self	84	41	85	45	83	31
Others	14	9	13	15	11	4
Joint	3	50	2	40	6	65
Mymmensingh: first loans						
Self	88	36	85	34		
Others	6	18	7	25		
Joint	5	45	7	40		
Mymmensingh: second loans						
Self	86	36	83	35		
Others	5	20	8	27		
Joint	8	43	8	38		

interests and they saw it as irrelevant that the loan had been granted in their name: As F40 put it, 'I may have brought in the loan, but I did it with my husband.' For others, 'jointness' reflected their awareness of their reliance on male family members to carry out certain stages of production and hence their to need to ensure male cooperation. F40 offered the following explanation of how 'separate' and 'joint' areas of decision-making were determined within her household:

> We had cows and calves before, but they were my husband's. … I have bought cocks and ducks and goats with my second loan and with the third, I bought a cow and also gave my husband some money for his wood business …. My husband takes decisions to do with looking after the cow, but with the goats and poultry, I decide. You see, the cow has to be taken out in the morning and brought back in the evening, and if some man comes to buy the milk, well, I am a woman, I can't go in front of him, my husband has to do the talking and running around. He has a role in it. I may get my husband to take my goats to the bazaar for sale, but I make all the decisions about it.
>
> (F40)

Finally there were those who had been previously been disenfranchised in household decision-making processes. They associated the transformation of their marginal role to one of joint decision-making to their access to credit and the resulting improvements in their earning capacity: 'My say has increased now that I know how to earn. I did not used to say much before but now I am malik (mistress) of my own shongshar (household economy).'

The third group of women, those who described themselves as primary decision-makers, were analytically the most interesting from our point of view since they appeared to go against the cultural norm. Here again, a number of different factors were at play. The first and most predictable category in this group were women heads of households whose primary decision-making role occurred by default. A second and less expected category were those who explained their key role in household decision-making in terms of their superior entrepreneurial competence, an opinion that was usually shared by other family members. F11 was an example of this category. She pointed out:

> The money from our business stays with me. When my husband needs it, he asks for it. He is not so good with accounts, so it all stays with me … I memorize the accounts, I can't read or write. 7,000/- worth of business is not so much that you need to write it down. … My husband knows whatever I do. He will never stop me from doing anything, whatever I say, he goes along with. I take all the business decisions. I keep all the hisab. If I tell him not to go to the bazaar today, he will not go.
>
> (F11)

An important point to make about the women in this category is that while access to loans may have expanded their sphere of decision-making, many of them were already exercising considerable voice within their own households on the basis of recognized managerial skills. This should not negate the importance of credit in their lives since it allowed them to realize their hitherto suppressed entrepreneurial potential, but it does mean that the extent of voice they exercised cannot be attributed solely to their access to credit.

A final category of women in the primary decision-making category were those who had extremely conflictual relationships with their husbands. While violence within marriage appeared to be a fairly widespread phenomenon, a certain degree of empathy characterized women's accounts of such violence when it was seen as an outcome of household poverty, and of the struggles of the male breadwinner to make ends meet. Exceptional violence, on the other hand, differed in that it was not explained in terms of the shared suffering of the poor, but in terms of the husband's character (abusive and foul-tempered) and habits (alcohol and drugs). There were three women out of the 50 in our qualitative sample who reported being married to such men. They had not left their husbands, but had effected a form of 'divorce within marriage,' using their loans to create a parallel economy for themselves which gave them considerable financial independence of their husbands.

F48 had used her loans to set up her own livestock business and then to purchase a rickshaw which she registered in her own name but which her son pulled. She was on her fourth loan when we interviewed her. By this time, she was managing the household budget, her relationship with her husband had improved and she had used her current loan to set him up in his own transport business. Here was how she described the changes in her relationship with her husband:

> My husband is working well now, he gives his earnings to me. Before he did not used to give it to me regularly. Now he doesn't drink any more and he has even reduced his biri smoking. I have cut it down, I have said I don't want to see you smoking, but he steals a little money and still smokes a bit – he can't do without it. And he used to drink in the beginning but not now .... And he has not raised his hand to me for the past three or four years. Not since the loan. His anger has subsided. Scarcity creates a lot of problems .... If woman kind has no money in her hand, mankind tolerates her less. When I had no money in my hand, he gave me no regard. Now he sees the woman has money in her hands, so that now if anything happens to me, it is his head that hurts. That is how it seems.
>
> (F48)

In F29's case, her husband's violence toward her had diminished when he had lost his legs, but not his abusiveness. While she used some of her loan money to improve his business, her relationship toward him remained antagonistic and it was in her son that she invested most of her affection and efforts. She related with satisfaction her ability to ignore her husband's abuse and go her own way, now that she was economically self-reliant:

> Now I am eating out of my own effort, I don't have to go to him for a single paisa .... If before I said, we need money, he would get angry, now he can't. If he gives me money, then he gives it and if he doesn't give it, then he doesn't. It is all the same to me. My son is now doing his training in Dhaka so I don't have to cook for him at present. If my husband gives me money for the bazaar, I will cook for him, if he doesn't, I won't.
>
> (F29)

As a footnote to this discussion, I should point out that the in-depth interviews with the 20 male loanees confirmed that women were far more marginal to household decision-making in their households and also helped to illuminate why. They reminded us that men did not rely on female family labor input in their enterprises in the critical way that women relied on men. In any case, men could take women's assistance in certain activities associated with their enterprises for granted on the basis of their authority as household heads: cooking for extra workers; adding the finishing touches to a garment; assistance with pottery or weaving. Consequently, they had neither practical nor normative imperative to take steps to ensure women's cooperation. Male loanees saw themselves as the primary and usually sole breadwinners of their families. Many were not only against their wives taking up income-earning activities but had explicitly forbidden them to take out their own loans. By and large, this group gave fairly unequivocal descriptions of male dominance within their households:

> I take the decisions about the business, she does what she understands, she doesn't get involved in extra jhamela (hassle). She has neither hisab or kitab [literacy or numeracy]. I take all the decisions around the house.

Once again, however, there were exceptions in that a number of male loanees did report making decisions jointly with their wives. A common factor appeared to be women's ability in these cases to make a contribution beyond that prescribed by the traditional gender division of labor. In some cases, women in male loanee households had taken out loans of their own, from organizations such as Grameen Bank or BRAC so that we were observing the effects of their access to credit on household decision-making. In others, it was their education which allowed them to assist their husband in keeping household accounts, particularly in cases where the husband was himself poorly educated.

(d) Transformatory investments: assets and education

The increase in women's voice in household decision-making processes was important in its own right for those who had been previously disenfranchised.

It had an added significance in a context where access to loans had led to an increase in household income. While it proved difficult to calculate precise returns to loan-funded activities,[2] what can be said with confidence is that most loanees reported satisfactory levels of profit – less than 5 percent reported a loss – and repayment was not generally regarded as a problem. The finding that access to loans generally increased levels of household income, and that women's access to credit enhanced their voice in household decision-making, also supports similar findings reported by some of the evaluations cited earlier, giving credence to the idea that expenditure patterns within the household were differentiated by the gender of the loanee. By and large, we found that male loanees were more likely than female to reinvest part of their profits in their businesses, that better-off women loanees (in Faridpur) were more likely to invest in some form of savings and that poorer ones (from Mymmensingh) were most likely to spend their profits on purely consumption needs.

Here I would like to focus not so much on gender differences in allocational priorities per se but on those which had the potential for addressing some of the inequalities which underpin women's subordinate status. My findings reaffirmed the finding, reported by both Pitt and Khandker (1995) and Hashemi *et al.* (1996), that women's access to credit had allowed a number of them to accumulate assets of their own. Table 8.3 reports on savings patterns of male and female loanees while Table 8.4 looks at patterns of owned and purchased homestead land. It will be seen that 'secret' savings, a longstanding practice by which rural women in Bangladesh ensured some degree of economic autonomy for themselves, persisted among women loanees. It will also be seen, however, that women loanees in both districts, but particularly the better-off ones from Faridpur, were also engaging in the less traditional practice of opening bank accounts in their own names.

Table 8.4 offers both direct evidence that women's exclusion, at least from homestead land, was beginning to break down, and indirect evidence that women were using their loans to purchase homestead land in their own names. Homestead land has a particular significance for women given the home-based nature of their enterprises.[3] Although women are entitled to half their brothers' share of parental property under Islamic law, most have not claimed land, waiving it voluntarily

Table 8.3 Saving patterns by gender (%)

	Faridpur		*Mymmensingh*	
	Male	*Female*	*Male*	*Female*
Cash at home	18	16	17	23
Bank account	25	20	20	9
Saving society	13	18	3	4
Lent on	–	1	–	6
Secret saving	–	12	–	6
No saving reported	44	45	61	54

Figure 8.4 Acquisition and registration of homestead land (%)

	Faridpur		*Mymmensingh*	
Acquisition	*Male*	*Female*	*Male*	*Female*
Inherited	67	61	54	56
Purchased	29	34	34	31
Both	2	2	9	10
Registration in own name	74	19	64	29

(as well as involuntarily) in favor of their brothers so as not to alienate their support should their marriages break down. Given the greater likelihood of male inheritance of land, the greater percentage of male loanees in the sample who reported that some or all of their homestead land was registered in their names is to be expected. But women loanees were as likely as male loanees in each district to report the purchase of some or all of their homestead land and, furthermore, 19 percent of those in Faridpur and 29 percent of those in Mymmensingh reported that some or all of it was registered in their names.

There are understandable reasons why women have not generally sought to assert individual property rights within the family in the past. There is also a broad cultural association between men and property. Moreover, given men's collective responsibility for household welfare, including the welfare of women, investment in male assets can be seen as an investment in the most widespread form of social capital available to women, their familial networks. In addition, certain assets such as rickshaws, irrigation pumps and tractors tend to be considered 'male' because they are almost invariably used by men. For a woman to register such an asset in her name, particularly when she had a husband, meant going against the grain of local notions of masculinity. As F13, who had purchased a rickshaw with her loan money, explained, 'He told me to put it in my name, but the thing is that the rickshaw has a signboard with the owner's name and if people see it has a woman's name, they will say, "Look at that fellow, he pulls a rickshaw but it is in a woman's name." I found that shameful.'

Whatever the rationale, it remains the case that the investment of women's loans in assets registered in men's names did little to alter customary gender asymmetries in the distribution of resources. For the purposes of our analysis, therefore, the more interesting cases were those where women's investment strategies did represent a departure from past practice and consequently evidence of the exercise of new kinds of choices. It was most often in conflictual marriages that women sought to separate out their asset holdings. In such cases, the practice of clandestine savings became a covert declaration of independence rather than an attempt to retain some control over purchasing power. These savings were no longer the traditional minuscule amounts, the residual income after basic needs had been met, or the fistful of rice accumulated painstakingly on a daily basis, but substantial sums of cash. F29, for instance, kept her finances separate from her husband's and chose not to let him know about her various savings:

> I have two DPS accounts in the bank and I save with our market samity [cooperative]. I also have saved 60,000/-, my husband knows nothing about that. I lend it to other business men and I get 50/- for 1000/-monthly. We are ignorant people, our money does not earn in the bank, but if I lend outside, I earn 250/- in 5 months for every 1000/- I lend.
>
> (F29)

It was also in situations of conflict that women were registered 'male' assets in their own names. Both F15 and F48, who had suffered extreme violence in the past at her husband's hands, registered the rickshaws they purchased with their loans in their own names. F15 hired out her rickshaw in return for a daily rent while F48 registered it in her own name 'so that no one could sell it off,' but gave it to her son to pull and took a daily contribution from his earnings. F4, whose husband had moved out to live with his second wife, registered her rickshaw in her own name – 'I bring in the loan, I will be the one to make the repayments' – but handed it over to her son to run as his business and collected her repayment money from him.

In other cases, it was a sense of generalized insecurity which led women to invest in some assets of their own. This motivation tended not to be openly discussed because it appeared to cast doubts on the reliability of family networks. F39 was one the few female loanees who referred explicitly to the insecurities which underpinned her desire to save in her own name. She had adopted a two-pronged strategy of investing in 'joint' assets (life insurance policy and mortgaged-in land) in her husband's name but also in a second life insurance account in her own name, both safeguarding family loyalty but also creating an independent resource for herself:

> I have saved what I could and made a life insurance policy, it is in his name and I am the nominee. That was for 50,000/-. I also took some mortgaged land with the loan money for 15,000/-. That is in my husband's name. Now I have raised 30,000/-, they have given 20,000/-. I put some in my own life insurance. It is for 30,000/-. Women have to look after themselves, can a husband and son do everything for them? These days, the left and right hand must work separately, they can't work together. Suppose something happens in future, where will I go? I don't want to have to suffer. Understanding this has determined my actions. He knows about the second account, but it is in my name. I didn't take the mortgage in my name, I have a husband, I have children – won't they be upset if I put it in my name? They will say, "Look we work to feed and clothe our mother, and she puts the land in her name."
>
> (F39)

It is also worth noting that while the registration of land in women's names can be seen as an important strengthening of their fall-back position, most women tended to explain it as a decision taken on their behalf by their husbands as an act of love and gratitude. But, its other significance was explicitly acknowledged by one of the male loanees we interviewed, a man who had registered one acre of the four acres he had purchased in his wife's name, both as recognition of her labor contributions to the household economy, but also to strengthen her bargaining position in the future, when he was no longer around:

> We have both worked hard. That is why I have put some of the land in her name, she has struggled along with me. If I die, my sons may not look after their mother or when they marry, their wives might misbehave with her. Now my sons will know she has property, their wives will know that their mother-in-law has property, they will give her importance. They will say, come and eat with us ....
>
> (Male Loanee)

Along with material assets, the other form of investment reported by women loanees which had the potential for transforming gender relations in the long-run related to girls' education. In many cases, children, particularly those with educated parents, were already attending school prior to loanees' access to credit. It was also clear, however, that access to loans, and the enhanced income levels which it generated, made education affordable for many households who could not previously have afforded it. This sometimes introduced a birth-order factor in educational differentials: education levels tended to be lower among older children whose school-going years coincided with the pre-loan phase of the household lifecycle and higher among younger children who reaped the benefits of credit access.

Of greater significance from the point of view of this paper is the fact that loan access also introduced a gender dimension to the decision to invest in children's schooling. Table 8.5 reports on mean 'gross enrollment rates,' measured as boys and girls aged 6–18 within a household currently attending school as a percentage of boys and girls aged 6–18 present in that household. In both districts, gross enrollment rates for boys were higher on average than for girls among male loanee households than female (although the difference was negligible in Mymmensingh) while in both districts, gross enrollment rates for girls were consistently higher than for boys in female loanee households. It is worth noting that a similar pattern was reported by Pitt and Khandker (cited in World Bank, 1995, p. 36). Not only should such results be welcomed in the light of the longstanding gender gap in education in Bangladesh but also on the grounds of the various transformatory effects attributed to female education by a wide-ranging body of academic findings, and also by the female loanees themselves.

Many of the rationales given by the women loanees for wanting to educate their daughters reflected a change in attitudes that appeared widespread and were often also expressed by male loanees: the idea that education enabled girls to marry more educated, and hence better-behaved, husbands; that less dowry would be asked of an educated bride; that husbands would respect a working woman; that it was no

Table 8.5 'Gross enrollment rates' for children aged 6–18 (%)

	Faridpur		*Mymmensingh*	
	Boys	*Girls*	*Boys*	*Girls*
Male loanee households	77	69	79	78
Female loanee households	71	77	55	62

longer acceptable for women to be uneducated. There was also evidence, however, of a gender-specific rationale in the particular stress that women loanees put on the need for women to 'stand on their own two feet,' both within marriage or in case the marriage failed. This was often based on their own bitter experiences of what it meant to be totally dependent on husbands for their every need, particularly at a time when marriage was no longer a very secure option.[4] Some women made a very explicit equation between female education, greater self-reliance within the marriage and reduced likelihood of abuse and violence: 'I will educate my daughter as far as is within my means. The reason is that these days if you don't educate girls, you marry them off to some no-good boy who will beat them. Why should I get my daughter beaten?' This belief does of course receive some statistical backing from the Schuler *et al.* finding cited earlier that women with some education were less likely to report having been beaten.[5]

(e) Program-specific impacts

It will be seen that there were many convergences between the impacts reported for the SEDP and those described in relation to poverty-oriented micro-credit interventions, suggesting that certain impacts can be attributed to access to credit per se rather than to specific models of credit delivery. At the same time, it is important to highlight two important divergences in findings which appeared to reflect specificities of organizational practice. First of all, there was general agreement among SEDP loanees, including those who had previously borrowed from BRAC and Grameen, that there were greater stresses and strains associated with repayment of loans from poverty-oriented programs. These often spilt over into conflict, sometimes between husband and wife, as noted by Goetz and Sen Gupta, sometimes between 'irresponsible' loanees and other group members worried about their future creditworthiness (this was also noted by Montgomery *et al.*) but most often between loanees families and program officers seeking to recover repayments. The testimonies of the loanees pointed to some of the programmatic differences between SEDP and poverty-oriented organizations which they believed accounted for the difference.

First, SEDP tended to target women and men with some prior entrepreneurial experience. Many of the tensions reported in connection with poverty-oriented lending occurred between program staff and loanees who were having trouble meeting their weekly repayments because of the failure to use loans profitably. Second, the larger size of SEDP loans also made a difference. As one woman said in relation to Grameen lending: 'They only give you 1,000 takas, what can you do with that?' SEDP loans were large enough for women to invest in their own enterprises, hence enhancing the value of their own contributions to the household and still be able to share them with male household members, thereby reducing potential resentment and ensuring joint benefits.[6] Finally, and perhaps most important, SEDP loans were given on easier terms: subsidized interest rates, monthly repayment and possibility for postponement of repayments in times of trouble.

The discipline built into poverty-related lending, which gave rise to the stresses remarked on by the loanees, reflected a concern with loan recovery and with long-term sustainability on the part of these programs. SEDP could afford to run a more relaxed lending regime because a concern with sustainability had not been built into program design while its loan recovery efforts were backed up by the perceived authority of a government bank. It was one of the constant ironies thrown up by the fieldwork that relatively well-off households could access loans at subsidized interest rates with greater flexibility built into their repayment schedules while all around us, poverty-focused credit organizations were lending far smaller sums of money to much poorer sections of the population at much higher interest rates with far more inflexible weekly repayment schedules. Indeed, the pressures of meeting weekly repayments were mentioned as the single most important source of the tensions generated by poverty-oriented lending. As F18 said bitterly, having experienced the repayment discipline imposed by Grameen Bank:

> If you take say, 1000/- from Grameen, you have to repay 10/- takas a month or the members of your samity will have to make it up for you. The cashier refuses to get up and says to you, "Until you have given your repayment, I will not leave." With SEDP, they allow you to give it two months late. In Grameen, your samity members will come and sell whatever is in your house to repay your loan. Grameen says, even if your husband or your son has died, even then you will have to make sure that you have made your repayment.
>
> (F18)

What was missing from the testimonies of the SEDP loanees was the kind of political awareness and mobilization documented by Hashemi *et al.* in the context of BRAC. This is not surprising since, aside from a brief initial training which covered both social and economic issues, SEDP did not set out explicitly to 'empower' women in the way that some of the other credit programs did. Most of its practices, including its training, were geared to enterprise development. The difference between the lessons offered by SEDP training and those offered by a local, explicitly feminist development organization was spelled out by F46 who had experience of both:

> Training is good for women … Before I joined Saptagram, you could say I was stupid … I was like a child. Saptagram taught me to think for myself.

> With SEDP training, I also learnt something new, how to do business … Which is better? Both are important.
>
> (F46)

But there was little evidence among SEDP loanees of a concern with wider political issues or with challenging the larger structures of gender subordination. Indeed, the practice of some of the loanees of lending out the profits from their loans to other sections of the community at the kind of usurious interest rates that the SEDP had rescued them from, while a sound use of their money from the micro-perspective, raises questions about the possible widening of the gap between those who were able to borrow from these organizations and those who could not.

8.3 CONCEPTUALIZING AND EVALUATING EMPOWERMENT: SOME LESSONS

Evaluations are attempts to document, assess and weigh up the social and economic significance of changes attributed to a particular intervention. Which particular changes are given significance in an evaluation will depend on the intervention in question but also on whose understanding of reality is given priority. My own evaluation of the SEDP prioritized the understandings of the loanees themselves and consequently used their testimonies as the basis of the analysis. This stress on personal testimonies should not be taken as a negation of other more objective forms of data. The quantification of findings plays a valuable role in providing some idea of their incidence and magnitude, helping to distinguish between those which are widespread and those which are relevant only to a minority. Qualitative methodologies can be used to place personal testimonies in their larger context. I chose to rely on personal testimonies because empowerment contains an irreducibly subjective element, but I sought to interpret my findings on the basis of my understanding of this larger context and to support with quantitative evidence, either from the household survey or from the secondary literature.

The first part of this paper discussed the very contradictory conclusions arrived at by a number of evaluations which set out to explore the empowerment impact of credit to women. Although these various evaluations, including my own, were conducted at different points in time (from the mid-1980s to the mid-1990s) and represent somewhat different models of credit delivery, I would suggest that the differences in their conclusions do not reflect either differences in timing of evaluation or in specifics of program delivery. Indeed, conflicting conclusions were evident for evaluations of the same set of programs carried out within a year or two of each other. Conversely, my own evaluation, while relating to a different model of credit delivery than the rest, nevertheless converged with some of their findings. Instead, I suggest that the main reasons for these conflicting evaluations lie in the questions asked, and the interpretations given to the answers, both of which reflect the underlying model of intra household relationships which underpin these evaluations.

Some of the evaluations prioritized structural aspects of intra household relations, the norms of female seclusion, and the gender division of labor which they legitimized. Others focused on more individual aspects, such as welfare outcomes and decision-making roles. Some evaluations conceptualized households as sites of gender conflict while others tended to stress their cooperative aspects. The particular model of gender relations which emerged out of the testimonies of the loanees interviewed in my study drew attention to the relations of unequal interdependence which underpinned the specific configuration of 'cooperative-conflict'[7] which characterized intra household relations in the Bangladesh context. Interdependence within the household was partly emotional. Family members who have shared adversity and faced the humiliations of poverty together, who were working toward common goals, are likely to develop ties of affection and loyalty toward each other. Interdependence also had a material basis, deriving from the division of roles and responsibilities within the family. Cooperative endeavor was a logical outcome of such interdependence. Interdependence within the family was also highly unequal. Gender asymmetries in relation to resources and opportunities made women far more dependent on men than men were on women. It gave them a much stronger stake in strengthening cooperation, and minimizing conflict within the family, than men and hence less able to bargain for their own needs and priorities.

Unequal interdependence within the family, and women's greater vulnerability outside it, explain why the women loanees sought greater equality within the family as a result of their access to credit rather than greater independence from it. It explains, for instance, the significance they invested in their ability to bring a valued resource into the household and to contribute directly to household income. It also explains the value they attached to improvements in the quality of family relationships as a result of the increase in their perceived economic contribution to the household. Some experienced this change as an increase in the affection, love and consideration that they received, others as a reduction in the tensions and violence within the household which arose out of men's frustrations at their inability to fulfill their obligations as primary breadwinners. As women took on a greater share of this responsibility, they also reported greater 'voice' in household decision-making, sometimes in the context of joint, sometimes individual, decision-making.

While these changes reflected cooperative solutions to household inequality, women's attempts to strengthen and democratize household relationships, a different pattern of behavior was reported by those in exceptionally conflictual marriages, conflicts which were often associated with male irresponsibility as breadwinners and hence the partial breakdown of interdependence. These women utilized their loans, not so much to leave their husbands whom they continued to rely on for social protection, but rather to effect a form of 'divorce within marriage.' They separated out their finances, made decisions about loan use independently of their husbands, although generally to the benefit of their children, and they retained control over loan-assisted activities. They were more likely to report independent decision-making and to register assets, including traditionally male assets, in their own names. Thus individualized forms of behavior often signaled greater conflict within the household rather than greater 'empowerment' for women. Nevertheless it was women's independent access to loans that allowed new forms of both cooperative as well as conflictual solutions to emerge.

The first key point that emerges out of the discussion in this paper is therefore the need to ground the conceptualization of empowerment in an understanding of the relationships of dependence, interdependence and autonomy which characterize gender relations in different cultures, the structures of risks, incentives and opportunities which they generate and therefore the particular trajectories which processes of empowerment are likely to take. A second important point is that, even within the same context, empowerment is a complex, rather than a simple, phenomenon. It has multiple dimensions and can occur through a multiplicity of routes. By way of illustration, I have summarized below the various impacts attributed to credit by the various evaluations discussed in this paper, making a rough distinction between those which relate to process and those which focus on outcomes (Table 8.6).

By and large, 'process'-related changes are the hypothesized pathways through which empowerment is believed to occur, while 'outcome'-related impacts relate to those achievements associated with access to credit which have transformatory implications for gender relations. There is however, no straightforward cause-and-effect relationship between process and outcomes. Nor is it always clear when a change is cause and when effect, when process and when outcome. Some impacts are means to valued ends, others are valued ends in themselves but also a necessary precondition for achieving yet other valued ends. Some outcomes may be conditional on hypothesized prior processes while others occur independently of them. Thus women were still able to achieve valued impacts in their

Table 8.6 The impacts attributed to micocredit by various evaluations

Process	*Outcomes*
Decision to access loans	Enhanced sense of self worth
Access to loans	Increase in perceived economic contribution
	Enhanced role in minor decisions
Decisions about loan use/repayment	Enhanced role in major decisions
	Exercise of purchasing power
	Mobility in the public domain
Decisions about loan-funded activities	Political participation
Labour contribution in loan-funded activities	Reduction of domestic violence
Marketing of loan-funded products	Increase in women's savings and assets
Accounting control	Reduction of gender gap in well-being
	Reduction in gender gap in education
Training	Greater social inclusion
Group participation	Self-reliant livelihoods

lives as a result of their access to credit, regardless of who managed their loan-funded activities or who kept the accounts. We also saw that where women used at least part of their loans to enhance their own productivity, they were more likely to experience such impacts. At the same time, a growth of women's self-confidence, in their knowledge of their rights, their willingness to participate in public action and even the reduction of domestic violence may have occurred as a result of women's participation in the new forms of social relationships embodied in credit organizations; they bore little relationship to the productivity of their loans.

The third point, which is an extension of the second, is the importance of avoiding narrow, unidimensional conceptualizations of empowerment which feed into dichotomous models of change: women are judged to be either empowered or not empowered on the basis of how closely they conform to a particular indicator. If instead we see empowerment as an expansion in the range of potential choices available to women so that actual outcomes reflect the particular set of choices which the women in question value, it becomes possible to make sense of what appear at first sight to be rather contradictory findings in my study. It becomes possible, for instance, to reconcile the finding that many of the women who subscribed most strictly to notions of purdah as a matter of family honor and female propriety were also some of the most successful entrepreneurs in my sample, women who not only managed and made a financial success of their enterprises but also described themselves as the main decision-makers in their households. It also allows us to make sense of women loanees who registered assets purchased with their loans or with their hard-earned incomes in their husband's rather than their own names and yet displayed enormous physical courage and initiative on occasions when their property was under threat.[8] It also explains why women who had previously ignored the norms of gender propriety, working as agricultural labor in the fields or taking their own goods to the market withdrew from these public forms of activity as soon as their increased prosperity allowed them to and opted instead for self-employment within the confines of their homes.

This suggests, as a fourth point, that we need to make a distinction between forms of change which have been prioritized in the feminist or in the developmental literature and forms of change valued by those whose lives an intervention is seeking to transform. Many of the impacts reported by the women and men in my study were also identified by 'etic' approaches to the evaluation of loan impact: the reduction in domestic violence, increased voice in decision-making and enhancement of their asset base. There were some aspects highlighted in the women's testimonies which were not reflected in these other evaluations, while others were given a significance not shared by the women themselves. The stress that women placed on their own sense of enhanced self-worth as economic actors, of being able to make a contribution to household livelihoods and the value they attached to both their own as well as husbands' ability to move out of demeaning forms of waged labor into their own enterprises, all of these are forms of social change with implications for intra household inequality which had no place in the evaluations cited earlier. Indeed, the women appeared to give a very different interpretation to the increase in their work associated with their access to credit to that given by some of the external analysts. The fact that this increase was a product of their enhanced ability to contribute to household livelihoods and the consequent mitigation of their status as dependants led many to describe it as a valued transformation of the meaning of work rather than an intensification of their work burdens.

On the other hand, they did not attach quite the same degree of value to individualized forms of control over resources that featured in some of the evaluations cited earlier. Although most did seek to utilize some part of their loans themselves, sharing their loans with husbands and sons did not necessarily carry connotations of loss of control. It was the ability to participate in making decisions about how loans were used and how the income from loans was to be used that mattered; this ability was valued whether exercised jointly or individually. As far as the ability to move around freely outside the home was concerned, the picture was mixed. Most women did not see this as a particularly valued aspect of change in their lives. The value they gave to working in a self-employed capacity on their own homesteads is not hard to understand when we consider the pittance that they earned as agricultural wage laborers and the arduous and demeaning conditions under which they worked. There was also near-unanimous antipathy among women loanees to the idea of marketing their own produce in rural bazaars or haats because of what such action signaled to the rest of the community. Consequently, the idea that women are excluded from the market place, and need transport and protection to overcome this exclusion, misses the point that many women exclude themselves from this arena and that they do so on the basis of what people might say rather than what men might do. Such self-imposed exclusion is likely to continue as long as the alternative is equated with poverty and with the absence or failure of male protection.

The final point to make is a variation on one often made by feminist scholars. Women are not a homogenous category. While this point is generally made to highlight the relevance of class, caste, race and culture in differentiating women's needs and interests, I want to make it here in relation to women as individuals. There is no reason to expect women, even those from the same class, to respond identically to new opportunities. Our understanding of the processes of empowerment needs to bear in mind the important distinction between women as a socially subordinate category and women as a highly diverse group of individuals. We have to allow for the fact that different women will experience and act on new opportunities in ways that reflect some combination of their structural positioning and their own unique individual histories. On the one hand, this means that even the best planned intervention is unlikely to be automatically empowering for all women. At best, it can create the kind of environment or provide the kind of resources which are most likely to help as many women as possible to empower themselves. But there are always likely to be some women who will not, or are not permitted to, take up the possibilities on offer. What we are likely to observe at any point are distributions of responses to these different possibilities.

On the other hand, however, the individuality of women also means that not all evidence of empowered behavior on their part can be ascribed to a particular intervention. The tendency to do this rests on a version of the dichotomous model of empowerment noted earlier where it is assumed that prior to the intervention, the women in question were cowed, fearful and mute while after it, they became articulate, entrepreneurial and active. Interviews with both men and women in my sample made it abundantly clear not all women had been passive or silent actors within their households prior to the arrival of SEDP. Indeed I found many examples of women who were already exercising considerable entrepreneurial initiative and playing key roles in managing their households. Some of this can be traced to their recognized individual competence relative to male household members. In addition, it can also be traced to some of the major social changes in Bangladesh in the past decade or so which have effected what has been called a 'quiet revolution' (Chen, 1983) in the ideas and practices of gender relations. The greater availability of such loans for women, and women's willingness to take them up, can be seen as both an effect of this revolution as well as contributing to further changes. Here is F18's account of these larger changes:

> We village girls, we understood less before, we never went into the town or city. Before this area was idle, there was very little education. It was jungle here, there was no decent road. But when the CNB road came, people became smarter. Before you could not sell a marrow here for 2 or 3 takas. Now since the road, you won't get less than 20 or 25 takas. This is how we have prospered .... I want both my son and daughter to study till IA. I hope she can get a job in family planning .... Many girls even in the villages are working now, they become cashiers with samities [cooperatives], they get paid. Before women did not go out of the house because people might say something. Before we were idle, now if there is money to be made, we are no longer idle .... Since independence women in towns got more opportunities, but since the first woman prime minister, women in the countryside are also getting more opportunities.
>
> (F18)

8.4 CONCLUSION

Let me conclude by making a general point about microfinance and women. While the recent questioning of the empowerment potential of loans to women helps to counter the earlier, somewhat single-minded preoccupation with 'repayment rates,' the recommendations which come out of the more negative evaluations cited in this paper carry the danger of overloading microfinance organizations with empowerment-related goals to the extent that their ability to deliver effective and sustainable financial services is likely to be seriously undermined. This point is made more generally by Rutherford (2000) who suggests that many NGOs promoting microcredit in the South Asian context have failed to develop effective financial services for the poor 'because they are not primarily interested in financial services but in much wider social issues' (p. 9).

There are multiple rationales for lending to women, apart from empowerment. The fact that women are much more likely to share their loans with male household members than men are with women, in my view, merely strengthens the argument for lending to women. The entire family is much more likely to benefit economically, and women are much more likely to benefit personally and socially, when loans are directed at women rather than men. Loans to men do little to challenge the internal gender inequalities of households, and indeed appear to reinforce them by giving men an affordable base from which to prevent their wives from engaging in their own income-earning activities.

There are other arguments as well. It is one of the injustices of the way that society is organized in Bangladesh that extremely able women, even those from better-off households, are unable to realize their entrepreneurial potential because their gender acts as a barrier to gaining access to the necessary resources. Men, even poor men, have always had more choices in terms of accessing economic opportunities than women from an equivalent class. Women's higher repayment records do not merely reflect their socialized compliance in the face of the instrumentalist authority of NGO or government officials, as the more negative evaluations tend to suggest, but also the compliance which comes with having few choices. If purposive interventions can help to direct resources to women, thereby overcoming past barriers which have led to the suppression of their entrepreneurial potential, then they must be welcomed on grounds of efficiency and equity. If greater efficiency and equity help to lay the grounds for women to tackle other aspects of injustice in their lives, then we will have found a different and perhaps more sustainable route to women's empowerment.

Notes

1 I would like to acknowledge the support provided by NORAD in carrying out this evaluation and to the staff of SEDP for their cooperation in the field. Reprinted from *World Development*, 29 (1), pp. 63–84, 2001.

2 Clearly, impact was likely at least partly to reflect returns to loan-related investment, but these proved extremely difficult to calculate. Loanees were at different stages of their loan cycle and loans were often repaid from sources other than the loan-funded enterprise so that profit calculations required calibration between costs and returns to more than one enterprise. See Kabeer (1998).

3 A nationwide participatory poverty assessment by the United Nations Development Programme (UNDP 1996) found ownership of homestead land the second most important priority identified by rural women, second only to productive opportunities.

4 I found a similar value attached to daughters' education as a route to greater self-reliance by women workers in the garment industry whom I interviewed in the context of a study exploring the impact of wages on women's empowerment. See Kabeer, (2000).

5 It is also supported by studies from other parts of the world; see Kabeer (1999).

6 Schuler *et al.* (1996) found that while access to credit by itself appeared to have some

effect in diminishing violence against women, women's economic contribution appeared to only start to have an effect once it had reached a certain level. The significance of loan size also crops up in the study Goetz and Sen Gupta: they found that while very few women in their sample received loans greater than 4000/-, those that did were much more likely to make some use of their loans themselves.

7 See Sen (1990).

8 One example was the women who had registered the rickshaw purchased with her loan in her husband's name and refused to let him write his land over into her name despite his desire to do so. Yet she, together with another woman, had sat guard, with machetes in their hands, over this land all night for several nights while her husband was away because she feared that their newly planted rice might be run over with a tractor by another family which was disputing their claim to the land. She told us: 'Afterwards my husband wanted to register the land in my name but I said, "It is your father's property, what will people say?" But he said, "You have struggled so hard for it." I said, "It is enough for me that you want to register it in my name but as long as I have a husband, the land will be there and if I don't have a husband, what use is the land to me?"'

References

Ackerly, B. A. (1995). Testing the tools of development: credit programmes, loan involvement and women's empowerment. *IDS Bulletin*, 26(3), 56–68.

Chen, M.A. (1983). *A quiet revolution: Women in transition in rural Bangladesh.* Cambridge MA: Schenkman.

Dreze, J. and Sen, A. (1995). *India, economic development and social opportunity*. Oxford: Oxford University Press.

Goetz, A. M. and Sen Gupta, R. (1994). Who takes the credit? Gender, power and control over loan use in rural credit programmes in Bangladesh. *World Development*, 24(1), 45–63.

Hashemi, S. M., Schuler, S. R. and Riley, A. P. (1996). Rural credit programs and women's empowerment in Bangladesh. *World Development*, 24(4), 635–53.

Kabeer, N. (1998). *Can't buy me love? Re-evaluating gender, credit and empowerment in rural Bangladesh*. IDS Discussion Paper No. 363. Institute of Development Studies, Sussex.

Kabeer, N. (1999). Resources, agency, achievement: reflections on the measurement of women's empowerment. *Development and Change*, 30(3), 435–64.

Kabeer, N. (2000). *The power to choose: Bangladeshi women and labour market decisions in London and Dhaka*. London: Verso.

Montgomery, R., Bhattacharya, D., and Hulme, D. (1996). Credit for the poor in Bangladesh. In D. Hulme, and P. Mosley (Eds), *Finance against poverty*. London: Routledge.

Pahl, J., (1989). *Money and marriage*. London: Macmillan.

Pitt, M., and Khandker, S. (1995). *Household and intrahousehold impacts of the Grameen Bank and similar targeted credit programs in Bangladesh*. Paper presented at workshop on credit programs for the poor: household and intrahousehold impacts and program sustainability by the Education and Social Policy Department, Washington, DC and Bangladesh Institute of Development Studies, Dhaka.

Rahman, R. I. (1986). *Impact of Grameen Bank on the situation of poor rural women.* BIDS Working Paper No. 1, Grameen Evaluation Project. Dhaka: Bangladesh Institute of Development Studies.

Rutherford, S. (2000). *Self-help groups as microfinance providers: how good can they get?* Paper presented at workshop on 'Best practices in group dynamics and micro-credit.

Organized by the Micro-credit Bureau, Department of Women and Children, Government of India. Delhi February 15–17.

Sen, A. K. (1990). Gender and co-operative conflicts. In I. Tinker (Ed.), *Persistent inequalities: Women and world development*, pp. 123–49. Oxford: Oxford University Press.

Schuler, S. R., Hashemi, S. M., Riley, A. P. and Akhter, A. (1996). Credit programs, patriarchy and men's violence against women in rural Bangladesh. *Social Science and Medicine*, 43(12), 1729–42.

UNDP (1996). *A pro-poor agenda: poor people's perspectives*. Report on Human Development in Bangladesh. Dhaka: UNDP.

World Bank (1995). *Toward gender equality: the role of public policy*. Washington, DC: World Bank.

9

MAKING MICROFINANCE MORE CLIENT LED[1]

Monique Cohen

9.1 INTRODUCTION

Six years ago the microfinance industry viewed its clients as a given. The general attitude among many of the experts was that 'we have the products, demand is unlimited and the clients will come.' Experts saw clients as statistics, measured in terms of repayment and repeat borrowing rates. Clients entered the discourse, if at all, through impact assessments that were largely the domain of the donors and researchers. These two partners formed an alliance: donors funded the impact assessments, researchers performed them. Microfinance institutions (MFIs) and their clients were the objects of these studies but they were rarely owners of the results.

Today, much of this has changed. The microfinance agenda is now increasingly client or market driven. Much of the current interest in clients is driven by the industry's focus on competition and dropouts. Competition, together with MFI policies of requiring clients to take increasingly large loans each cycle, has tempted some clients to take out multiple loans, to assume too much debt and at times end up defaulting on some of their microfinance credit. Dropouts have raised operational costs, a situation few MFIs can afford.

As a result, new attention is being given to clients and products, how to attract and keep clients. As this market driven microfinance agenda emerges, its component elements are taking shape. While the client-product nexus is important, it is only part of the agenda. It also includes linkages between clients and institutions and the client's financial landscape. Thus, we can discern three levels which define the new framework: the *client*, the *institution* and the *market.*

- The *client-product* nexus cuts across the issue of customer access to appropriate products and services. The agenda moves from one in which the institutional approach to clients was 'catch as catch can' to a market focus with specific products attracting particular market niches.
- *Institution-client linkages* differentiate between the internal need for mechanisms to provide institutions with a client database that can be used for product

development, marketing or service delivery and the larger question of what the appropriate institutional mechanisms are for serving large underserved markets like Brazil or Nigeria, and the self excluded (both the extreme poor and vulnerable nonpoor).[2]

- The *client's financial system* landscape challenges the attitude among many MFIs that they are the only game in town. The client's portfolio of financial services, formal and informal, determines not only how the client uses microfinance but also the role of microfinance within the financial market.

9.2 THE AVERAGE CLIENT AND THE AVERAGE PRODUCT

The client driven microfinance agenda has moved the industry discourse from its traditional focus on quantity to one that includes both quantity *and* quality of the services delivered (Chao-Beroff, 2001). This requires a greater in-depth understanding of clients, something that until now many MFIs have ignored or relegated to impact studies and dismissed as having no operational relevance. While impact studies have been primarily focused on seeking to determine if microfinance makes a difference to clients, today's renewed interest in clients begins with two other, equally basic questions:

- Who are the clients?
- How do the clients use financial services?

Turning to the first question, it is clear that even though most MFIs serve a wide range of clients, the majority are clustered just above and just below poverty line (see Figure 9.1). While poverty targeted programs tend to reach a higher percentage of lower income clients, significant poorer populations self exclude or are denied access. They include the destitute and to a lesser extent, the extreme poor (Sebstad and Cohen, 2001).

The similarity of clients, which extends across a wide range of methodologically different institutions, has been paralleled by a similarity of products. Indeed, microfinance can be viewed as a limited product industry, whose principal products are short-term working capital loans and involuntary savings. A few programs provide fixed asset loans. These features have been at the core of the 'microcredit for enterprise' approach that has dominated microfinance for the last two decades. A smaller number of MFIs offer voluntary savings services, some loan insurance, while an even smaller minority have attempted to address other insurance needs, such as health, disability, life or property insurance.

Not pressured to be responsive to demand, the industry has been able to deliver products that have worked in what until recently have been largely monopoly markets. The average product, the peer lending working capital loan, was an appropriate first choice for an industry in its infancy: homogeneity keeps costs down,

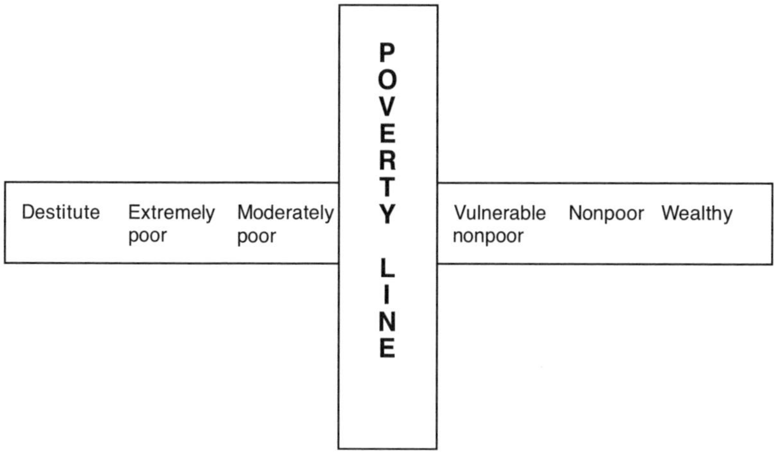

Figure 9.1 Defining the clients.

simplifies management systems and can be readily replicated. Moreover, short-term lending to existing businesses reduces risk to the MFI. In what was judged as a large untapped market, it was a safe bet to go for as many clients as possible.

Absent from this picture was a recognition that poor people often do not want to borrow all the time nor automatically increase their loan size. By misjudging these factors, which were assumed to be incentives for clients staying with a program, credit focused MFIs never bothered to develop other ways of retaining contact/ interaction with their clients, for example voluntary savings.

For the clients with no alternative sources of formal finance, MFIs fill a clear niche. It is cheaper than much informal finance, it is accessible, and it offers a relative certainty of supply over time. With little influence over the design of the products, the borrowers simply adapted the financial service to the most appropriate need at the time. Loans, ostensibly borrowed for micro enterprise development, are many times used to meet a multiplicity of other needs (Sebstad and Cohen, 2001).

Clients are demonstrating the imperfect nature of the products by voting with their feet. Dropout rates of anywhere from 13 to 60 percent in Uganda attest to this. Some clients, after participating in microcredit programs, often choose to 'rest' and/ or look for alternative services because the transaction costs are found to exceed the benefits (Wright *et al.*, 1999). While a minority dropout for reasons of default, the preference is to repay at all costs so that future access will not be denied, if and when the need arises (Sebstad and Cohen, 2001). These trends suggest that this industry is clearly not in tune with its clients. Furthermore, competition and client dissatisfaction are putting pressure on institutions to be more responsive to demand. MFIs have much to gain from designing new products and services or refining old ones. Among the benefits are an increase in market share, higher levels of client retention and lower operational costs.

However, such innovation is not readily realized. As Hulme and Mosley (1997) have noted, this requires designers of financial services for poor people to acknowledge that 'the poor' is not a homogeneous group with broadly similar needs. However, recognizing the heterogeneity of the poor clearly complicates matters for scheme designers. Homogeneity may be good for keeping delivery costs low, but is it not necessarily good for institutional sustainability if high dropout rates result.

Broadening and deepening outreach, as well as retaining more of the existing clientele, means *attracting* both new and old customers with products and services that better correspond to their preferences. That is, client preferences with regard to cash flow cycles across the year, their need for diverse sources of cash flow as well as their need for lump sums of cash for anticipated and unanticipated expenses (Rutherford, 2000a, b; Sebstad and Cohen, 2001). Furthermore, a look at the household's demand for financial services over its lifetime is a reminder that for clients (or potential clients) the use of financial services can take many forms, serve many purposes and also changes significantly over time. Figure 9.2 not only illustrates this, but also emphasizes the limited range of products offered by most MFIs. The imperfect fit between product and clients is obvious. Is it so surprising that people manage their finances using whichever products are available to them? As the industry matures it is clearly time to direct attention to product differentiation, albeit cautiously (Wright *et al.*, 2001).

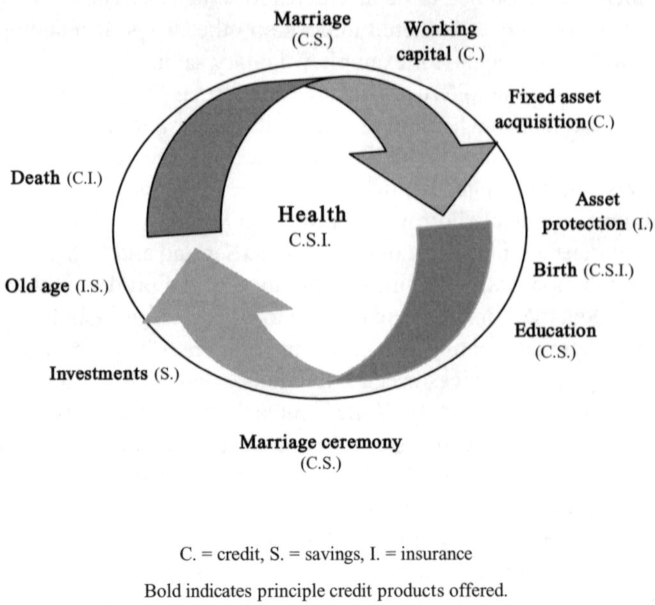

Figure 9.2 Household life-cycle financial needs.

The argument for a market driven agenda for microfinance takes place within a framework of long-term institutional sustainability. Without losing sight of the discipline of best practice financial performance, one needs to also go beyond defining the industry only in terms of the financial ratios which dominate today's measures of success. We should think in terms of how to efficiently gather client information, how to store it in a management information system (MIS), and how to use it effectively for clearly operational objectives.

Much of the current discourse on new products for existing clients (as well as new clients) assumes products will be delivered within existing organizational structures. But are these products and institutional structures necessarily the path to expanded scale and low-cost service delivery? Delivering more client responsive financial services to broader segments of the populations may require more than simply different products, it may also call for rethinking the existing organizational models in terms of built in mechanisms for listening to clients. Creative options can also be explored with respect to different institutional delivery models which can lower operational costs.

Lastly, a client led agenda for microfinance should recognize the role of MFIs within the larger financial system. The distinction between formal, informal and semi formal institutions may make sense when we consider the regulatory environment for financial services, but does this differentiation matter in terms of the client's reality? For most of the poor, access to microfinance services are but one of a range of financial services, formal and informal, which are available to them. None of these services is used in isolation. On the contrary, clients mesh these financial services in a way that best minimizes risk and enables them to better manage their money. Seen from this perspective we can gain an understanding of the niche market occupied by 'the average product' that MFIs deliver.

At this point, we shall examine in greater detail a few key aspects of the three levels described above: the client-product nexus, client-institutional linkages and the financial system from a client's perspective. We will explore how each can influence the design and implementation of a client led or market driven microfinance agenda.

9.3 THE CLIENT-PRODUCT NEXUS

In advocating for a more client oriented microfinance system, the need for more flexible financial services has become a mantra. Rutherford's documentation of SafeSave made the case for flexible financial services, services that more effectively respond to the cyclical flows and cash requirements of poor households (CGAP(18), 2001). Outside of Rutherford's work, the argument for flexible financial services has been typically limited to support for savings as a complement to credit. However, flexible services are more than new services like savings and insurance. They could also include money transfers or mutual funds which are currently still at a very experimental stage within the industry. They should also cover the refinement of existing products and the introduction of different credit products such as housing or emergency loans. Such an approach has been followed by some of the more creative MFIs such as SEWA Bank and BURO.

To identify more appropriate and flexible financial products, one can argue, as Wright does, that product design begins with understanding client use of financial services. Sebstad and Cohen's (2001) report on *Microfinance, Risk Management and Poverty* draws directly on the poor's experiences with microfinance to demonstrate how the industry's financial services are used by clients to manage risk. The use of loans to expand the household's sources of income, to build and diversify assets, and to improve money management are global strategies pursued by the poor to mitigate risk prior to a shock. By contrast, the current array of microfinance services is less likely to be used to cope with losses after they occur. What are offered by most MFIs are products that lack the capability to respond to emergencies by delivering small amounts of cash quickly in the face of crisis. It is worth noting that when an institution does offer emergency loans for the poor, this product has proven to be immensely popular. This was the case for the CVECA[3] programs in the Dogon region of Mali (Cohen and Sebstad, 1999).

In a field in which attention to clients has been limited, poor people's financial behavior has been an enigma for too long. Using information collected in four countries, Sebstad and Cohen (2001) argue that if microfinance services are to be more effective in helping the poor manage financial risks, then we need to think in terms of:

- matching products to clients' needs
- matching repayment amounts and cycles to clients' needs
- matching loan size to clients' needs, and
- matching financial flows and repayment cycles.

A better understanding of these factors provides a firmer basis for determining how old products might be tweaked or new products designed. From the recent AIMS[4] study conducted in India, it is apparent that the poor, including those fortunate enough to be SEWA Bank clients, are highly indebted. When expenditures and borrowings over a year are compared for 12 SEWA Bank clients, only 45 percent of their needs are met from cash flow and savings. The balance of their annual requirements (55 percent) is met by borrowing from the formal and informal sectors combined. However, only one-third of borrowed funds come from SEWA Bank (Chen and Snodgrass, 2001).

Clearly these poor live in a world of debt. It is also shows the limited contribution of microfinance. SEWA Bank offers its clients one product: a 2–3 year loan with a maximum of 25,000 rupees (Rs). This is a sizeable amount of money relative to income and represents the Bank's upper limit of what they think their clients can afford. However, because it is often less than what they need the informal finance sector remains a big player in clients' lives.

Rutherford (2000a, b) has noted that poor people need lump sums of money to reduce their vulnerability, to meet anticipated and unanticipated needs, and to take advantage of opportunities as they arise. Household cash flow is rarely sufficient to cover big expenses, health costs, school fees or basic recuperation after a shock. Despite the repeated stated purpose of a loan for micro enterprise development, client behavior attests to their tendency to use loans for these purposes. But is this the same as flexibility? Let's look again at SEWA loan product. On the face of it there seems to be a lack of flexibility – the loan period is long and the size of the loan provides only partial coverage for the big expenses such as marriage costs and housing, the two dominant uses of SEWA loan. However, from the client's perspective, maybe the picture looks different. This loan works when clients have a sizeable expenditure. This is where the general market offers few, if any, alternative options. However, because the largest loan size of Rs 25,000 will not cover the full amount of the cost of most weddings, acute illnesses, accidents, housing or business investments, the clients must still resort to 'patching' funds together. Yet the SEWA loan does give the borrower an important advantage. It lowers transaction costs by reducing a client's needs to access a multiplicity of informal sources for big anticipated expenses.

> A young boy whose mother was a SEWA Bank member needed 70,000 rupees (Rs) for a heart operation. His mother took a Rs 25,000 loan from SEWA Bank, borrowed Rs 5,000 from relatives, and accessed an additional Rs 5,000 from a moneylender at 60 percent interest per annum. The son raised the balance over several months from charities (Chen and Snodgrass, 2001).

With their average loan term of six months the product line of Pro Mujer, a communal banking institution in Bolivia, is weakest in providing its clients with a means to access significant lump sums of capital (see Box).

> Maria, a vendor who sells food at fiestas and outside her house, used her eighth loan (7,000 bolivianos (Bs)) to facilitate the purchase of a car for her husband. As a deficit still existed the balance was funded with savings. From renting a taxi, her husband now drives his own taxi, thus he has been able to increase his net income as a chauffeur by 50 percent.
>
> Anna produces and sells knitted goods. She has used her loans primarily as working capital to build up her business. However, her fifth and sixth loans (4,000–5,000 Bs) were invested in the materials and labor to construct her family's new house. This complemented the heavy dollar debt they had already incurred for the initial investments by borrowing US$1000 and US$500 from family and friends. Repayments were stressful but feasible because the loan enabled them to save money by no longer paying rent and using their home as their place of business (Cohen, 1999).

Typical of many clients' behavior, Anna and Maria must cope with available financing options provided by the MFI and the market at large. These women live in a world where they must 'patch' together scarce sources of attractive and accessible funds. Clients must incur high charges and transaction costs to invest in long-term assets. Indeed, in a country where there are multiple MFIs such larger loans relative to demand have been a relatively scarce commodity.

At the same time the shortness of the loan term can also play to a client's advantage (Cohen, 1999). Among 11 Pro Mujer clients, only three consistently used the loan funds for a single purpose, in all cases to purchase stock or inputs for their micro enterprises. Others split the use of their loans between inventory or partial investment in assets (including investments such as education fees, improvements to a market stall, land acquisition or the purchase of the husband's taxi). For these clients, the loan works much like a consumer loan. As long as repayment capacity exists within the household the funds are completely fungible. The internal account of the village bank, which can be (and is) accessed by members in good stead, can be used to cover outstanding debt and unanticipated expenses, such as health costs or funeral costs (Cohen, 1999). However, for some households, even a six-month term is too long, and repayment creates even more stress when household repayment capacity is constrained.

The same pattern has been seen in Africa amongst Uganda Women's Finance Trust clients (Wright *et al.*, 1999).

> A client with two businesses, snack food sales and the production and sales of borders for polleras took her first Pro Mujer loan of 500 Bs in 1996. At the time of her fifth (1,000 Bs) loan, 18 months later, her son, who had helped her in her business, died and her husband, formerly salaried, was paralyzed. Her business, which had generated a steady return with profits of about 200 Bs/month over the intervening period, was totally decapitalized. She was forced to draw down the inventory to pay for the funeral as well as the medical needs of her spouse. In addition, she withdrew funds from the internal account to pay off her loan balance. Six months later, clear of debt, her association gave her a second chance to get on her feet by giving her 500 Bs, her initial loan size. This was divided between 60 percent for borders for polleras, 20 percent for the purchase of used clothes for resale and the balance allocated to her property taxes. Slowly she is rebuilding the business and her income is rising (Cohen, 1999).

9.4 INSTITUTION-CLIENT LINKAGES

It is striking how many MFIs are largely top down in their flows of information. In such institutions, the opportunity for the client to be heard or the client to participate in institutional decision making is constrained. Yet if the voice of the client is heard and then further utilized to influence the functions of a MFI, it can significantly improve the effectiveness of services. Again, take the example of SEWA Bank, in which the clients also serve as members of its Board. In addition, SEWA organizers in their regular interaction with clients offer another vehicle for its members to be heard. A final mechanism is the specially trained Bank team that reaches out to individual clients to advise them on financial management practices, particularly when times are tough. Taken together, these conduits of information permit SEWA Bank management to gain client input and managers are held accountable for decisions that directly and indirectly affect the clients. Institutionalizing such information flows fits well with the basic developmental approach taken by SEWA Bank and other similar organizations throughout South Asia. Priority placed on organizing and empowering women as a necessary step in enabling them to get their demands heard and, by extension, recognized.

SEWA is not unlike the many older MFIs, which informally (if not formally) continue to work at keeping bottom up lines of communications open. When one asks many newer MFIs if, how, and why they collect information about clients, the frequent answer is either 'we don't' or 'we include 4–10 indicators in our MIS system.' While we have moved beyond the scant client monitoring documented by Dearden and Hyman (1996), confusion remains. In many client MISs, much of this information sits idle in databases, with ill-defined objectives for the use of the data. Moreover, the more data there are, the more difficult they are to manipulate. Two important exceptions are Freedom From Hunger (FFH) and ADEMI. The client monitoring system being developed by FFH to track program movement towards the achievement of both sustainability and social goals has clear operational objectives. Since the early 1980s ADEMI in the Dominican Republic has been regularly collecting three enterprise indicators from their clients: enterprise revenues, assets and employment. This information is used to determine the size of a repeat loan and to ascertain at what time business advisory services might be appropriate.

In some MFIs, learning from clients, both formally and informally, has retreated into the background. Having learned the mechanics of microfinance, some have adopted client tracking systems as part of their MIS. However, some MFIs, particularly the newer ones, have omitted means to integrate mechanisms for listening to clients. It may be that for the older MFIs it was so intuitive that it was never written down in the operations manual!

Many MFIs have set up client/customer consultative groups, which typically involve regular consultations with group leaders, e.g. Pride-Tanzania; LAPO-Nigeria; BURO-Tangail, Bangladesh. However, their effectiveness in both transferring information up through the chain of command and having managers act on the information does not always take place. CETZAM, a relatively new MFI in Zambia is considering another approach. Run by two ex-bankers, they recognize that a successful financial services provider, like all businesses, must be in tune with its customers. They wish to change CETZAM's organizational culture, which is top down and directive. This plus the prevailing culture make it difficult for lower level staff to question top down lines of authority. CETZAM is exploring the institutionalization of focus group discussions around client satisfaction and other issues. Loan officers and field managers will receive training in interview techniques and steps will be taken organizationally to legitimize the channels of communication that flow from the bottom up to senior management. At the same time, regular market research/customer surveys will be outsourced on a regular basis.

The institutionalization of listening to clients appears to have disappeared from view for many MFIs. Yet, nothing can replace the voices of the clients and the importance of ongoing and upward flows of information to enable institutions to be more responsive. This practice will require greater staff interface with clients, as well as staff training in appropriate listening skills. This shift creates changes in how business is conducted, something institutions may be reluctant to consider. It is costly, and requires new systems for the careful collection and transmission of information. However, it also brings benefits that can improve the bottom line.

In 1999 Pro Mujer in Bolivia undertook a client assessment using the AIMS/SEEP Tools. Findings from the application of the client satisfaction and other tools suggested that the clients found the MFI staff to be patronizing. The staff tended to decide what was 'good' for the clients and ignored any client input which could have ensured that the services were more responsive to the clients. Upon review of the assessment results Pro Mujer set about restructuring its human resources system, introducing new loan officer incentives which would encourage listening to clients and result in greater client loyalty and in turn retention.

Much of what is being discussed in terms of clients and products presumes the introduction of new products or refinement and relaunching of old products in existing institutions. But is it sufficient to assume that the existing institutions are the only ones that can deliver microfinance sustainability? The time has come to consider the restructuring of existing institutions or even the introduction of alternative delivery systems to attract non clients, the poorer ones who self exclude, the vulnerable non poor, the dropouts or others that have chosen not to access microfinance services.

9.5 THE CLIENTS' FINANCIAL LANDSCAPE

Wright *et al.* (2001) have noted that a common belief among MFIs once established or wishing to enter a market is that they are 'the only game in town.' Yet, this is rarely if ever the case. Many clients simultaneously belong to informal financial institutions such as ROSCAs or savings clubs that deliver lump sums of cash at regular intervals. Donors also have a long history of projects intended to increase the poor's access to financial services using banks and cooperatives. Whatever the financial institution, inevitably it will influence how clients use any new financial services that are introduced into the mosaic. For most clients microfinance appears to have a clear niche and rarely, if ever, displaces other financial services. An understanding of this panoply of services (i.e. the competition) is key to any client led agenda.

In the research undertaken to determine the market and design of an insurance product in Nepal, the financial landscape of a group of savings and credit

Table 9.1 Rural women's financial landscape, Nepal (Kavre District)

Financial service	*Number of members*	*Interest rate per annum*	*Loan size (Rs)*	*Term of loan*	*Repayment rate*	*Ease of access to funds*
Nepal Bank Savings[a]	n.a	5%	n.a	n.a	n.a	n.a
Savings and Credit Organization (SCO) Credit[b]	1,700	15–17%	Starts at 5,000	1–2 years	96%	High
Savings		5–11%[c]	n.a	Festival savings are for one year only	n.a	Low
Revolving funds[d]	n.a	n.a	n.a	n.a	n.a	High
Social sector loan	n.a	16%	15,000–17,000[e]	Up to 2 years	n.a	High
Emergency fund	n.a	5%	5,000	3 months	n.a	n.a
Mother's group						
Credit	45	20%	600–5,000	2 months	n.a	High
Savings	No interest	50/mo	n.a	n.a		Very timely
Landowner						
Credit[f]		50% of crop share	n.a	n.a	n.a	High
Money lender						
Credit	n.a	24%–36%[7]	Loan amount based on trust and asset base	Short term and long term	n.a	High
Women's group						

(continued)

Table 9.1 Rural women's financial landscape, Nepal (Kavre District) (*continued*)

Financial service	*Number of members*	*Interest rate per annum*	*Loan size (Rs)*	*Term of loan*	*Repayment rate*	*Ease of access to funds*
Credit	12	18%	10,000–18,000	1 year	100%	n.a
Family and friends						
Credit	n.a	No interest		Less than 1 week	n.a	High

Source: Simkhada et al. (2000).

Notes

a Women had opened these accounts as part of a donor project in the 1990s. When the SCOs were established many groups preferred not to close the accounts but retain minimum balances that could be activated in time of emergency.

b Includes group loan at 15% interest and individual loan at 17% interest.

c Includes: Festival savings at 9%; Daily savings at 10%; Education savings for children up to 16 years at 5%.

d This fund is used to buy back member's shares when they leave the cooperative.

e Minimum 5,000Rs and maximum 50,000Rs.

f For loans of less than 100Rs, a 5% service charge is deducted at the time of the loan.

organization (SCO) clients was reviewed (see Table 9.1). The financial landscape in rural Nepal is composed of formal and informal sources of finance, each with a different advantage. Ease of access varies, as do entry requirements. However, aside from the charges assessed by moneylenders and landowners, interest rates across services show little variation. SCO members have access to a range of funds savings and credit from cooperatives, mothers' groups, women's groups, money lenders and banks. While many of these institutions deliver small units of cash in a timely manner, transaction costs are high, especially when a large expenditure requires combining multiple sources of funds.

> Early in 2001 I shared the Nepal table with MFI managers attending a meeting in Zambia of the Association of Microfinance Institutions. All operate in Lusaka offering similar products to similar clients. The ensuring discussion was very revealing. They admitted to having forgotten about all the 'other' players and what that means for the debt-carrying capacity of their clients. This was particularly salient given the problems of repayment they seem to be encountering. The MFIs' donors that had justified their investments in microfinance by arguing that there was a large untapped market for working capital loans based on some guestimate of the size of the informal sector had similarly forgotten about other players.

Getting access to a lump sum of money when a crisis occurs brings with it one set of stresses, but the process of repayment creates other strains. Loans from moneylenders have extremely high interest rates and are very risky for the poor, especially when a house or land is required as collateral. In addition, loans are hard to come by if the family is already indebted. Some require mortgaging assets, which are hard earned gains for the poor that take a long time to replace. In general, poor women find it difficult to obtain 'lump sums' of money which are needed when the poor find themselves faced with a large loss, a major life event or the purchase of major assets, for example, a roof for the house or equipment for farming or an enterprise. In times when a major expenditure cannot be deferred, the poor are forced to 'patch' together small units of money from different sources. Hence, there exists a need to have many financial services into which one can tap (Simkhada *et al.*, 2000).

> When some one dies in Nepal, community members donate a small amount of money and rice which families use during the 13-day mourning period. However, this covers no more than 25 percent of the likely costs. To cover additional costs related to death (Rs 5,000–35,000) people use savings, or sell grain or other small assets.
> (*Source*: Simkhada *et al.*, 2000).

The importance of having access to multiple financial sources, formal and informal, is never lost on the clients. A review of clients' financial landscapes elsewhere is proof of this. Discussion with the poor in Peru, India and Zimbabwe suggest that both active and inactive accounts are maintained carefully, each having its particular use (see Table 9.2). Ingenuity in juggling various options is exercised by clients as well as lenders everywhere. For example, informal traders in Peru provide services to their clients that permit them to have the use of the cash installments until the product is paid in full. Only then do the traders go out and purchase the product for their clients. Perhaps the documentation of the clients' financial landscape is old news. Still, a client led agenda must bear in mind that microfinance loans are only one component of the debt burden of many households. Indeed, initial research suggests that microfinance debt might consist of a small percentage of the total owed by many households. Examination of a client's financial landscape can help inform MFIs about the gaps in the market, client behavior and product design.

9.6 THE CLIENT ASSESSMENT TOOLKIT

In view of our limited knowledge about clients, it is probably fair to argue that what MFI managers *think* clients want is not always what they want. To change this requires a means of gathering client information. Fortunately the microfinance industry has begun to build up a set of tools appropriate to the task. We already have the AIMS/SEEP Practitioner led Client Assessment Tools and MicroSave Africa's

Table 9.2 Financial landscapes of clients in Peru, India and Zimbabwe, 1999

	Peru	*India*	*Zimbabwe*
Number of informal financial services	ROSCAs (juntas)	ROSCAS (VCs)	ROSCAs
	Layaway for customers	Money lenders	Money lenders
	Money lenders	Pawning	
Formal credit	MiBanco	SEWA Bank	Zambuko Trust
	Other banks	Other banks[a]	Banks
	Other MFIs		Other MFIs
	Communal bank		
	Cooperative		
			Hire purchase
	Consumer credit		
	Housing materials bank		
Other sources of credit	Supplier credit	Supplier credit	
		Employer credit	Employer credit
Family	Spouse	Family and friends	Family and friends
Savings	Cooperative bank	SEWA	Banks
			Building societies
			POSB

Source: Dunn and Arbuckle (2001); Chen and Snodgrass (2001); and Barnes (2001).

Note a Three participants only.

Market Research for Microfinance qualitative tools. The two are complementary (see Appendices 9.A and 9.B).

However, gathering the information on clients is only part of the process, albeit the one that has received the most attention. The subsequent issue, whether the data are used appropriately and regularly is less discussed. One answer is through the new product development process. But that means that most of the attention within an institution is primarily focused on the client product nexus and by extension the marketing department of the institution, to the extent that it exists. However, as this paper has suggested a broader perspective is needed, one that integrates client information across an institution and may involve not only changes to the products but also to the systems used to deliver these products.

9.7 CONCLUSION

The ideas presented in this paper are designed to direct the arena of discourse towards a more holistic market driven or client focused microfinance agenda. Currently, the debate on market driven microfinance is primarily framed by the 'problems' of competition and dropouts among established MFIs. The solutions to the problems are defined in terms of more responsive products, the creation of new products, and the restructuring of existing ones. Appropriate products will not only benefit the operations of an institution they will also have a positive impact on the wellbeing of the client, reducing the risk of borrowing and the poor's vulnerability.

This client-product nexus is a necessary part of the client led agenda, but it is not the only part. It is critical to clarify the role of the institution within an integrated financial system, which extends from the formal to the informal; the next priority is thinking through alternative institutional options that will internalize a client led agenda at all management levels.

In presenting current thinking on a client led agenda, this paper finds itself in a precarious position in the midst of this debate. Client led models are still in their infancy and when this author began to focus on clients in microfinance six years ago, the notion that clients deserved a voice in the design and delivery of services was dismissed out of hand. High repayment rates were thought to confirm client satisfaction with the product on offer. It was a time when there was little, if any, concern with dropout rates. They were masked by the high growth of demand or simply ignored.

As greater realism enters the microfinance market place, the notion of being customer friendly is increasingly being accepted as good business. Indeed, it is difficult to see how the MFIs as they now operate will stay in business if they are not responsive to their clients. Just as all businesses in the last two to three decades have moved from product to market led approaches so too must MFIs. If nothing else competition will force their hand. Practitioners of microcredit must move forward towards further exploration and formulation of a truly client led microfinance paradigm. However, in doing so they must step with caution balancing carefully costs and benefits of moving in this new direction. For the institution sustainability must be the objective goal. Having institutions that provide low cost appropriate services with a measure of certainty are what will keep the customer happy.

ACKNOWLEDGEMENTS

The views here are those of the author and do not reflect those of USAID. The author wishes to acknowledge the contributions of Ayesha Nibbe.

Notes

1 This article was originally presented at the Marriott School Microfinance Research Symposium 'The Second Microfinance Revolution: Creating Customer-Centered Microfinance Institutions,' Provo, Utah, USA, 5 April, 2001. This article is a US Government work and is in the public domain in the USA.

2 The vulnerable nonpoor are clients who are above the poverty line but vulnerable to slipping into poverty; moderate poor clients are in the top 50 percentiles of households

below the poverty line; the extreme poor are in households in the bottom 10 to 50 percentiles of households below the poverty line; and the destitute are in households in the bottom 10 percentiles of households below the poverty line (Sebstad and Cohen, 2001).

3 Caisses Villageoises d'Epargne et de Crédit Autogérées, which is French for self reliant village savings and credit banks .

4 This is the acronym for the USAID project Assessing the Impact of Micro enterprise Services.

References

Barnes C. 2001. Microfinance Program Clients and Impact: an assessment of Zambuko Trust, Zimbabwe. AIMS Paper. Management Systems International: Washington, DC.

Barnes C., Keogh E. 2000. An assessment of the impact of Zambuko Microenterprise Program in Zimbabwe: baseline findings.

Chao-Beroff, R. 2001. Understanding microfinance clients: advances in impact assessment and applications for market research. Keynote Speech, AIMS Conference, USAID, May 2001.

Chen M., Snodgrass D. 2001. Managing resources, activities, and risk in urban India: the impact of microfinance. AIMS Paper. Management Systems International: Washington, DC.

Cohen M. 1999. Bolivia: loan use by Pro Mujer clients. Field trip report. USAID, Office of Micro enterprise Development. Mimeographed: Washington, DC.

Cohen M, Sebstad J. 1999. Microfinance and risk management: a client perspective. Paper presented at the 3rd New Development Finance Seminar. Frankfurt, Germany.

Dearden K., Hyman E. 1996. A review of the impact information systems of NGO micro enterprise programmes. AIMS Paper. Management Systems International: Washington, DC.

Dunn E., Arbuckle, J. G. Jr. 2001. The impacts of microcredit: a case study from Peru. AIMS Paper. Management Systems International: Washington, DC.

Hulme D., Mutesasira L., Sempangi H., Mugwanga H., Kashangaki J., Maximambali F., Lwoga C., Wright G. and Rutherford S. 1998. Client drop out (exits) from East African MFIs. MicroSave-Africa: Uganda.

Hulme D., Mosely P. 1996. *Finance Against Poverty, Volume I: Analysis and Recommendations*. Routledge: London.

Rutherford S. 2000a. *The Poor and Their Money*. Oxford University Press: New Delhi.

Rutherford S. 2000b. Raising the curtain on the 'microfinancial services era'. CGAP Focus Note, No. 15: Washington, DC.

Sebstad J., Cohen M. 2001. *Micro-finance, Risk Management and Poverty*. CGAP, World Bank: Washington, DC.

Simkhada N. R., Gautam S., Mishra M., Acharya I. and Sharma N. 2000. *Research on risk and vulnerability of rural women in Nepal*. Center for Microfinance: Kathmanadu, Nepal.

Wright G. 2001. Market research and client responsive product development. (Mimeo.) MicroSave-Africa: Kenya.

Wright G., Kasente D., Ssemgerere G. and Mutesasira L. 1999. Vulnerability, risks, assets and empowerment the impact of microfinance on poverty alleviation. (Mimeo.) MicroSave-Africa: Uganda.

Wright G., Brand M., Northrip Z., Cohen M., McCord M. and Helms B. 2001. Look before you leap. (Mimeo.) MicroSave-Africa: Kenya.

APPENDIX 9.A

Participatory rapid appraisal for microfinance from the Microsave-Africa market research for microfinance tools

Assembled and developed by Graham A. N. Wright, Shahnaz Ahmed and Leonard Mutesasira with help from Stuart Rutherford, Monique Cohen and Jennefer Sebstad.

1 Seasonality analysis of household income, expenditure, savings and credit is used to obtain information on seasonal flows of income and expenditure, and the demand for credit and savings services. This analysis also provides insights into some of the risks and pressures faced by clients and how they use MFIs' financial services to respond to these. This tool also provides insights into the financial intermediation needs of the community and what products the MFIs can design in response to these.

2 Seasonality analysis of migration, casual employment and goods/services provided by the poor looks at the availability of cash to the people in the community and examines how far they might have to migrate to find work (when it is available). This has important implications for their ability to make regular savings and loan repayments.

3 Life cycle profile to determine which of the events require lump sums of cash; to examine the implications of these for household income/expenditure; to establish current coping mechanisms; and then finally to discuss how access to MFI financial services can help the household respond to these. The information gathered is useful for designing financial products that match the various needs expressed at different milestones during a person's life cycle.

4 Venn/Chapati diagram allows analysis of financial service groups/organizations within the community and their roles and to understand more about the social capital accumulated by participants.

5 Simple ranking can be used to a explore a wide variety of issues when an understanding of the relative importance/desirability etc. is needed (e.g., for understanding the relative importance of different elements of products interest, rate, opening balance, grace period etc.).

6 Relative preference ranking is used to see how clients and potential clients perceive the financial service providers and components of the financial

services they provide.

7 Pair-wise ranking is used to examine in detail how clients and potential clients compare and contrast critical components of financial services, and why those elements are important for them.

8 Simple wealth ranking provides a rapid way of segregating a community into three basic categories, and is useful in situations where there are many households in a community. This is useful for targeting. This exercise can also be useful in impact assessment, and for examining the socio-economic characteristics of people who chose to join (or don't join) the MFI and also those who leave or whose accounts become dormant.

9 Detailed wealth ranking provides an understanding of in what way and why rich people are wealthy and the poor are poor, and a 'ranking' of the households in the village, from the most wealthy to the least wealthy, as seen by the members of the community.

10 Cash mobility mapping provides an understanding of where the community goes to acquire or spend cash (markets, waged labor, cooperatives, informal financial organizations etc.) and to lead into discussions of which financial service institutions they trust or value and why. The exercise also provides initial insights into potential income generating ventures/projects that the clients might get involved in.

11 Time series of sickness, death, loss of employment, theft, natural disaster etc. (this year, last year, 5 and 10 years before) provides an opportunity to learn from the community about how it views change over time in various areas related to a series of crises. It also allows the research team to integrate key changes into the community profile, which will simplify problem identification; and to begin to organize the range of opportunities for improved delivery of financial services.

12 Time series of asset ownership (this year, last year, 5 and 10 years before) is useful in determining what 'productive' and 'protective' assets (in a broader sense) are valued the most and thus the potential for designing or refining corresponding financial products including leasing, contractual savings deposits (e.g., for housing, education, health insurance etc.).

13 Financial services matrix is useful in determining which financial services are used by which socio-economic or socio-cultural strata of society and why, and thus the potential for designing or refining appropriate financial products.

14 Financial sector trend analysis is useful in determining which financial services have been used over time by which socio-economic or socio-cultural strata of society, and thus for understanding the changes in the use/availability of a variety of financial services over time, and why participants used them.

15 Financial landscape analysis is useful in determining the types of competition that are operating in the area as well as the rates they charge/offer etc. The tool also provides insights into the use/availability of a variety of financial services and why participants use them. It can also provide important insights into how poor people's perceptions of financial services sometimes vary substantially from the actual terms and conditions being offered.

APPENDIX 9.B

Learning from clients: assessment tool for microfinance practitioners

– The AIMS/SEEP Tools –

Candace Nelson, Barbara MKnelly, Carter Garber, Elaine Edgcomb, Nancy Horn, Gary Gaile, Karen Lippold.

1. IMPACT SURVEY

The objective of the survey is to assess the impact of micro enterprise programs at the community, household, enterprise and individual levels. This quantitative tool which comprises seven modules that can be combined in different ways in response to specific program hypotheses, takes between 45 and 60 minutes. It uses standardized questions and pre-determined answer categories. Sample sizes have ranged from 140–490. The design is cross sectional and calls for a comparison group of income clients who have not received any program service.

2. EXIT SURVEY

The tool seeks to determine *why* and *when* clients leave the program, *what* clients think about the program (strengths and weaknesses) and *what* they perceive to be the program's impact. As above this quantitative survey uses standardized questions and pre-determined answer categories. However, the individual interview requires no more than 15–20 minutes to administer and sample sizes are smaller, ranging from 30–140 ex-clients.

3. USE OF LOAN, PROFITS AND SAVINGS OVER TIME

Using individual interviews this tool demonstrates how micro-entrepreneurs use financial resources to carry out their economic strategies for their businesses and their households. It can also provide insights into how clients cope with crisis. This qualitative tool takes 60 minutes to administer and uses a sample size of 15–30 clients.

4. CLIENT SATISFACTION TOOL

This qualitative tool not only identifies areas of client satisfaction and dissatisfaction with the program but also provides MFI managers with suggestions for change. The focus group discussion can use an optional group voting process and takes 60 minutes to administer. The recommended sample size ranges from 120 clients/110 groups to 214 clients/119 groups.

5. EMPOWERMENT TOOL

The objective of this tool is to identify changes in women's self esteem, control over resources, skills, household relationships, and status within their communities. A qualitative tool, it explores the client's perception of how s/he has changed since joining the program. It is best used with mature clients who have participated in the program for at least two years. Three methodological options are offered, administration takes 1–2 hours and the sample size is in the range of 25–48.

10

THE STORY OF THE GRAMEEN BANK

From subsidized microcredit to market based microfinance

David Hulme

10.1 INTRODUCTION

The Grameen Bank of Bangladesh holds an iconic position in the world of microfinance. It is credited with proving that 'the poor are bankable'; the Grameen 'model' has been copied in more than 40 countries; it is the most widely cited development success story in the world; and, its charismatic Founder-Director, Professor Muhammad Yunus was awarded the Nobel Peace Prize in 2006. At the end of February 2008 it had 7.4 million clients and outstanding loans of US$545 million. By any measure it is an organization that has impacted greatly on the lives of many poor people and on ideas about microfinance, poverty reduction and international development.

The group based lending model, targeted at poor, rural women, that is synonymous with the Grameen Bank contrasts markedly with the two other iconic microfinance institutions (MFIs), Bank Rakyat Indonesia and BancoSol of Bolivia (discussed in this volume by Marguerite Robinson). The original Grameen Bank model comes out of what Robinson calls a 'poverty lending' approach rather than the 'financial systems' approach that she, the Consultative Group to Assist the Poor (CGAP) and many US microfinance specialists prefer. However, unnoticed by many observers, the Grameen Bank made dramatic changes in its services around 2001 and 2002. Its new model (Grameen II), takes it much closer to a financial systems approach. Although Yunus continues to champion the idea of microfinance for poor women, most obviously through the annual Microcredit Summit, the Bank he directs increasingly lends to non-poor clients; has moved aggressively into savings mobilization; and is very much concerned with the overall profitability of the mix of its products. Grameen II reflects not so much a reform as a revolution in the Grameen's strategy. Rather than challenging the financial systems approach that Robinson promotes in her chapter of this volume, the contemporary Grameen Bank vindicates it. But, let's start at the beginning.

10.2 EARLY DAYS

As Yunus reports in his autobiography (Yunus, 1999), and as Fuglesang and Chandler (1986) record, the origins of the Grameen Bank lie in the dilemma that the young Yunus found himself facing in the mid-1970s. Having completed his PhD in the USA he had returned to Bangladesh to lecture in economics at Chittagong University. However, he found himself wondering what relevance the economic theory he taught had to the immediate needs of the thousands of hungry and deprived people he saw in rural Bangladesh. The country was slowly recovering from a vicious war of independence that had destroyed its infrastructure and its productivity and murdered much of its intelligentsia. The damage caused by the war had been amplified by the famine of 1974 and the country was dependent on food aid. Human suffering on a vast scale could be witnessed in any town or village.

Yunus could try to help people by giving them charity, but he wondered whether some of his economic theory could be applied in the field. His training postulated that if people got access to credit they could increase their profitability, or diversify their economic activities, in ways that would allow them to raise their incomes. So, if he could lend some poor people his money they could improve their lives and pay him back: then, he could lend the money to other poor people and thus assist many more people than could be achieved by simply giving his money away.

It was an interesting theory but his initial experiments seemed to show it was invalid. Quite a few of the men and women he lent to did not repay their small loans (sums of US$10 or $20). He thought that this was because they had either used the money unwisely (for consumption or poorly planned microenterprises) or were not trustworthy. As a result he began to experiment with ways of (i) approving and supervising loans to ensure they would be used for productive investments, and (ii) selecting trustworthy clients and managing them so that they would repay their loans.

Eventually he came up with a model that worked. This had a number of features:

- Lending to poor, rural women (as they were less likely than men to use loans badly and were more reliable for repayment).
- Organizing women into cells of five that took collective responsibility for each other's loans (creating social collateral and a peer screening process).
- Establishing *Kendro* (centres) where six cells (i.e. 30 women) met at a set time each week to apply for loans and make repayments.
- Charging a higher rate of interest than government schemes and non-governmental organization (NGO) loans programs.
- Requiring clients to make compulsory microsavings each week (to create

financial discipline and generate financial collateral for groups) and to make promises about their social conduct.
- Simple, standardized products that required regular, small repayments.
- Recruiting and training bright, young graduates to administer services (to minimize corruption).

There were many other carefully designed elements of this 'Grameen Model' (see Fuglesang and Chandler (1986) for details). It certainly appeared to work and Yunus was able to persuade the state run Bangladesh Krishi Bank (BKB) to finance and house the experiment. Donor agencies, such as the Ford Foundation, became involved.

10.3 EXPANSION AND INSTITUTIONALISATION

The early success of the Grameen model was matched by Yunus's personal energy and enthusiasm. But, to expand the Bank he needed more finance and a robust organizational structure. The finance was not too much of a problem. In the early 1980s there were many foreign aid agencies in Bangladesh facing a big problem: most of the grants they made to government agencies were only weakly accounted for and they appeared to achieve little development impact. A bright, young social entrepreneur who was gaining a reputation for assisting the poor and who monitored his program's impacts was just what they needed. For the next decade or so Yunus would be able to rely on the financial support of the Grameen Bank Donor Consortium.

Achieving an effective organizational structure was, perhaps, more challenging. If Yunus stayed with BKB then as the Grameen Bank expanded it would be likely to take on the characteristics of the country's nationalized commercial banks: nepotistic staff recruitment and promotion, financial corruption, the politicization of the loan portfolio and an offhand attitude towards clients. The alternatives – registering as a Bank or as a cooperative – were not attractive. So, with great insight and careful politicking, Yunus negotiated the passing of a Grameen Bank Ordinance in 1983. Quite how this was done has never been fully explained but Yunus was a well connected member of the country's small elite and General Ershad, the country's new military dictator, was looking for ways of promoting a more popular image of his regime. The Ordinance established the Bank as a parastatal agency overseen by a Board comprised of Yunus, a small number of state officials and a larger group of Bank clients. This gave Yunus firm personal control of the organization and the flexibility to modify its services and staffing as the Bank evolved.

Over the 1980s and early 1990s the Grameen Bank steadily expanded with large inflows of donor funding. By 1991 it had more than one million clients and a growing range of products – housing loans, agricultural loans and others. Alongside this, both the profiles of the Bank and of Yunus became increasingly international.

The Bank was able to accommodate itself to the ascendancy of neo-liberal ideas of this era and to criticisms of those ideas. Yunus's eloquent narrative presented the poor as 'micro-entrepreneurs' who could seize market based opportunities once they had access to microcredit (then seen as loans of around US$50 to $200). But this was moderated: the Bank promoted women's empowerment (sometimes Yunus presented this as the poor's empowerment), collective action by groups and social development. In effect, the Bank's narrative allowed it to present itself as extending the benefits of capitalism down to the poor whilst, at the same time, being an alternative to orthodox capitalism.

10.4 INTERNATIONAL TRANSFER REPLICATION

As the 1980s progressed an increasing amount of Grameen Bank senior management time was devoted to exporting the Grameen Bank model. I first became acquainted with the Grameen model in 1987 while researching rural finance in Sri Lanka. At the time it seemed that almost every NGO and donor project I visited had staff who had recently returned from a visit to the Grameen Bank. Most of these staff were very impressed with what they had seen and talked of 'replicating' the model. The Asian Development Bank, desperate to approve loans to Sri Lanka, dressed up its rural finance proposals as building on the Grameen Bank's success – even though they were not using the Grameen model!

The Bank moved from mounting *ad hoc* visitor programs to regular programs for replicators. It targeted not only developing countries and was proud to announce Grameen transfers to the USA and Canada. By the mid 1990s Yunus was increasingly spending his time travelling overseas: sitting on the boards of Grameen replicas (such as Amanah Ikhtar Malaysia), visiting aid donors, and addressing academic, policy and public audiences. He energetically promoted microenterprise credit as a panacea for poverty reduction (something that intensely annoyed me as it was so wrong) and eloquently spoke of the agency and energy of the poor (something I deeply appreciated, given that many analysts fail to point out that most poverty reduction is done by the poor themselves).

The idea of replicating the Grameen Bank around the world crystallized when the US-based group RESULTS (which runs campaigns promoting microcredit) and its Director, an experienced lobbyist, came up with the idea of a Microcredit Summit. Since 1990 the UN had convened a set of global summits that had set goals for poverty reduction, education, gender equality and other issues. The 1997 Microcredit Summit was not a UN event – it was organized by RESULTS – but, it presented as a global summit with claims of 'microcredit is a human right' and speeches from heads of state. It set a goal of mobilizing US$21.6 billion so that 150 million households would be able to access Grameen Bank-type loans by 2005. Some within the Microcredit Summit movement pushed for a focus on microfinance and a broader range of services but that did not suit RESULTS' campaigning style. It needed a simple message. The Grameen Bank was a panacea, the world should replicate it!

10.5 CAN THE GRAMEEN BANK GO BUST?

As the Grameen model was 'exported' overseas during the 1990s the Bank continued to grow in Bangladesh. Client numbers grew steadily but the portfolio grew more quickly as clients took bigger ordinary loans and new types of loans (especially housing). Those of us working in Bangladesh increasingly heard that repayment rates were falling, but that branch managers were massaging their performance figures by issuing new loans to defaulters. These were immediately used to pay off the outstanding loan and hide the problem of non-repayment. There were also criticisms of the gender achievements of the Bank: did it merely get women to take loans that they gave straight to their husbands? Then, there were criticisms of the idea that Yunus propounded of every Grameen Bank loan being used for microenterprise, and every microenterprise being successful. Independent fieldwork showed that Grameen Bank clients used their loans for many different purposes – business, food consumption, health, education and even dowry. Grameen loans did not go to micro-firms for a single, specific investment; rather they went into the complex financial portfolios of low-income households.

Long time researcher on microfinance in Bangladesh, Stuart Rutherford, was one of those able to see what was going on. Grameen Bank clients paid the *kisti* (weekly repayments) on their loans not from a single microenterprise but from patching together earnings from casual employment, self employment, remittances and a variety of loans from other sources. But, as clients stayed with Grameen Bank they were under pressure to take bigger, ordinary loans alongside new housing loans. As a result, they took on levels of debt they could not service from their income. To stop them from defaulting, they were issued with larger loans by Grameen branch managers to repay earlier loans. In Dhaka, rumors circulated of a meeting at which Yunus asked his senior staff to tell him the true level of repayment and the scale of the 'hole' in the Bank's finances. The severe floods of 1998, and the collapse of the Bank's recently introduced agriculture loans, exacerbated the repayment problem.

Things moved from being a problem to being a crisis in 2000 when Daniel Pearl, a journalist on *The New York Times*, published an article saying that the Grameen Bank was virtually bankrupt. For believers in the Bank this was either heresy or the end of the world. For proponents of the non-subsidized, financial systems approach it showed the validity of their ideas.

But, a mere financial crisis was not enough to sink the Grameen Bank. An authoritative independent account of how the Bank survived is not available, but I believe a three-pronged strategy was used to stabilize and reshape it. The first prong of this strategy involved Bank staff in carefully going through the entire portfolio at the local level and screening outstanding loans to raise repayment rates, reschedule loans and, when necessary, write-off loans that could not be recovered from borrowers or their centers. This meant that the entire Bank had to recognize significant losses. These could be absorbed by writing off parts of the Bank's asset base but a second prong of strategy helped reduce this 'hit' on the Bank. Yunus was partially able to mobilize grants form aid donors to offset these losses. Again, it is unclear precisely how this was done but some commentators suspect it was by presenting the Bank's financial problems as being due to the floods of 1998, rather than being more systemic. The third prong of the strategy was to redesign the Bank's products so that they became more profitable and could compete with the many other providers of microfinance in the country (many of which had prospered in the wake of Grameen's initial breakthrough). This led to what Yunus has called Grameen II.

10.6 FROM GRAMEEN I TO GRAMEEN II

The problems faced by Grameen Bank in the late 1990s led to its senior staff piloting a number of experiments with new products and new ways of managing service provision. By early 2001 these had been consolidated and Yunus announced the launch of 'Grameen II' – the replacement of the Bank's earlier products by a new range on different terms. The components of Grameen II were designed so that (i) they should meet client demand, and (ii) they should be profitable for the Bank. Between March 2001 and August 2002 all of the Grameen's 1,200 branches were shifted from Grameen I to Grameen II products and systems. Accounts of this process and the practice and outcomes of Grameen II are provided by Rutherford *et al.* (2006) and Dowla and Barua (2006).

The main elements of Grameen II are:

- A major focus on savings from members and the public. This included voluntary savings, term deposits and the Grameen Pension Scheme (GPS) a long-term savings program.
- The provision of flexible 'basic loans' to members (rather than the standardized Grameen I 12-month loans). These are for variable amounts, can be repaid over 3 to 36 months, have negotiable repayment schedules and interest rates are determined by loan type (size, length, grace period, etc).
- The abandonment of joint liability (and the idea of social collateral).
- A poverty focused 'struggling members' program that provides small, subsidized loans to beggars and encourages them to join Grameen Bank centers.

The results have been staggering. The Bank has not only been able to stabilize itself but has, in effect, relaunched itself and its trajectory. While it took the Grameen 25 years to reach a client base of 2.5 million, it took only 3 years, from 2001, to recruit the next 2.5 million clients (Rutherford *et al.*, 2006). Over the period 2002 to 2005 the Bank tripled the deposits (US$478 million) it held and doubled its portfolio of outstanding loans. The Bank's loans portfolio became smaller than its savings portfolio. It built up a large fund for bad loan provision and profits rose from 60 million taka in 2002 to 442 million taka (US$7 million) in 2005. This growth meant that physical expansion became essential and the Bank opened 500 new branches, so that it had more than 1700 branches, by late 2005.

While the Bank still proclaims its mission of poverty reduction my personal observations lead me to believe that its clientele is less economically deprived than was the case in the 1980s and 1990s. This is partly because clients have done well (perhaps through Grameen membership) and partly because of the product redesign and the drive for expansion and profitability. Many of its clients would be classed as non-poor or moderately poor by Bangladesh's official poverty line. A much smaller proportion are extremely poor (the targets for Grameen I over 1975 to 2000). The 'struggling members program' is targeted at the extreme poor but by December 2005 it had only 56,000 clients, against more than 25 million extremely poor people in the country. Average loan size for these members was only US$6 and their average savings were US$1 (Rutherford *et al.*, 2006). While many poor and extremely poor people may benefit indirectly from Grameen II (through employment, increased demand for products, greater availability of local level charity) the struggling members program appears to be either failing or tokenistic.

10.7 THE FUTURE OF THE GRAMEEN BANK

The Grameen Bank looks as though it has a secure future as an MFI in Bangladesh and should remain a major player in the microfinance market, alongside other big players such as ASA and BRAC. It also seems set to remain a global icon although there is real confusion about the message that the Bank (and Yunus) project. Internationally, it is still perceived as a micro-lending institution focused on extremely poor women, despite the fact that it has adopted a market based, 'financial systems' approach since 2001.

The confusion could be a cause for concern but my personal analysis is more positive. Within Bangladesh the Grameen Bank now plays an important role as a substantial MFI that meets client needs and helps to promote competition within the financial markets. Its viability is essential for this internal role but also very important for its external role. Had the Grameen Bank collapsed then optimism about the feasibility of poverty reduction and international development would have been dented. While the international message associated with the Bank – microenterprise credit for extremely poor women lifts them out of poverty – is now inaccurate, the broader thrust of this message – of hard working poor people using their personal agency to overcome the problems they face – is highly appropriate for the publics and politicians of rich countries. It helps the citizens of the rich world understand that poor people are active agents in the processes of development and not passive recipients of food aid and humanitarian relief as the media (in the USA, Europe, Japan and the Middle East) usually stereotype them. The Grameen Bank today is a very different organization than it was 20 years ago but it still serves as an inspiration for those trying to help poor and low-income people in their own efforts to improve their lives.

References

Fuglesang, A. and Chandler, D. (1986), *Participation as Process: What Can We Learn from the Grameen Bank, Bangladesh*, Oslo: Norwegian Ministry of Development Corporation.

Rutherford, S. with Maniruzzaman, S. K. Sinha and Acnabin and Co. (2006), 'GRAMEEN II – The First Five Years: 2001–06', *Grameen II Briefing Notes* for MicroSave, http://www.microsave.org/.

Dowla, A. and Barua, D. (2006), *The Poor Always Pay Back – The Grameen II Story*, West Hartford: Kumarian Press

Yunus, M. (1999), *Banker to the Poor: Microlending and the Battle Against Poverty*, New York: Public Affairs.

11

MICROINSURANCE – THE RISKS, PERILS AND OPPORTUNITIES

Warren Brown[1]

11.1 INTRODUCTION

There is a rising tide of microfinance institutions (MFIs) wanting to develop insurance products for the low income market. The rationales they give for this interest include: protecting poor clients from risks, reducing an MFI's loan defaults and earning additional income for an MFI's loan portfolio. While there is no question that the poor are highly vulnerable to a wide variety of risks, this vulnerability cannot necessarily be translated into a demand or need for insurance. Moreover, the mere existence of vulnerability says nothing to the question of whether MFIs are suitably equipped to provide insurance. In fact, most are not.

Insurance is a risky business that, in many developed markets, commercial lenders are prohibited from entering. Though potentially complementary, banking and insurance products can also be mutually destructive. Just as loan losses can erode the reserves required to meet insurance claims, losses in insurance operations can deplete depositor assets and an MFI's loan capital in a single catastrophic event.

Before launching insurance initiatives, MFIs and the donors who support them should understand the risks and be certain that the required resources and skills are in place to manage them. This assessment should be frank. Few MFIs have reached financial sustainability and even fewer have successfully integrated a savings component into their product line. Most continue to rely on compulsory savings, and these are often managed irresponsibly or illegally. Some MFIs forthrightly admit their use of savings products to fund doubtful loan books; many more do the same but attribute their actions to rationales that donors find more attractive.

This article attempts to assist organizations in assessing (1) whether there is a potential market for microinsurance; (2) how that market can be served through strategic partnerships; and (3) the resource requirements that dictate why most insurance products are more than most MFIs can reasonably manage on their own (this article is a summary version of a more detailed report by Brown, Green and Lindquist, 2001). Figure 11.1 lays out these sets of questions in decision tree format.

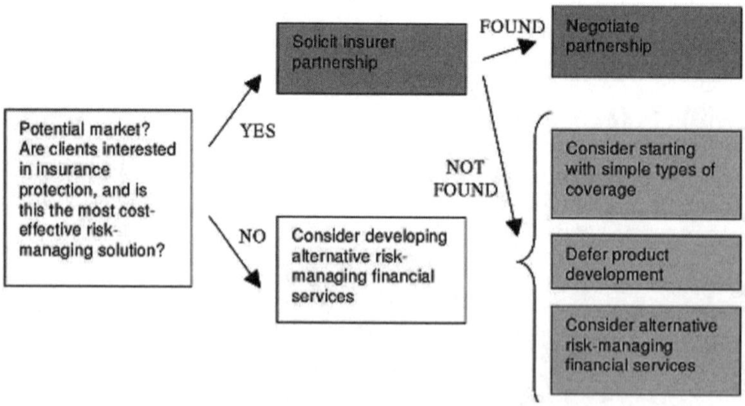

Figure 11.1 Decision-tree for microinsurance product development.

Defining microinsurance

The term 'microinsurance' is growing increasingly familiar in the microfinance industry. There are two parts to the definition of 'microinsurance' used in this article. First, 'insurance' refers to a financial service that uses *risk pooling* to provide compensation to individuals or groups that are adversely affected by a specified risk or event. Risk pooling involves collecting large groups, or pools, of individuals or groups to share the losses resulting from the occurrence of a risky event. Persons harmed by such an event benefit from the contributions of those who are not affected and, as a result, they receive compensation that is greater than the amount they have invested in the insurance policy. Thus, products that only allow an affected individual to receive up to the amount they have contributed are considered savings products, not insurance. 'Micro-' indicates that we are discussing insurance products designed to be beneficial to, and affordable by, low income individuals or groups.

11.2 PART I: VERIFYING THE POTENTIAL MARKET FOR MICROINSURANCE

Before jumping on the insurance bandwagon, MFIs and donors should consider three basic questions regarding the potential market for microinsurance:

Do clients want assistance in reducing vulnerability to risks through insurance?

- Is insurance the most appropriate financial service for providing this protection?
- Are clients willing and able to pay a price at which the insurance can be delivered profitably?

Is there client interest in reducing vulnerability to risk?

One can easily create a compelling story about how an insurance product will protect the poor against devastating losses or smooth households' volatile incomes. However, this scenario can overshadow the more fundamental question of whether an MFI's clients actually *want* insurance to reduce their vulnerability against certain risks. If a household does not want the kind of protection that a specific type of insurance provides, no matter how compelling the rationale to MFI managers and funders, there is no justification for developing the product. As Box 11.1 illustrates, poor households are not interested in insurance protection against *all* risks.

The Groupe de Recherche et d'Echanges Technologiques (GRET) has operated a microcredit program in Cambodia for many years. In the process of pilot testing a health insurance scheme, GRET conducted market research to test households' satisfaction with the plan. The results of this research confirmed that clients appreciated the benefits provided by the insurance and that even those that had not become ill were satisfied in knowing that the protection was available and that they had helped others in the community.

This same market research uncovered that, in addition to healthcare costs, losses resulting from the untimely death of livestock were a significant threat to many households. However, when asked if they would be interested in property insurance on their livestock, the majority of the respondents said 'No'. While they were satisfied with participating in a health insurance scheme, they preferred to manage losses relating to livestock death on their own, stating that 'In the case of the animal's death, the meat is still edible' and 'the animal's death is the sole responsibility of the owner'.

Box 11.1 Assessing client interest in different types of insurance in Cambodia.

It is the responsibility of the MFI to ensure that a proposed product is of interest to clients, particularly if the insurance is to be made mandatory for all borrowers or savers.

To be sure that they have addressed this question, MFIs can use tools like MicroSave Africa's PRA methodology (for details, visit the website http://www.uncdf.org/sum/msa) to test clients' level of interest in insurance. If their response is positive, the MFI should go on to consider the remaining questions in this paper. If it is negative, the MFI should consider other ways it might assist its clients in managing risk.

Is insurance a potential solution?

The second question in establishing whether a potential market exists for micro-insurance has two parts. The first asks whether insurance can, from a technical perspective, be feasibly offered against the proposed risks. The second considers whether other financial services, particularly savings, might be a more effective alternative.

What can and cannot be insured? MFIs should verify that their proposed coverage meets the following basic insurance principles:

- *Large numbers*: Insurance works by sharing risk across a large population. If the pool of policyholders is too small, volatility in the number of claims can quickly exceed the plans' reserves, leading to bankruptcy. Although no precise minimum number of policyholders can be established, less than 1,000–2,000 are likely to create undue risk for the provider.
- *Specified risks only*: Insurance can only be designed to protect against specific risks for which the chance of loss can be calculated. Despite the attractive 'development benefits' of blanket insurance coverage against all or an unspecified set of potential causes of loss (e.g. building insurance against all causes of damage), coverage of this type provided by MFIs and governments, has consistently failed when unexpected claims overwhelm premium income and the insurer is faced with the difficult and unpopular choice of folding the plan or arbitrarily reducing the benefits paid out in order to keep claims expenses within the plan's means.
- *Not covariant*: Risks covered by insurance should only be able to affect a relatively small portion of the total insured population at any given time. Covariant risks, such as a flood or HIV/AIDS, are likely to cause similar damage to a large portion of an MFI's clients at the same time. If a client base is concentrated in a single community, an epidemic or disaster can quickly bankrupt the insurance plan.
- *Controls on moral hazard*: Policyholders' ability to influence whether the risk actually occurs must be limited or controlled. If a policyholder can control the timing or likelihood of loss, claims can quickly increase beyond expectations, leading to bankruptcy. These risks are especially high in the provision of health and property insurance.
- *Balance of risk/controls against adverse selection*: The pool of insured households should include both high and low risk cases so that the average risk occurrence within the pool is similar to the average in the population at large. Adverse selection occurs when low risk policyholders opt-out of purchasing the coverage or high risk policyholders opt-in in greater numbers than expected. Controls need to be in place to ensure that high risk policyholders do not overwhelm the pool.

To improve the ability of rural farmers to repay loans from agricultural development banks (ADBs), many governments developed crop insurance programs in the 1970s and 1980s. These programs typically provided loan repayment and occasionally income supplements to farmers suffering crop yields below an established minimum. Similar programs were developed in countries as diverse as Brazil, India, the Philippines and the USA. In each country the results were disastrous, with expenses (administrative and claims) totaling 2 to 5 times revenues in any given year. The failure of these programs was, in large measure, the result of trying to provide insurance in uninsurable conditions:

- *Unspecific coverage*: By guaranteeing a minimum crop yield, these programs were essentially insuring against all possible causes of poor crop yield, a virtually endless list of risks.
- *Covariant losses*: Many of the programs were bankrupted when a drought or other natural calamity hit the region in which the program operated, affecting most of the insured members at the same time.
- *Moral hazard*: Farmers were less likely to follow sound husbandry practices because all severe yield losses were protected, leading to an increase in claims.
- *Balance of risks*: Coverage was often focused in specific geographic regions and only provided for poor farmers, essentially covering only the highest risks.

Box 11.2 The dismal history of crop insurance.

A good example of the potential consequences of insuring against risks that do not meet the above criteria is outlined in Box 11.2 (adapted from Hazell, 1992).

What should and should not be insured? In addition to risks that simply cannot be insured against, there are some risks where insurance is technically possible, but may not be the most appropriate tool for clients to manage risk. For example, dowries and school fees – events that cause financial stress, but which occur with greater certainty – can often be more effectively covered through access to savings rather than insurance. In developed markets, people tend to use savings or credit before insurance against most risks. Why should poor households be any different? If an MFI's clients don't yet have access to flexible savings and credit, MFIs and donors should consider that providing insurance may be premature, particularly in the light of recent evidence showcasing the success of innovative savings products and collection systems (Rutherford, 1999; and Wright, 1998). Moreover, MFIs are more likely to have the expertise and resources to offer savings products. Insurance, as Part III of this article describes, is another matter altogether.

Can coverage be provided that is both affordable and financially viable?

Even in situations where these first two criteria have been met (clients are interested in reducing their vulnerability and the cause of the vulnerability is insurable), MFIs may experience challenges in designing coverage that is both affordable for clients and financially viable for the institution. Confirming affordability can be difficult, as clients will often say that they 'cannot' afford the full cost of a product when it is described to them in general, but are willing to pay when they are presented with a product that meets their needs and demonstrates clear value to them.

If an MFI can confidently answer the preceding three questions in the affirmative, there probably is a potential market among their clients for a certain type of insurance. It does not necessarily follow, however, that the MFI should meet these needs on its own. For most MFIs and most types of insurance, there is a strong logic to form a partnership with an established insurer to deliver insurance benefits to their clients. This is the focus of Part II, which describes the rationale for these partnerships and identifies how an MFI can negotiate with potential partners to obtain the best coverage possible.

11.2 PART II: RESPONDING TO CLIENT DEMAND THROUGH PARTNERSHIPS

If demand for insurance has been established, the challenge is to determine the most effective strategy to create, deliver, and manage the product for long-term profitability and client satisfaction.

The most common mechanism used by formal insurers to get insurance products into the hands of consumers is through agents. Agents act as an intermediary between an insurance company – mutually owned, private or public sector – and its market. They perform the sales and servicing activities of the insurer to improve efficiency for both the consumer and the company. This model has proven effective in developed insurance markets with the entire range of products, including life, health, disability and property insurance. More recently, several MFIs have successfully used this model to provide insurance benefits to their clients (McCord, 2000).

In an MFI/insurer partnership, the MFI acts as the *agent*, marketing and selling the product to its existing clientele through the distribution network it has already

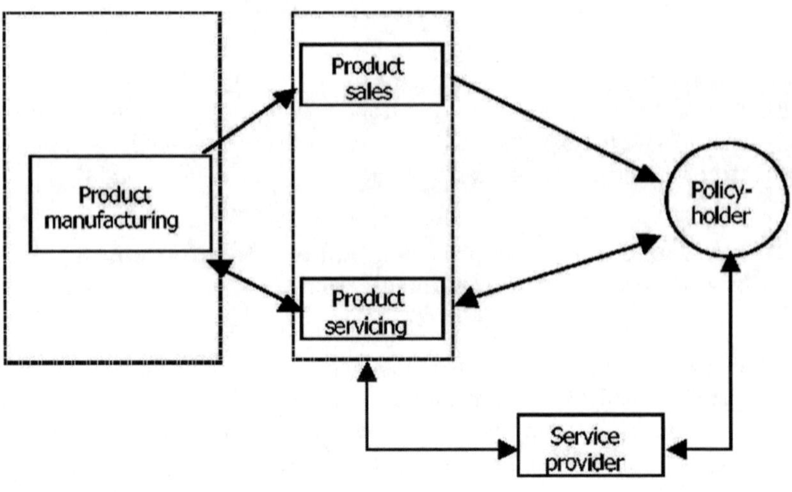

Figure 11.2 The partner-agent model of insurance delivery.

established for its other financial services. The insurance provider acts as the *partner*, providing the actuarial, financial and claims processing expertise, as well as the capital required for initial investments and reserves as required by law. The partner also generally manages the relationship with external service providers involved in claims provision (e.g. healthcare provider, funeral home). Figure 11.2 illustrates a partnership arrangement.

The experiences of a number of MFIs suggest that partnering can be beneficial not only to the MFI, but to their partners and clients as well.

MFI benefits. For the MFI, the potential benefits of partnering include:

- limited initial capital investment and low variable costs;
- rapid product launch and scaling-up;
- compliance with legal and regulatory requirements;
- potential for stable revenue stream from commissions; and
- opportunities to learn the business without taking on the risk.

Partner benefits. For insurance companies that partner with MFIs, there can also be a variety of benefits:

- access to new markets;
- access to clientele with verifiable financial records;
- reduced transaction costs in serving a new market;
- improved political or public image; and
- compliance with licensing requirements in some countries (e.g. in India), which stipulate that an insurer maintains a certain portion of its portfolio in low income areas.

Client benefits. Low income clients who traditionally have not had access to insurance protection may be the greatest benefactors of the partner/agent model. Preliminary evidence suggests that this model allows greater insurance coverage at a lower cost than if an MFI designs and provides the coverage on its own. For example, of the insurance schemes studied by the author, most of the MFI designed programs that provide their own life insurance tied to their loans limited the coverage to just the outstanding loan balance, occasionally offering small additional benefits (US$25–$100). The cost of this coverage ranged from 0.5–2 percent of the loan value. In contrast, the products offered through an MFI/insurer partnership provided larger additional benefits (US$800–$1,000), often against a greater number of risks, for premiums of 0.35–0.5 percent.

Challenges of the partner/agent model

The partner/agent model is not, however, without its challenges. Several factors may limit or prevent an MFI from partnering with an established insurer to provide coverage to its clients.

Limited availability of potential partners. In some markets, there may be few or no insurers available or interested in partnering with an MFI, although an increasing number of formal insurers are becoming interested in the area. The challenge for MFIs is to understand how to communicate the opportunity to potential partners in a way that will be meaningful and understood by organizations unfamiliar with the development sector.

Coverage of more complex risks. Most existing partner/agent relationships tend to provide the least complex form of insurance: basic life coverage. Until they have more experience with the low income market, potential partner insurers may be reluctant to provide coverage against more complex risks.

Before selecting a partner insurance provider, an MFI should consider the following list of questions. While they are not 'hard and fast' requirements for selection, they do provide good talking points with which to begin a conversation with a potential insurance provider.

- What is the national reputation of the insurance provider?
- How is the insurer currently financed? Does it have a stable, conservative asset portfolio?
- What is the claims experience of the insurer and their history of claims payouts? Are they willing to guarantee a fast turnaround on claims from MFI clients?
- How interested is the insurer in serving the low income market?
- Will the insurer adjust their products so that they are responsive to the needs and preferences of low income households?
- Are they willing to make a medium- or long-term commitment to the MFI?
- Are they willing to pay a commission to the MFI for performing the agent role?
- Are there issues related to regulatory compliance?
- Will the insurer give the MFI responsibility for verifying claims?
- What can the insurer do to minimize the number of exclusions, without jeopardizing the sustainability of the plan?

Box 11.3 Due diligence checklist for selecting a partner.

Difficulties ensuring rapid repayment of claims. Given the relative size of the claims, partner insurers may place little importance on processing claims requests, unless a specific process is established for processing microinsurance claims.

Difficulties in negotiating an equal partnership. Because most MFIs know little about what they should attempt to negotiate in establishing a partnership with a formal insurer, the MFIs often end up with less than ideal partnerships. MFIs should, at a minimum, carefully consider the commissions to be paid to the MFI, the exclusions from the policy and the information requirements for submitting a claim to ensure that a formal insurer's offer is congruous with the realities of low income policyholders and beneficial to the MFI. Box 11.3 provides a brief set of guidelines to assist MFIs in selecting a partner. Equally important to the development of productive partnerships is for MFIs to improve their abilities to market their services to potential insurer partners. MFIs are more likely to attract established insurers and to negotiate a rewarding partnership if they are:

- conversant with the details of insurance operations;
- confident in their understanding of clients' needs and preferences for insurance coverage. (Other publications that will assist MFIs in conducting market research and understanding the insurance business include Brand, 2000, and Brown and Churchill, 2000); and
- convincing in demonstrating their capacity to sell and service insurance policies professionally.

11.2 PART III: AN INSURER'S CAPABILITIES

In spite of the arguments against doing so, we recognize that, driven by a lack of suitable partners or the desire for greater premium revenues, some MFIs will elect to develop and manage insurance products on their own. Consequently, Part III summarizes the prerequisites to the provision of insurance in seven areas, highlighting common problems for MFI run insurance schemes. These can be thought of as pre-conditions that MFIs ought to satisfy before developing a self managed insurance product. It is important to note that the level of complexity and required resources and skills for the following activities are much greater for health and property insurance than for life insurance.

(1) Actuarial analysis (pricing)

For an insurance scheme to be viable, premiums must be high enough to cover future claims and, consequently, managers need to be able to predict, with a reasonable degree of accuracy, what future claims will be. If these predictions prove to be inaccurate, unexpectedly high insurance claims can decapitalize an institution. MFI designed and managed programs tend to encounter difficulties in three areas:

Estimating future losses. Although experience can often provide a reasonable estimate of potential future losses, few MFIs use this information to set prices. Where reasonable historical information is not available or where historical averages are not likely to reflect future losses – in many countries HIV/AIDS, for example, is radically changing the average death rates – pricing should incorporate a sufficient margin of error to reflect the uncertainty in future claims behavior.

Establishing reserves. In addition to covering claims and administrative expenses, insurance premiums need to establish reserves. Reserves are funds set aside each year to protect the insurer against unexpectedly high claims. If claims expenses exceed annual premium revenues, claims are paid out of the reserves and the scheme remains solvent. For this reason, insurance regulations typically require a new insurer to provide a minimum initial amount of capital before starting operations. MFIs however, typically have limited liquid reserves, leaving them exposed to unexpectedly high losses, particularly during the early years.

Reinsurance. Reinsurance is the shifting of part or all of the insurance risk originally written by one insurer to another insurer. Formal insurers use reinsurance to limit this risk in both new and established lines of business. To date, no such reinsurance is available to MFIs that offer insurance on their own (except for an experiment being conducted by the ILO's Social Finance Unit, supported by the World Bank, in creating a reinsurance scheme for community based health insurance schemes). This leaves them highly exposed to small fluctuations in claims expenses.

In order to market its health insurance, GRET designed a multistage information session approach. Before making insurance available in a village, GRET uses two 'promoters' to generate interest in the insurance and answer questions. These promoters, in agreement with the commune head, organize a group meeting for all commune members (usually about 2,000 members) to explain the basics of the insurance. Using a graphics-intensive presentation, the promoters explain what insurance is, how GRET's system works, and how benefits will be provided.

A week after this initial meeting, the promoters return to the village to have conversations with individual families. At the end of these conversations, the families are informed that the insurance agent – who is responsible for selling policies and collecting premiums – will return the following week to ask if they want to purchase a policy.

Box 11.4 Multistage marketing at GRET.

(2) Marketing

Marketing of microinsurance involves more than just selling policies. Experience indicates that for a program to be successful, the MFI must also educate prospective clients about the potential benefits and cost of the product and ensure that consumers know how to 'use' it (e.g. how to make claims). Marketing of insurance is also less straightforward than credit or savings because clients must be willing to continue to pay premiums even when they are not receiving any direct benefits. With this in mind, MFIs should consider the following marketing related questions:

- Do the staff that will be marketing the product have the training, materials, knowledge and time required to sell, educate and train clients? Marketing insurance can be a multi stage process (see Box 11.4). Even if the insurance is to be mandatory, training is needed to ensure that loan officers feel comfortable marketing the product and can answer clients' questions and guide them through the claims process.

- How will the MFI ensure that clients are not being coerced or unduly pressured to purchase the proposed product, particularly if the product is to be mandatory for all borrowers or savers? Several private insurers, particularly in different parts of Africa, have become profitable by selling a good volume of policies to poor households. However, in many cases these new policyholders did not understand what they were purchasing or how to make a claim. Without mechanisms to monitor client satisfaction, MFI-offered insurance policies that are mandatory for borrowers or savers run the risk of exploiting MFIs' existing relationships with clients, and potentially damaging the MFIs' loan or savings portfolios.

(3) Underwriting

Underwriting is the process of verifying whether insurance coverage should be provided to a particular potential policyholder. Typically this involves confirming that the potential policyholder meets the eligibility criteria determined by the MFI. For example, if a life insurance policy excludes deaths due to pre existing illnesses, the underwriting process needs to document all illnesses existing when a policy is purchased. MFIs need to consider the following questions:

- *Can the MFI check or confirm the accuracy of the information provided by the prospective client?* If prospective policyholders can misrepresent their age, health status or other relevant information, an MFI may unknowingly change the risk profile of its portfolio. In a small program, the inclusion of even a handful of high risk policyholders may lead to serious unexpected losses.
- *Can the MFI monitor changes in the characteristics of the market and its portfolio, which may change the nature of the risk it has assumed?* If the characteristics of the market and the insured portfolio change over time, this may change the nature of the risk that has been insured. For example, if the average age of policyholders in a life insurance portfolio increases from 35 to 40 over time, the probability of claims will also increase.
- *To avoid adverse selection, will a large percentage of the market be insured?* If the insured population is only a small percentage of the potential market (as would be the case for most MFIs, given their small size), stronger underwriting procedures are needed to avoid adverse selection.

(4) Investment management

While the majority of premium income is needed to cover administrative and claims expenses, the difference in time and value between receipt of premiums and payment of claims and expenses gives an insurance plan the opportunity to earn investment income. The investment manager must balance the desire to earn greater investment returns and the need to maintain sufficient liquidity to meet claims and expenses. With this in mind, MFIs should ask the following two questions:

- *Are any of the insurance premiums or reserves intended to be invested in the MFI's capital fund?* Many MFIs are tempted to use insurance premiums as an additional source of capital to fund their loan portfolio. Initially, this may seem like a wise decision: funds invested in an MFI's loan portfolio may bring in more revenue than funds invested in a savings account or similarly liquid instrument. However, unless an MFI is fully operationally sustainable, funds invested in its loan portfolio will actually shrink rather than grow over time. In addition, if an MFI needs to use its insurance reserves to pay unexpected claims, it cannot quickly call in the illiquid loans it has made with the policyholders' premiums. Furthermore, in many cases, using insurance reserves for on-lending is illegal.
- *How will the insurance plan deal with inflationary cost increases, particularly in high inflation environments?* This is a particularly thorny issue for health and property insurance that promises to provide certain services or replacement assets in the future in exchange for taking a premium today. If the premiums received today are not earning a real rate of return, they will probably be insufficient to cover the higher cost of claims in the future.

(5) Claims management

The systems and staff responsible for verifying whether a claim should be paid out and for ensuring that claims are processed quickly are key. Verification ensures that fraudulent claims are not made, while processing time is a key factor in policyholders' satisfaction with the product. Key questions to consider in assessing an MFI's capability to manage claims include:

- *Have processes been developed to verify that only claims covered by the insurance are paid out?* Do the staff responsible for verification have the knowledge and information needed to assess the validity of claims with accuracy and consistency? For life insurance claims, the MFI must have procedures to handle situations in which the body is not available and to ensure that local staff cannot collude with clients to 'verify' fraudulent claims. For health and property insurance, the difficulties in verifying claims are greater. For health insurance, claims verification involves a whole range of checks, including, for example, photo ID verification to confirm that a patient is indeed insured and detailed tracking information to ensure that certain doctors or patients are not making an unusually high number of claims. Verification of property insurance claims can also be problematic because the cause of the loss is not always readily apparent. For example, it is difficult for an MFI to determine whether a fire that destroys an insured asset was an accident or deliberate.
- *Can the MFI reasonably ensure that claims will be processed in a timely fashion?* Based on current experience, a turnaround time of two weeks or less for life insurance claims is reasonable. The fastest performers pay out claims the same day. For health insurance, payments are often made monthly between

the health care provider and the insurance plan. If clients are reimbursed by the insurance plan for medical expenses incurred, claims processing times need to be less than a few days if the coverage is to be truly valuable to clients. Standard claims processing times for property micro insurance have yet to be established; however standards of 1–3 weeks should be a reasonable objective.

(6) Product management and administration

Coordination and communication among all of the activities mentioned thus far is crucial to the smooth operation of an insurance product. Without effective management and administration of this communication and information sharing, insurance plans can quickly run into financial difficulties. Two areas where many MFI's lack the capability to manage the full range of activities involved in offering an insurance product include management information systems and management time/expertise:

- *Does the MFI have the IT and management systems required to collect and generate the information needed to manage an insurance plan effectively?* Access to up-to-date, accurate information is crucial to the success of an insurance plan. Particularly for health and property insurance, even a one- to two-month lag in access to claims information can hide potential problems long enough for them to become serious. Manual accounting systems and processes, while simple and cost effective, are probably inappropriate for all but the most basic forms of insurance.
- *Does MFI management have the additional time and knowledge necessary to manage effectively a new insurance product?* In addition to the time and effort needed to develop a product, MFI management will need to dedicate time to manage the product once it has been launched. If an MFI is currently having difficulties with its credit portfolio, for example, management's time may be better spent focused on that issue rather than on a new product.

(7) Regulatory compliance

Can an MFI provide insurance legally? Insurance regulations mandate that providers maintain substantial reserves, report regular financial results and have trained underwriting and sales staff. Given the small size of microinsurance policies, these regulations can unintentionally restrict an MFI's ability to provide insurance profitably to the low income market. Therefore, many MFIs offer their insurance products at the margins of the law. While there are differing perspectives on this activity, all MFIs thinking about offering insurance should consider the following questions:

- *Does the plan for the proposed insurance product at least comply with the 'spirit' of the insurance regulations, if not the actual regulations themselves?* Minimum capital requirements and other regulations may be inappropriately high for an organization serving a low income market, but an MFI should still be able to demonstrate that it has sufficient capital and reserves to cover any reasonable, unexpected losses. Insurance regulations also typically require that insurers provide regular reports on their financial status to the relevant body; there is no reason why MFIs should not be able to do the same. In addition, MFIs should be able to demonstrate that policies are being sold in an open and fair manner and that clients are not being misled in the sales process.

- *If an MFI does plan to operate an unregulated insurance product, is it reasonable to assume that local regulators will allow this to happen? For how long?* Some MFIs may be able to avoid regulations if they are only offering basic life insurance tied to their loans, but will this ability continue indefinitely? What will happen if they want to offer more coverage? The deregulation of the insurance industry in India has recently forced SEWA to decide whether to formalize their insurance offerings or find an alternative way to provide this coverage.

11.3 CONCLUSION: A FUTURE FOR MICROFINANCE

There is little doubt that many of the risks faced by the low income clients served by MFIs are insurable, and, in these cases, well designed microinsurance products can have an important development impact. The challenge is to ensure that the product being developed (1) is appropriate for the needs and preferences of the households, (2) is financially viable and (3) is provided through institutions that have the resources and expertise to manage the finances and the risk inherent in the product.

MFIs possess some, but not all, of the resources required to get the job done. With the possible exception of life insurance, most MFIs lack the key expertise and resources needed to provide these microinsurance products sustainably and profitably. Fortunately for MFIs interested in entering the microinsurance market, the most likely source for these resources and expertise – established insurers – lack the client knowledge and distribution network in the micro market that MFIs possess, creating the opportunity for win-win partnerships.

Experience suggests that if an MFI is to develop an insurance product, it is best to start with a very limited product, developed and managed in partnership with an established insurer. Over time, as the MFI develops experience in handling insurance products and collects information on utilization, they may consider taking the product in house. In general, however, complex health and property products should be avoided by individual MFIs unless a suitable partner is available.

The questions in this paper should encourage donors to assess frankly the ability of an MFI to manage a proposed insurance product, particularly if the MFI has no partner with whom the risk can be shared. Donors should also question the opportunity cost of an MFI's focus on insurance product development, particularly if there are existing problems with the institution's portfolio quality or operational efficiency.

Note

1 Much of the work incorporated in this article took place while Warren Brown was with Calmeadow as a Microfinance Research Specialist. The author is indebted to many people for their assistance, including: Colleen Green; Gordon Lindquist; Monique Cohen; Peg Birk; Michael McCord; Zan Northrip; Craig Churchill and USAID's Microenterprise Best Practices Project for their support to produce the longer paper on which this is based, Brown and Churchill (2000). Reprinted from *Small Enterprise Development*, 12 (1), 11–24, 2001.

References

Brand, Monica (2000), 'The MBP guide to new product development', prepared for the USAID Microenterprise Best Practices Project, Development Alternatives, Inc. Bethesda, MD.

Brown, Warren and Craig Churchill (2000), 'Providing insurance to low-income households: Parts I and II', Microenterprise Best Practices Project, Development Alternatives Inc. Bethesda, MD (http://www.eldis.org/go/topics/resource-guides/education&id=11564&type=Document).

Brown, Warren, Colleen Green and Gordon Lindquist (2001), 'Cautionary note for MFIs and donors considering developing microinsurance products', USAID's Microenterprise Best Practices (MBP) research facility.

Cohen, Monique and Jennifer Sebstad (2000), 'Microfinance and risk management: A client perspective', AIMS Paper, USAID, Washington, DC

Hazell, Peter B. R. (1992), 'The appropriate role of agricultural insurance in developing countries', *Journal of International Development*, Vol. 4, No. 6, pp. 567–82.

McCord, M. J. (2000) *Microinsurance In Uganda: A Case Study of an Example of the Partner-Agent Model of Microinsurance Provision*, Micro-Save Africa.

Rutherford, Stuart (1999), *The poor and their money: an essay about financial services for poor people*, Department for International Development (DFID), New Delhi, India.

Wright, Graham (1998), *Beyond basic credit and savings: developing new financial services products for the poor*, Micro-Save Africa.

12

REGULATING FOR DEVELOPMENT

The case of microfinance

Thankom Arun[1]

12.1 INTRODUCTION

In recent years, the discussion on regulation has broadened our understanding of the extent to which the realities of the political economy influence the regulatory policy choices of different institutions. Traditionally, the need for regulation of economic activities is justified in the economics literature as a policy instrument to minimise the effects of market failures, and the issue has gained substantial attention recently, particularly in the course of reform measures in developing countries (Armstrong, Cowan, and Vickers, 1994; Majone, 1996). In broader terms, regulation refers to a set of enforceable rules that restrict or direct the actions of participants and as a result alter the outcomes of this action (Chaves and Gonzalez-Vega, 1994). The financial crises in various countries have indeed brought the issue of regulation to the forefront of financial sector reforms, which is primarily about ensuring systemic stability and protecting depositors. Nevertheless, appropriate regulation of financial markets depends very much on the country-specific characteristics such as level of development and institutional capacities. Recently, the debates on regulatory policies have focused on how to provide appropriate linkage between economic and social objectives on the one hand and the connection between the political and economic system on the other (Cook and Minogue, 2003). In other words, regulation is seen more often as an agreed set of rules to promote developmental objectives along with competitiveness and consumer interests.

This paper discusses regulatory issues in the microfinance sector, which caters to the needs of those who have been excluded from the formal financial sector, largely through reviewing the sector specificities, and existing practices of regulation. Although no conclusive findings are available on how to regulate microfinance institutions (MFIs), the answer to the regulatory concerns of the microfinance sector lies in the special nature of these institutions, which is explored in the next section. The paper then considers the main issues related to the existing regulatory approaches and their impact on the microfinance sector. After exploring the rationale for regulation in the microfinance sector, the paper elaborates on the nature of different types of regulation in this sector. Section 12.4 explores the role of state in the regulation of this sector, while some conclusions are drawn in the final section.

12.2 MICROFINANCE – SALIENT FEATURES

During the post colonial period, subsidised agricultural credit was considered an appropriate development strategy to reach the poor. Most governments followed this strategy, with relaxed requirements for collateral and subsidised interest rates. Over the years, this particular approach seemed to be failing due to higher transaction costs, interest rate restrictions, corrupt practices and high default rates, which have resulted in the phenomenal growth of informal financial markets. The reasons for poor loan recovery are related to inappropriate design features, leading to incentive problems, and politicisation that made borrowers view credit as political largesse (Lipton *et al.*, 1997).

The main providers of informal financial credit services are (i) lending by individuals on a non-profit (and often reciprocal) basis; (ii) direct but intermittent lending by individuals with a temporary surplus; (iii) lending by individuals specialised in lending, whether on the basis of their own funds or intermediated funds; (iv) individuals who collect deposits or 'guard' money; and (v) group finance (for a detailed discussion on these various categories see Matin *et al.*, 2002). Informal providers are ready to accept collateral in different forms that are unacceptable to formal providers, and are part of a localised scale of financial intermediation which has much better information regarding the activities and characteristics of borrowers. The experience of formal and informal financial markets has highlighted the gap in terms of methodology and approach to reaching out to the poor, particularly in developing countries.

The failures in reaching out to the poor had stimulated a set of innovative financial institutions in several countries such as Bolivia, Bangladesh and Indonesia. These MFIs share a commitment to serving clients that have been excluded from the formal banking sector. The real innovations in these schemes are concepts such as group lending contracts, character based lending, short-term repeat loans and incentives for loan repayments. The group lending methodology is based on 'private ordering' which is defined as 'the conformity of members of the group to expected norms and the influence of social pressures for deviations from expected performance of members' (Rao, 2003, p. 53). Repayment incentives may include several devices, including larger repeat loans, access to loans for other group members and cash back facilities for clients who repay on time. The flexibility in repayment options allows borrowers to repay out of existing income, freeing the borrower to invest the loan in relation to their needs. These features made MFIs different from small scale commercial and informal financial institutions and from large government sponsored schemes, and they are either independent of government and/or have a high degree of autonomy from bureaucrats and politicians.

The primary clientele of these institutions are those who face severe barriers preventing them from accessing financial services. MFIs work on the premise that what households need is access to credit, not cheap credit. Many MFIs permit people to access useful lump sums through loans and allow borrowers to repay the loans in small, frequent and manageable instalments, which is further supported by quick access to larger repeat loans. Most of these institutions are successful financially due to high repayment rates and an enhanced awareness of the levels of subsidy. In brief, MFIs have underlined the inability of the poor people to engage in income generating activities due to inadequate provision of savings, credit and insurance facilities.

In the early stages, these institutions had concentrated their activities only on microcredit, but this changed to providing a range of services in due course (Matin *et al.* 2002). However, even after two decades, a better understanding of the financial service preferences and behaviours of the poor is still needed to expand the scope of microfinance initiatives addressing the concerns about the welfare implications of MFIs (Gulli, 1998 and Morduch, 2000). Along with the loan provision, opportunities for opening savings accounts and deposit services are also important. In the 1990s, a debate emerged around two leading views of microfinance services available to the poor – the financial systems approach and the poverty lending approach, both of which share a commitment to making these services available to the poor. The poverty lending approach focuses on credit and other services funded by donor and concessional funds as an important mechanism for poverty reduction. On the contrary, the financial systems approach focuses on commercial financial intermediation with an emphasis on a self sustaining institutional framework. The research findings are inconclusive and the major difficulty concerning the trade-off between reaching the poor and achieving financial sustainability persists. After a detailed analysis of various MFIs, Hulme and Mosley (1996) provide evidence of the existence of a trade-off between outreach and sustainability which is contrary to the findings of the study by Christen *et al.* (1995). The so-called failure of MFIs in attracting the lowest strata of the poor may be due to the limited understanding regarding the mismatch between demand-side constraints and supply-side limitations (Arun and Hulme, 2003). This argument emphasises the better understanding of the demand for financial services by the poor and their behavioural patterns which is important in the process of refocusing the operations of MFIs towards the poorest of poor.

12.3 RATIONALE AND THE NATURE OF REGULATION IN MICROFINANCE

The issue of regulation and supervision has attracted a growing interest in the microfinance sector akin to that in the formal financial sector. The regulation in the formal financial sector aims to maintain a balance between shareholder and debtor/depositor interests, and arises from information asymmetries that are due to the peculiar nature of the assets of the banking firm (Chaves and Gonzalez-Vega, 1994; Stiglitz, 1994). Financial institutions such as depository intermediaries/banks may increase expected returns for shareholders while undertaking excessively precarious positions, which can lead to an interest clash between shareholders and depositors. This moral hazard problem is mainly due to the asymmetric distribution of information in favour of insiders such as bank owners and managers who have an informational advantage over outsiders such as depositors and creditors. This could lead to agency problems such as the inability of the depositors to monitor the decisions of financial institutions.

Further, in a competitive market scenario, other competitors would be forced to accept the high interest rate offered by one institution, which would eventually lead to an excessive risk to the system as a whole. Similarly, the failure of one institution normally leads to panic and massive withdrawals within the system which could affect even the most prudent institution. These spillover effects of opportunistic behaviour by one institution could endanger the financial system as a whole. In many countries, government ownership of banks can be viewed as an instrument for assuring the safety of the system which is normally accompanied by economic regulations such as asset and activity restrictions, and interest rate controls.

In developing economies, the recent financial reforms have led to the removal of economic regulation, and the introduction of a prudential approach to regulation which focuses on capital adequacy requirements and supervisory controls through on-site and off-site monitoring. It is believed that capital requirements help control bank risk taking, although risks are complex to define in the context of developing countries. Monitoring is also relatively difficult due to the lack of trained personnel and high quality accounting systems. The model of prudential regulation in developing countries simply followed a best practice package developed elsewhere, mainly in developed countries. A recent study by Barth *et al.* (2001) found that the implementation of international best practices did not minimise the probability that a country would suffer a banking crisis. The reform experiences in developing countries, particularly in East Asia, suggest that a gradual approach to financial sector reforms is important, mainly due to the fact that developing countries in general do not have in place sufficient institutional arrangements to permit the prudential approach to bank regulation required to ensure banking stability (Arun and Turner, 2002, p. 435). These experiences shed light on the politicisation of the regulatory process and the difficulty in enforcing legal/bureaucratic regulations in developing countries.

There are concerns as to whether regulation is really needed in the microfinance sector and, if it is needed, what the different options are beyond merely emulating the practices from the formal sector. Although MFIs serve a large section of the population and have contributed to financial deepening over the years, they have not achieved adequate market penetration to pose any systemic risk to the financial system as a whole (Wright, 2000). The arguments for regulation in the microfinance sector seems to be justified when we consider the level of uncertainty to which clients are subjected to, such as innovative procedures and high operating costs. Also the financial failures in the microfinance sector could have a serious impact on the financial system by affecting the commercial banks (who lend to MFIs) and on public confidence.

The arguments for no regulation in microfinance are based on the small size operations of microfinance and on the assumption that the cost of developing and implementing regulations exceeds the benefits accrued from them. For instance, a recent study on Ghana observed that supervision of MFIs is costly relative to their potential impact on the system (Steel and Andah, 2003). Although small financial institutions may be costly to regulate and supervise, financial deepening combined with the development of a competitive market structure spreading across various financial services and client groups is imperative for the growth of the sector. However, the conclusions of a study on 12 regulated MFIs in Latin America reported that the benefits of regulation exceeded the cost (Theodore and Loubiere, 2002). The benefits included greater access to commercial sources of funds for equity and debt, increased ability to provide diversified products, higher standards of control and reporting, and the enhanced legitimacy of the operations.[2]

The idea of internal/self regulation is also discussed in the literature, although the concept is not that appealing in the context of diversified activities by the MFIs. Under this idea, the primary responsibility for monitoring and enforcing regulation lies within the organisation or an apex organisation. This cost effective mechanism may be appropriate for relatively smaller MFIs or those who are in the early stages of growth. However, the likelihood of success in the context of diversified operations and objectives is limited (Kirkpatrick and Maimbo, 2002). In South Africa, the Association of Micro Lenders sought the self regulation of the microfinance sector in 1996. The impetus behind this move was the existence of inappropriate regulation which prevented the improvement of refinance facilities available to the members and the enhancement of the public status of microlenders. However, Staschen (1999) notes that over the years, the South African experience illustrates that self regulation neither promotes consumer protection nor safeguards the financial system. The ineffectiveness of the self regulation approach may be due to the conflict of interests between various stakeholders within the institution. The enforcement and governance rests primarily on member motivation in this type of approach, which was not effective in many cases.

There are certain instances where the regulatory authorities contact a consulting firm to perform regulatory functions. This is a useful approach when supervisors do not have adequate interest in, and the capability to, regulate MFIs. Although the regulatory agency maintains legal responsibility of the supervised institutions, it delegates regular monitoring and on-site inspections to a different agency. For instance, in Indonesia, Bank Rakyat uses its rural branch offices to supervise a large number of tiny municipal banks (Badan Kredit Desas). In Peru, the Bank Superintendent has delegated day-to-day overseeing to a federation of municipal savings and loan institutions which assists the monitoring process, with the technical assistance of a German consulting firm. This hybrid approach is considered logical since microfinance portfolios require different approaches and skills compared to those needed for commercial bank supervision (Berenbach and Churchill, 1997). An alternative view is that regulation in the microfinance sector can be achieved through the existing legal and regulatory framework. However, most of the legislation in the formal sector needs to be reframed in the context of MFIs for their effective application. For instance, in Zambia, the Banking and Financial Act (1995) fixes separate minimum capital requirements depending on the nature of the institution (banks, leasing companies and other non-bank institutions), in addition to a risk weighted capital adequacy ratio of 10 per cent, applied to all institutions on a sliding scale which incorporates their size, profitability, diversification and other relevant characteristics (Meagher and Wilkinson, 2001). The reality is that this scheme as does not accommodate MFIs and only explains the definitional rigidities followed in the formal systems.

MFIs are significantly different in their risk profiles (such as risks on credit, interest and liquidity), which provides a further argument for regulation and rapid integration with practices such as prudential regulation.[3] The policy justification for prudential regulation is that it minimises the risk profiles and provides protection for small investors. The observance of sound risk management is crucial, whether the MFIs are subject to external regulation or not (Greuning *et al.*, 1999). One needs to accept that the volume and nature of MFIs' activities raise the question of how applicable the set of rules prevalent in the formal financial sector are to them. Christen and Rosenberg (2000) observed that unlike formal financial institutions, it would be difficult in the case of MFIs to provide additional capital at the time of distress. In the formal financial sector, at the time of distress, regulators can instruct institutions to stop lending without affecting the debt collection process. However, in the microfinance sector, an action of this nature will seriously affect the repayment of outstanding loans, and the cost of collection may be more than the value of the outstanding loans in many cases.

There is also the point that regulated MFIs must be more conservative in prescribing the financial indicators for risk management such as higher risk weighted capital adequacy ratios which reveal the financial strength and the ability of the institution to absorb losses. The fact that portfolio assets of MFIs come under the high risk category indicates the potential danger in permitting these institutions to self leverage. For instance, in Latin America and Caribbean countries, studies have found that the general principles of financial regulation are not entirely appropriate for MFIs (Jansson and Wenner, 1997). It is imperative that regulators take into account the differences among the various classes of borrowers and the methodologies employed to reach these borrowers. Regulators must understand the dynamics of the system and allow sufficient flexibility with regard to issues such as documentation and legal procedures.

Similarly, loan loss provisions/classifications are expected to match up with the value at risk in a loan portfolio, which has an impact on the income statement and the balance sheet of the institution. Microfinance loans are considered as consumer loans which prescribe the minimum loan loss provisions based upon the number of days the loan is overdue. Most of these loans have shorter repayment frequencies and even a couple of months' arrears may be a big problem for clients. Also, once these loans fall into the arrears category, it is difficult to recover them. Although the conservative practices may affect the return on assets and equity of MFIs, these are essential for sustaining the industry. All these discussions on the need for sector-specific regulations emphasise the distinctiveness of the sector.

The special regulations may facilitate an environment which allows MFIs to mobilise savings and also reduce the problems in enforcing normal banking regulations. However, there is a consensus in the literature that prudential regulation needs to be implemented only in those MFIs which accept deposits for the purpose of lending (elaborated on in the next section). Also, it is imperative to incorporate country specificities in the regulatory approach due to the varied macroeconomic environments and different stages of development.

12.4 MICROFINANCE, REGULATION AND GOVERNMENT

MFIs are mostly registered as NGOs which are not generally included under the financial regulation followed by the central banks and do not have a legal charter to engage in financial intermediation. In many countries, deposit taking from the public is an activity restricted to licensed financial institutions only. Most of the MFIs are dependent on subsidies and are unable to operate profitably enough to pay a commercial cost for a large portion of their funds (Christen and Rosenberg, 2000). This restricted status has prohibited most of the MFIs from accessing deposits from the public or engaging in any type of banking operation, such as providing savings services for the poor, which is a way of obtaining a long-term source of capital at a reduced cost. There are no other possible avenues for these institutions to raise resources to sustainably deliver an increasing variety of financial services to the poor. In this scenario, adequate regulation may allow these institutions to attract deposits from the public which may in turn allow them to grow in a sustainable way. Regulation may also bring about greater linkages with the banking sector, an improved operating network and higher standards of control and reporting.

The nature of contract between depositors and financial organisations could also provide windows for opportunistic behaviour by the financial institution[4] which justifies the need for regulation further. However, one needs to be definite that excessive regulation will not lead to repression of innovation and flexibility in providing services, both of which are imperative to the growth of MFIs (see Section 12.2). Also, whether the regulatory mechanisms facilitate existing providers in enlarging their activities or not and to what extent they encourage the entry of new providers in the sector is also important. The experiences of Indonesia and Philippines show that the availability of legal charter with lower capital requirements has brought private rural banks into the microfinance sector.

Although some governments are concerned about the high interest rates, the Latin American experience shows that non-involvement by government has helped the MFIs immensely in their early stages (Christen and Rosenberg, 2000). Most of the countries in Latin America had legally permissible lower levels of interest rates, which were not enough for sustainable MFI operation and which compelled them to operate as non-governmental organisations (NGOs). Over the years, governments have seen the enhanced demand for high interest rate loans and this becomes a non-issue in the licensing of MFIs later on. The governments are also keen to regulate these institutions to protect depositors' interest, particularly in the case of those MFIs which are already taking deposits. Most of the depositors are poor and unorganised. In Bangladesh, many poor people lost their savings due to the incompetence or fraud of unregulated and little known institutions (Wright, 2000). Nevertheless, most of the governments which have followed a *laissez faire* approach to MFIs so far have been changing recently. The governments are considering this as an opportunity for them to engage with MFIs, mainly due to the high political profile of these institutions. Since governments have the legal power to make economic agents conform to regulations, the role of government in regulation is significant. However, the ambiguities in legal and policy frameworks could affect the operational environment of MFIs as well. For instance, in Russia the ambiguous and uncertain policy environment had left MFIs vulnerable to regulatory discretion in the interpretation of the legal basis for lending activities (Safavian *et al.*, 2000). The study observed that since MFIs are neither mentioned nor authorised in any of the legislation in Russia this has given a discretionary power to the local enforcement agencies to apply some of the existing laws unevenly and unpredictably to MFIs.

The Indian experience offers a solution to this situation through a dialogue dominated approach between NGOs and government agencies in developing an appropriate regulatory framework (Titus, 2000). The study found out that this approach is cautiously taking steps in the right direction and creating a space for MFIs to grow further, which is very different from the passive attitude followed by the government towards the microfinance sector over the years. Although this approach takes time to evolve, it provides an opportunity for MFIs to set common priorities for the development of the sector, particularly when countries have different operating models.

Both donors and governments expect that regulation will speed up the emergence of sustainable MFIs. However, the process of integrating MFIs in a licensed environment should be a gradual one due to the unfamiliarity of the regulatory process in the microfinance sector (Christen and Rosenberg, 2000). Because of the variety in the type of MFIs, it has been suggested that institutions be fitted into a tiered structure which clearly defines how the types of institutions are regulated and by whom (Meagher, 2002). The advantages of a tiered approach are that it provides opportunities and incentives for MFIs to graduate between tiers and that it creates appropriate regulatory requirements for different types of institutions.

The tiered approach has benefited the development of sustainable microfinance in the Philippines and Ghana by clearly identifying pathways for MFIs to become legitimate institutions and gain access to financial resources from commercial markets (Gallardo, 2002). In Ghana, while the tiered approach has led to the growth of different types of MFIs, it has also permitted the easy entry of institutions with weak management and internal controls. This experience demonstrates the difficulty in balancing entry and innovation on the one hand and appropriate regulatory capacity on the other (Steel and Andah, 2003). If the tiers are not defined properly, this could lead to regulatory arbitrage, overlap and ambiguity (Staschen, 2003). There is a strong perception that regulation in a tiered approach must incorporate the basic features of the sector, such as management capacities, the nature of clients and transaction volume. The regulatory approaches must also consider diversity among institutional types and be consistent with the overall financial sector framework (Berenbach and Churchill, 1997). The approach to regulation of MFIs should be country-specific in nature and there is no single prototype that can be applied universally.

The regulation of microfinance needs to address the two emerging thoughts in the sector discussed in Section 12.2: reaching the poorest of the poor and the provision of a wide range of services. Both of these indicate the need to develop a flexible approach to the regulation of MFIs. In this context, it is imperative to discuss alternative models that are flexible and less costly compared to conventional forms of regulation, such as voluntary registration (proposed by Stuart Rutherford, see Wright, 2000), which would allow clients to compare different MFIs in relation to risk and benefits associated with these institutions. MFIs wishing to mobilise deposits must register with an institution and must provide details of their nature and area of operation, and of their ownership. This registration document must be distributed by the MFIs to all of their clients in the local language, and must be displayed at the local government office. Another innovative scheme is 'deposit insurance'. Under this scheme, government regulators allow banks to act as insurers to MFIs, and the role of the state is to define the minimum acceptable insurance contract that ensures the parties concerned have the capacity to undertake obligations, and to ascertain that the parties have appropriate legal standing for enforcement against them (Wright, 2000, p. 99). By insuring all the deposits this scheme is expected to result in the dispersion of risks. Kirkpatrick and Maimbo (2002) have identified some issues of concern in these innovative schemes. These schemes emphasise the categorisation of MFI clients in relation to their performance. Since there are no standard criteria for comparison, those clients – especially those who are from the lowest strata of the income category – who are using the voluntary register may not get the expected benefits out of it. There is also a tendency to minimise the involvement of the state by encouraging a risk based approach. MFIs will have to allocate more resources for regulation which may outweigh benefits in the large number of smaller institutions.

12.5 CONCLUSIONS

MFIs have received increased attention in the development literature due to their potential to contribute to the development of functional financial markets in rural areas for households, particularly those who were previously without proper access to financial services. Recently, these institutions have been moving towards a credit-plus era and have expanded their nature of activities by providing additional services such as savings and insurance. However, there is also a push for greater emphasis to be put on providing financial services to the poorest of the poor by these institutions. Both these changes indicate the need to develop flexible and less costly forms of regulatory practices in the sector.

In many countries MFIs are not usually included in the financial legislation which restricts access to deposits from the public. Most governments have followed a *laissez faire* approach in regulating MFIs which has affected these institutions' ability to obtain long-term sources of capital at a reduced cost. This paper underlines the importance of an appropriate regulatory framework to support the sustainable delivery of diversified microfinance services. The sector-specific regulations along with prudential reforms may facilitate an environment which allows MFIs to mobilise savings and also reduce the problems in enforcing normal banking regulations. The tiered approach has benefited the development of sustainable microfinance in many countries by identifying pathways for MFIs to access the resources from commercial markets. However, the regulatory approaches must incorporate the diversity among institutions and sector-specific requirements. Also, one needs to incorporate the specificities of countries in the regulatory approach and to take into account the varied macroeconomic environments and different stages of development.

ACKNOWLEDGEMENTS

The author acknowledges valuable suggestions from Dr Peter Vass, Director of the Centre for the Study of Regulated Industries (CRI) at the University of Bath, Dr Bernardo Mueller, Universidade de Brasilia, and other conference participants.

Notes

1 Reprinted from *The Quarterly Review of Economics and Finance*, 45 (2–3), 345–57, 2005.
2 However, the CGAP (2002) study estimates a higher cost of supervision in the first year (5 per cent of total cost) and 1 per cent in the following years.
3 Prudential regulation refers to the set of general principles that aim to contribute to the stable and efficient performance of financial institutions and markets (Chaves and Gonzalez-Vega, 1994). These regulations, such as accounting policies and standards of financial structure, are intended to protect the interests of depositors and encourage competition in the sector. However, there are certain non-prudential regulatory requirements which do not entail the government taking a position on the financial soundness of an institution, such as disclosure of ownership and control and publication of financial statements (Christen and Rosenberg, 2000).
4 The opaqueness of financial institutions such as banks makes it more difficult for diffuse equity- and debt holders to write and enforce effective incentive contracts, to use their

voting rights as a vehicle for influencing firm decisions, or to constrain managerial discretion through debt covenants (Capiro and Levine, 2002). In order to credibly commit to not expropriating depositors, banks could make investments in brand-name or reputational capital (Klein, 1974), but these schemes give depositors little confidence, especially when contracts have a finite nature and discount rates are sufficiently high (Goodhart, 1998).

References

Armstrong, M., Cowan, S., & Vickers, J. (1994). *Regulatory reform: Economic analysis and British experience*. Cambridge, MA: MIT Press.

Arun, T. G., & Hulme, D. (2003). Balancing supply and demand: The emerging agenda for microfinance institutions. *Journal of Microfinance*, 5, 2.

Arun, T. G., & Turner, J. (2002). Financial sector reform: The Indian experience. *The World Economy*, 25, 3.

Barth, J., Caprio, G., & Levine, R. (2001). *Bank regulation and supervision: What works best?* (World Bank Working Paper No. 2725). Washington, DC.

Berenbach, S., & Churchill, C. (1997). *Regulation and supervision of microfinance institutions: Experiences from Latin America, Asia and Africa*. Washington, DC: USAID.

Caprio, G., Jr., & Levine, R. (2002). *Corporate governance of banks: Concepts and international observations*. Paper presented in the Global Corporate Governance Forum Research Network Meeting, 5 April.

Chaves, A., & Gonzalez-Vega, C. (1994). Principles of regulation and prudential supervision and their relevance for microenterprise finance organisations'. In O. Maria & R. Elisabeth (Eds), *The new world of microenterprise finance for the poor*. Hartford, CT and London: Kumarian Press.

Christen, R. P., Rhyne, E., Vogel, R., & McKean, C. (1995). *Maximising the outreach of microenterprise finance: An analysis of successful microfinance program* (USAID Program and Operations Assessment Report No. 10).Washington, DC: USAID.

Christen, R. P., & Rosenberg, R. (2000). *The rush to regulate: Legal frameworks for microfinance* (Occasional Paper No. 4). Washington, DC: CGAP.

Cook, P., & Minogue, M. (2003). *Regulating for development* (Insights 49, id. 21). Institute of Development Studies, University of Sussex.

Gallardo, J. (2002). *A framework for regulating microfinance institutions: The experience in Ghana and the Philippines* (Policy Research Working Paper No. 2755). Washington, DC: World Bank.

Goodhart, C. (1998). *Financial regulation: Why how and where now?* London: Routledge.

Greuning, H., Gallardo, J., & Randhawa, Bikki K. (1999). *A framework for regulating microfinance institutions*. Washington, DC: World Bank.

Gulli, H. (1998). *Microfinance and poverty: Questioning conventional wisdom*. Washington: Inter-American Development Bank.

Hulme, D., & Mosley, P. (Eds). (1996). *Finance against poverty: Vols. 1 and 2*. London: Routledge.

Jansson, T., & Wenner, M. (1997). *Financial regulation and its significance for microfinance in Latin America and the Caribbean microenterprises*. Washington, DC: Sustainable Development Department, Inter-American Development Bank.

Kirkpatrick, C., & Maimbo, S. (2002). Implications of the evolving microfinance agenda. *Development Policy Review*, 20(2), 293–305.

Klein, B. (1974). The competitive supply of money. *Journal of Money, Credit and Banking*, 6(4), 421–53.

Lipton, M., de Haan, A., & Yaqub, S. (1997). Credit and employment for the poor. *Politica Internazionale*, 5, 153–66.

Majone, G. (1996). *Regulating Europe*. London: Routledge.

Matin, I., Hulme, D., & Rutherford, S. (2002). Finance for the poor: From microcredit to microfinancial services. Policy Arena on Finance and Development. *Journal of International Development*, 14(2), 273–94.

Meagher, P. (2002). Microfinance regulation in South Africa: A comparative perspective. *Development Bulletin*, 57, 48–52.

Meagher, P., &Wilkinson, B. (2001). *Filling the gap in South Africa's small and micro credit market: An analysis of major policy, legal and regulatory issues*. Mimeo, IRIS Center, University of Maryland.

Morduch, J. (2000). The microfinance schism. *World Development*, 28(4), 617–29.

Rao, P. K. (2003). *Development finance*. London: Springer.

Safavian, M. S., Graham, D. H., Gonzalez-Vega, C., & Whelan, D. (2000). The state of microfinance activity and regulation in Russia. *Small Enterprise Development*, 11, 4.

Staschen, S. (1999). *Regulation and supervision of microfinance institutions in South Africa*. Report prepared for Deutsche Gesellschaft fur Technische Zusammenarbeit (GTZ).

Staschen, S. (2003). *Regulatory requirements for microfinance: A comparison of legal frameworks in 11 countries worldwide*. Eschborn: GTZ.

Steel, W. F., & Andah, D. O. (2003). *Rural and microfinance regulation in Ghana: Implications for development and performance of the industry* (World Bank Africa Regional Working Paper Series No. 49). Washington, DC.

Stiglitz, J. E. (1994). The role of the state in financial markets. *Proceedings of the World Bank Annual Conference on Development Economics 1993*, 19–52.

Theodore, L., & Loubiere, T. (2002). The experience of microfinance institutions with regulation and supervision: Perspectives from practitioners and a supervisor. In D. Deborah & R. Elisabeth (Eds), *The commercialization of microfinance: Balancing business and development*. Kumarian Press.

Titus, M. (2000). Building the regulatory framework for microfinance in India. *Small Enterprise Development*, 11, 4.

Wright, G. (2000). *Microfinance systems: Designing quality financial services for the poor*. London: Zed Books.

13

IMPACT ASSESSMENT METHODOLOGIES FOR MICROFINANCE

Theory, experience and better practice

David Hulme[1]

13.1 INTRODUCTION

In recent years impact assessment (IA) has become an increasingly important aspect of development activity as agencies, and particularly aid donors, have sought to ensure that funds are well spent. As microfinance programs and institutions have become an important component of strategies to reduce poverty or promote micro and small enterprise development then the spotlight has begun to focus on them. But knowledge about the achievements of such initiatives remains only partial and is contested. At one end of the spectrum are studies arguing that microfinance has very beneficial economic and social impacts (Holcombe, 1995; Hossain, 1988; Khandker, 1998; Otero and Rhyne, 1994; Remenyi, 1991 and Schuler *et al.*, 1997). At the other are writers who caution against such optimism and point to the negative impacts that microfinance can have (Adams and von Pischke, 1992; Buckley, 1997; Montgomery, 1996; Rogaly, 1996 and Wood and Sharrif, 1997). In the 'middle' is work that identifies beneficial impacts but argues that microfinance does not assist the poorest, as is so often claimed (Hulme and Mosley, 1996 and Mosley and Hulme, 1998).

Given this state of affairs, the assessment of microfinance programs remains an important field for researchers, policy makers and development practitioners.[2] This paper reviews the methodological options for assessing the impacts of such programs drawing on writings on microfinance and the broader literature on evaluation and IA. Subsequently it explores ways in which IA practice might be improved. It views IA as being 'as much an art as a science' (a phrase lifted from Little, 1997, p. 2). Enhancing the contribution that IA can make to developmental goals requires both better science and better art. The scientific improvements relate to improving standards of measurement, sampling and analytical technique.

Econometricians and statisticians are particularly concerned with this field. Improving the 'art' of IA has at least three strands. One concerns making more systematic and informed judgements about the overall design of IAs in relation to their costs, specific objectives and contexts. The second is about what mixes of IA methods are most appropriate for any given study. The third relates to increasing our understanding of the ways in which the results of IA studies influence policy makers and microfinance institution (MFI) managers.

13.2 IMPACT ASSESSMENT: OBJECTIVES

IA studies have become increasingly popular with donor agencies and, in consequence, have become an increasingly significant activity for recipient agencies. In part this reflects a cosmetic change, with the term IA simply being substituted for evaluation. But it has also been associated with a greater focus on the outcomes of interventions, rather than inputs and outputs. While the goals of IA studies commonly incorporate both 'proving' impacts and 'improving' interventions, IAs are more likely to prioritize the proving goal than did the evaluations of the 1980s. A set of factors are associated with the extreme 'pole' positions of this continuum and these underpin many of the issues that must be resolved (and personal and institutional tensions that arise) when IAs are being initiated (Figure 13.1).

Behind the shift from 'evaluation' to 'IA' are a number of factors. These are not explored in any detail in this paper but they form an essential element for the understanding of IA and its potential contributions. Explicitly, IAs are promoted by both the sponsors and implementers of programs so that they can learn what

	PROVING IMPACTS ←-----→	IMPROVING PRACTICE
Primary Goal	Measuring as accurately as possible the impacts of an intervention	Understanding the processes of intervention and their impacts so as to improve those processes
Main Audiences	Academics and researchers Policymakers Evaluation departments Program managers	Program managers Donor field staff NGO personnel Intended beneficiaries
Associated Factors	Objectivity Theory External Top down Generalization Academic research Long timescales Degree of confidence	Subjectivity Practice Internal Bottom up Contextualization Market research Short timescales Level of plausibility

Figure 13.1 The goals of impact assessment.

is being achieved and improve the effectiveness and efficiency of their activities. Implicitly, IAs are a method by which sponsors seek to get more information about program effectiveness than is available from the routine accountability systems of implementing organizations. IAs are also of significance to aid agencies in terms of meeting the ever increasing accountability demands of their governments (in this era of 'results' and 'value for money') and for contesting the rhetoric of the anti-aid lobby. While recipient agencies benefit from this, they are one stage removed, and many are likely to see donor initiated IA as an activity that has limited practical relevance for program activities. To quote the director of a large Asian MFI that has received substantial amounts of aid financed IA consultancy and internal IA-capacity building, 'impact assessment studies keep donors happy … we don't use them very much.'

A final issue to raise in this section is whether the expectations of OECD based agencies about the feasibility of the accurate measurement of impacts in the difficult contexts of developing countries (limited numbers of professional researchers, few written records, illiteracy, communication problems etc.) are higher than in their own countries. My professional experience of EU financed 'small enterprise development' projects in Manchester has revealed a startling lack of concern with impacts: this is in marked contrast to my consultancy work in Bangladesh where donors criticize nongovernment organizations (NGOs) for failing to make IA a priority! If recipients perceive that the IA standards expected of 'them' are higher than donors expect of themselves then IA will be seen as an external imposition rather than a shared opportunity.

13.3 ASSESSING IMPACT: THE CHOICE OF CONCEPTUAL FRAMEWORKS

All IA exercises have a conceptual framework at their heart. In well planned and well resourced IAs with long 'lead in' times, such frameworks are usually explicitly identified (Khandker, 1998; Sebstad *et al.*, 1995 and Schuler and Hashemi, 1994). By contrast, in many smaller scale exercises the framework is implicit and may be seen as 'common sense.' There are three main elements to a conceptual framework:

- a model of the impact chain that the study is to examine,
- the specification of the unit(s), or levels, at which impacts are assessed, and
- the specification of the types of impact that are to be assessed.

(a) Models of impact chains

Behind all microfinance programs, and indeed virtually all aid financed initiatives,[3] is the assumption that intervention will change human behaviors and practices in ways that lead to the achievement (or raise the probability of achievement) of desired outcomes. IAs assess the difference in the values of key variables between the outcomes on 'agents' (individuals, enterprises, households, populations, policy makers etc.) which have experienced an intervention against the values of those variables that would have occurred had there been no intervention. The fact that no agent can both experience an intervention and at the same time not experience an intervention generates many methodological problems. All changes are influenced by mediating processes (specific characteristics of the agent and of the economic, physical, social and political environment) that influence both behavioral changes and the outcomes in ways that are difficult to predict (Sebstad *et al.*, 1995).

The impact chain is very simply depicted in Figure 13.2. A more detailed conceptualization would present a complex set of links as each 'effect' becomes a 'cause' in its own right generating further effects. For example, in a conventional microfinance project a package of technical assistance and capital changes the behavior (and products) of a MFI. The MFI subsequently provides different services to a client, most commonly in the form of a loan. These services lead to the client modifying her/his microenterprise activities which in turn leads to increased or decreased microenterprise income. The change in microenterprise income causes changes in household income which in turn leads to greater or lesser household economic security. The modified level of household economic security leads to changes in the morbidity and mortality of household members, in educational and skill levels and in future economic and social opportunities. Ultimately, perhaps, these changes lead to modifications in social and political relations and structures. The complexity of such chains provides the assessor with a range of choices about which link (or links) to focus on. For microfinance, it is useful to distinguish between two main schools of thought with regard to which link(s) in the chain to focus on. For convenience, these are termed the 'intended beneficiary'[4] school and the 'intermediary' school.

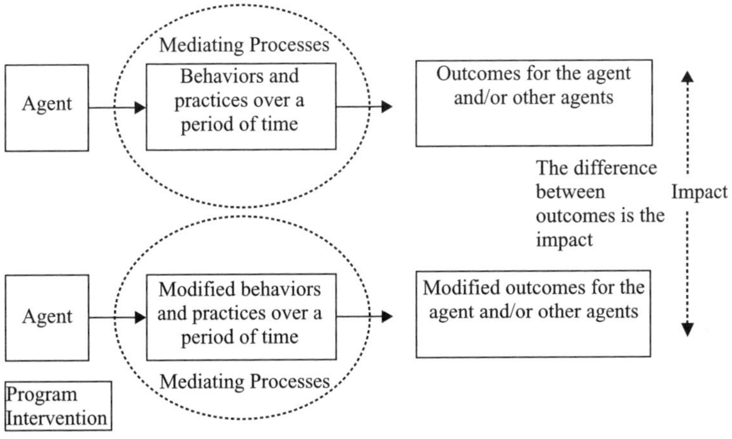

Figure 13.2 The conventional model of the impact chain.

The intended beneficiary school, building on the ideas of conventional evaluation, seeks to get as far down the impact chain as is feasible (in terms of budgets and techniques) and to assess the impact on intended beneficiaries (individuals or households). The intermediary school focuses purely on the beginning of the chain and in particular on changes in the MFI and its operations. Its roots are closely associated with the Ohio State University School's analyses of rural finance. Generally, two key variables are focused on: institutional outreach and institutional sustainability[5] (Yaron *et al.*, 1997). If both outreach and sustainability have been enhanced then the intervention is judged to have a beneficial impact as it has widened the financial market in a sustainable fashion. This is based on the assumption that such institutional impacts extend the choices of people looking for credit and savings services and that this extension of choice ultimately leads to improved microenterprise performance and household economic security. While this assumption can be supported by theoretical frameworks (if a set of further assumptions are made about perfect competition and other factors), it is an assumption which has proved invalid in a number of experiences.[6] In addition, it will not reveal borrower 'cross financing' of loans (Wiig, 1997) which may threaten the long-term viability of an MFI.

While the choice between these two schools can ultimately be seen as an ideological choice (does one prioritize contributions to improved welfare or to more efficient markets?), it is possible to recognize different strengths and weaknesses. The intended beneficiary school makes fewer assumptions about the impact chain and is better able to distinguish 'who' benefits and 'how.' It is, however, demanding in both methodological and cost terms. The intermediary school usefully incorporates notions of sustainability and provides an IA methodological framework that can be operated largely with pre-existing data. It is, though, very weak on 'who' benefits and 'how' (as illustrated by assessments of the USAID financed APPLE program).[7] Possible ways of strengthening the intermediary school approach have been suggested by Feinstein (1997) through the analysis of borrower transaction costs. He proposes the collection of longitudinal data on borrowers' transaction costs (p. 5) to assess whether an MFI has benefited borrowers, i.e. has reduced their total costs for accessing finance. This offers a potential 'bridge' between the two main 'schools,' if data on 'who' borrowers are also collected.

(b) Units of assessment

Following on from the design of a model of the impact path comes the choice of the unit(s) of assessment (or levels of assessment). Common units of assessment are the household, the enterprise or the institutional environment within which agents operate. Occasionally studies have attempted to assess impact at an individual level (Goetz and Sen Gupta, 1996 and Peace and Hulme, 1994), but this is relatively rare and has to take a qualitative focus. More recently some studies have attempted to assess impacts at a number of levels, such as Hulme and Mosley (1996) who looked

Table 13.1 Units of assessment and their advantages and disadvantages

Unit	*Advantages*	*Disadvantages*
Individual	– Easily defined and identified	– Most interventions have impacts beyond the individual – Difficulties of diaggregating group impacts and impacts on 'relations'
Enterprise	– Availability of analytical tools (profitability, return on investment etc.)	– Definition and identification is difficult in microenterprises – Much microfinance is used for other enterprises and/or consumption – Links between enterprise performance and livelihoods need careful validation
Household	– Relatively easily defined and identified – Permits an appreciation of livelihood impacts	– Sometimes exact membership difficult to gauge – The assumption that what is good for a household in aggregate is good for all of its members individually is often invalid
	– Permits an appreciation of interlinkages of different enterprises and consumption	
Community	– Permits major externalities of interventions to be captured	– Quantative data is difficult to gather – Definition of its boundary is arbitrary
Institutional impacts	– Availability of data	– How valid are inferences about the outcomes produced by institutional activity?
	– Availability of analytical tools (profitability, SDIs, transaction costs)	
Household economic portfolio (i.e. household, enterprise, individual and community)	– Comprehensive coverage of impacts	– Complexity
	– Appreciation of linkages between different units	– High costs – Demands sophisticated analytical skills – Time consuming

at microenterprise, household, community and institutional levels and USAID's Assessing the Impact of Microenterprise Services (AIMS) Project. Through a household economic portfolio model (HEPM) the latter seeks to assess impacts at household, enterprise, individual and community levels and thus produce a fuller picture of overall impacts (Chen and Dunn, 1996).

The relative advantages and disadvantages of different units of assessment are summarized in Table 13.1. As can be seen, a focus purely on the 'individual' or the 'enterprise' has such drawbacks that they could be viewed as discredited. The HEPM has much to recommend it – especially if institutional impacts are incorporated in the community level analysis. It does have the profound disadvantage, though, of making assessment demanding in terms of costs, skilled personnel and time. If used with limited resources it risks sacrificing depth for breadth of coverage of possible impacts.

(c) Types of impact

An almost infinite array of variables can be identified to assess impacts on different units. To be of use these must be able to be defined with precision and must be measurable. Conventionally, economic indicators have dominated microfinance IAs with assessors particularly keen to measure changes in income despite the enormous problems this presents. Other popular variables have been levels and patterns of expenditure, consumption and assets. A strong case can be made that assets are a particularly useful indicator of impact because their level does not fluctuate as greatly as other economic indicators and is not simply based on an annual estimate (Barnes, 1996, p. v).

The social indicators that became popular in the early 1980s (e.g. educational status, access to health services, nutritional levels, anthropometric measures and contraceptive use) have recently been extended into the socio-political arena in an attempt to assess whether microfinance can promote empowerment (Mayoux, 1997; Goetz and Sen Gupta, 1996; Schuler and Hashemi, 1994 and Hashemi *et al.*, 1996). This has led to the measurement of individual control over resources, involvement in household and community decision making, levels of participation in community activities and social networks and electoral participation. The bulk of this work has focused on changes in gender relations, but there are sometimes partially formulated assessments of class relations within it (Fuglesang and Chandler, 1993). These extensions to the types of impact assessed permit IAs to be more sophisticated and to shed light on developmental impacts at a time when the goals of development have also been extended. They do add, however, to the complexity of IA work and require the skills of assessors who are experienced at making judgements on social relations.

Sebstad *et al.* (1995) usefully distinguish between 'domains of change' (e.g. household income) and the specific 'markers of change' (e.g. amount of income, number of income sources and seasonality of income) within each domain. While not comprehensive, the detailed sets of domains and markers, produced in their paper provide an excellent checklist for impact assessors to consider at the IA design stage.[8] Often the exact markers used will be shaped by the methodology that is selected. This can cause problems for multi method IAs which may not be able to apply a single definition for a marker for each of the methods used. In addition, impact assessors should always seek to keep the number of variables they measure to a manageable number and not be tempted to go for a comprehensive approach that will impact adversely on data quality and study relevance.

13.4 THE THREE PARADIGMS OF IMPACT ASSESSMENT: PROBLEMS OF ATTRIBUTION AND FUNGIBILITY

The major methodological problems that confront the IA of microfinance relate to attribution and fungibility. At the heart of IA is the attribution of specific effects (i.e. impacts) to specific causes (i.e. interventions). From the vast literature on microfinance IA it is possible to draw out three very different paradigms by which authors seek to demonstrate attribution. The first is the conventional scientific method with its origins in the natural sciences. The second has its roots in the humanities and focuses on making a reasoned argument supported by theory and specific pieces of evidence. Although the former has tended to dominate discussions about microfinance IA (see, for example, the studies reviewed by Gaile and Foster, 1996), the latter tradition is being increasingly used by MFIs and researchers (Bouman and Hospes, 1994; Ardener and Burman, 1995; Remenyi, 1991 and Rutherford, 1999). The third part of this section explores a recent entrant to the field – participatory learning and action (PLA) – which offers a radical challenge to both conventional IA and to 'science' itself. Although these three approaches can be separated for analytical purposes, in recent practice many studies have woven elements of these approaches together (see Section 13.5 for a discussion).

(a) Scientific method

Scientific method seeks to ensure that effects can be attributed to causes through experimentation.[9] A particular stimulus to a particular object in a rigorously controlled environment is judged to be the cause of the observed effect. The experimental approach is virtually infeasible in the social sciences, because of the nature of the subject matter, and so the approach has been adapted into quasi-experiments (Casley and Lury, 1982). Quasi-experiments seek to compare the outcomes of an intervention with a simulation of what the outcomes would have been, had there been no intervention. One method for this is multiple regression, but this has rarely been used in microfinance IA because of its enormous demands for data on other possible causal factors and its assumptions (Mosley, 1997, pp. 2–3). A second approach is the control group method which has been widely used. This requires a before and after comparison of a population that received a specific treatment[10] (i.e. a microfinance program) and an identical population (or as near as possible) that did not receive the treatment. While this idea is elegantly simple a number of 'elephant traps' may befall its user. In particular, problems of sample selection bias, misspecification of underlying causal relationships and respondent motivation (see later) must be overcome.

Selection bias may occur because of:

i difficulties in finding a location at which the control group's economic, physical and social environment matches that of the treatment group,
ii the treatment group systematically possessing an 'invisible' attribute which the control group lacks (most commonly identified as entrepreneurial drive and ability),
iii receiving any form of intervention may result in a short-term positive response from the treatment group (the Hawthorne effect),
iv the control group becoming contaminated by contact with the treatment group (though this could be a long-term program goal!), and
v the fungibility of the treatment (e.g. when a loan is transferred from a borrower to someone else or when the loan is not used in the planned way).

Problems (i) and (iv) can be tackled by more careful selection of the control group. This applies particularly to controlling for access to infrastructure (which has a key influence on input and output prices as well as other variables) and ensuring that the control group is located far away from the treatment group. Problems (ii) and (iii) are more intractable, but in many cases they can be tackled by using program accepted 'clients to be,' who have not yet received microfinance services, as the control group (Hulme and Mosley, 1996, chapter 4). It must be noted, however, that this approach will not be valid when the take up of microfinance services is based on diffusion through a heterogeneous population.[11]

This leaves the problem of loan fungibility. This can be seen as an intractable problem as 'no study has successfully controlled for the fungibility of resources between the household and the assisted enterprise' (Gaile and Foster, 1996, p. 24). Using case study materials to crosscheck actual loan use against intended loan use and thus estimating 'leakage' is one possible approach to controlling for fungibility (Pulley, 1989 and Mosley, 1997). But for all studies except those that focus exclusively on 'the enterprise,' then a concern about fungibility may be irrelevant. For studies looking at the household, the community or the household economic portfolio (see Section 13.3b) fungibility is not a problem for the assessor, rather it is a vital strategy for the client. The best investment returns may be on 'consumption' (in terms of developing or maintaining human capital through school fees and doctors' bills, or buying food at a time of crisis when the credit terms on 'in-kind' borrowing from traders may be exceptionally high). From this perspective the task of the assessor is not to pretend that microenterprises are 'firms' whose inputs and outputs can be precisely identified and measured but to recognize that the impacts of microfinance must be assessed at a variety of levels. The assessor attempting to control for fungibility (to prove impact) has failed to recognize that fungibility is a process to be encouraged (to improve impact)!

The *misspecification of underlying causal relationships* arises most commonly because of the assumption that causality is a one way process (Figure 13.2). This may be a reasonable assumption in the physical sciences (though it does not go unchallenged by contemporary philosophers of science). For human activity it is commonly invalid, as causation may also run from impact back to intervention. Mosley (1997, p. 6) illustrates this with the example of a program whose field staff put pressure on a borrower to repay her loan; this may succeed in the short term but may induce the borrower to sell assets (machinery, land, trees) which reduce the probability of repayment in the longer term. Such reverse causation need not necessarily be negative and, from the perspective of more process oriented analytical frameworks, is essential if programs are to continually learn from their experience and improve (rather than prove) their impact.

Such problems can be overcome by the adoption of models that conceptualize causation as a two way process by the use of the two stage least squares technique and regression analysis (Mosley, 1997, p. 7). Such an approach is enormously demanding in terms of data requirements, technical expertise and costs. It will only be feasible on very rare occasions (for example, see Khandker, 1998). For most researchers adopting the scientific method, reverse causality is a problem to be coped with rather than overcome. The main means of dealing with it are tracing dropouts from both the treated and control groups; only conducting IAs on relatively mature programs; interim impact monitoring activities to gather qualitative information about the complexity of causality; and retrospective in-depth interviews with clients (Mosley, 1997, p. 6).

Table 13.2 Common impact assessment methods

Method	*Key features*
Sample surveys	Collect quantifiable data through questionnaires. Usually a random sample and a matched control group are used to measure predetermined indicators before and after intervention
Rapid appraisal	A range of tools and techniques developed originally as rapid rural appraisal (RRA). It involves the use of focus groups, semi-structured interviews with key informants, case studies, participant observation and secondary sources
Participant observation	Extended residence in a program community by field researchers using qualitative techniques and mini-scale sample surveys
Case studies	Detailed studies of a specific unit (a group, locality, organisation) involving open-ended questioning and the preparation of 'histories'
Participatory learning and action	The preparation by the intended beneficiaries of a program of timelines, impact flow charts, village and resource maps, well-being and wealth-ranking, seasonal diagrams, problem ranking and institutional assessments through group processes assisted by a facilitator

(b) The humanities tradition[12]

The broad set of approaches that fall under this heading have their roots in the humanities. Originally geography and rural sociology were the 'lead' subjects, but over the last 20 years anthropology has become most important. Its main features are an inductive approach, a focus on key informants, recording by notes or image, and the data analyst is usually directly (and heavily) involved in data collection.[13] This tradition does not try to 'prove' impact within statistically definable limits of probability. Rather, it seeks to provide an interpretation of the processes involved in intervention and of the impacts that have a high level of plausibility. It recognizes that there are usually different, and often conflicting, accounts of what has happened and what has been achieved by a program. The validity of specific IAs adopting this approach has to be judged by the reader on the basis of the logical consistency of the arguments and materials presented; the strength and quality of the evidence provided; the degree of triangulation used to crosscheck evidence; the quality of the methodology; and the reputation of the researcher(s). Whether 'standards' could be specified for such work – to help its users appreciate how rigorously designed they are – is an important issue that merits attention.[14] Commonly the bulk of data generated by such an approach is 'qualitative,' although at later stages of analysis such work often quantifies some data. The main types of methods used have been discussed in Section 13.4 (in particular see Table 13.2).

Although such work has been common in development studies for decades, it was only during the 1980s that its relevance for IA was recognized.[15] This recognition has arisen partly because of the potential contribution of qualitative approaches (especially in understanding changes in social relations, the nature of program staff beneficiary relations and fungibility) and partly because of the widespread recognition that much IA survey work was based on inaccurate information collected by questionnaire from biased samples (Chambers, 1993). Low budget and low rigor IAs claiming to adopt the scientific method were at best pseudo-science, but more often simply bad science, despite the sophisticated analytical tools that were applied to poor datasets.

IAs with their roots in the humanities have considerable difficulties with regard to the attribution of cause and effect. Such studies cannot usually demonstrate the causal link as they are not able to generate a 'without program' control group (although at times some researchers neglect to mention this to the reader and simply assume causality). Instead, causality is inferred from the information about the causal chain collected from intended beneficiaries and key informants, and by comparisons with data from secondary sources about changes in out-of-program areas. Problems also arise because not infrequently the labels 'rapid appraisal,' 'mini survey' and 'case study' are applied to work which has been done in an *ad hoc* manner and does not achieve a minimum professional standard in terms of informant selection and the rigor of data collection and analysis. Examples of this include: basing data collection only in program areas that are performing well, and surveying best clients; and inferring that the data collected in one area apply to all clients without explaining this assumption.

While such studies cannot provide the degree of confidence in their conclusions that a fully resourced scientific method approach can yield, my personal judgement is that in many cases their conclusions are more valid than survey based IA work that masquerades as science but has not collected data with scientific rigor. It is nonetheless becoming increasingly common to combine 'scientific' and 'humanities' approaches so as to check the validity of information and provide added confidence in the findings (Hashemi *et al.*, 1996; Hulme and Mosley, 1996; and Schuler and Hashemi, 1994). In the future, dealing with attribution by multimethod approaches seems the way forward.

(c) Participatory learning and action (PLA)

In the last five years participatory approaches to development planning and management have moved from being fringe activities onto center stage. While many donor agencies have simply added a bit of PLA to their existing procedures, it can be argued that this is inappropriate as conceptually participatory approaches challenge the validity and utility of the scientific method as applied to developmental problems (Chambers, 1997). According to this line of argument the scientific method fails as: it ignores the complexity, diversity and contingency of winning a livelihood; it reduces causality to simple unidirectional chains, rather than complex webs; it measures the irrelevant or pretends to measure the immeasurable; and, it empowers professionals, policy makers and elites, thus reinforcing the status quo and directly retarding the achievement of development goals. At heart, PLA theorists do not believe that ultimately there is one objective reality that must be understood. Rather, there are multiple realities and before any analysis or action is taken the individuals concerned must ask themselves, 'whose reality counts?' (Chambers, 1997). Their answer is that the perceived reality of the poor must take pride of place as, if development is about 'empowering the poor' or 'empowering women' (as virtually all development agencies now say), then the first step toward empowerment is ensuring that 'the poor' or 'women' take the lead in problem identification and analysis and knowledge creation.[16]

For IA the purist PLA line is damning: 'conventional baseline surveys are virtually useless for impact assessments .... The question now is how widely local people can be enabled to identify their own indicators, establish their own participatory baselines, monitor change, and evaluate causality' (Mayoux, 1997, p. 123). By this means two objectives may be achieved: better IAs, and intended beneficiaries will be 'empower[ed] through the research process itself' (Mayoux, 1997, p. 2). In practice, the art of participatory impact assessment (PIA) is in its infancy and a pragmatic rather than a purist approach has been common. Agencies such as Proshika in Bangladesh have begun to use PLA methods extensively for their assessment and planning exercises.[17]

The reliability of participatory methods varies enormously, as with 'scientific' surveys, depending 'largely on the motivation and skills of facilitators and those investigated and the ways in which informants' perceptions of the consequences of research are addressed' (Mayoux, 1997, pp. 12–13). Nevertheless, it is argued that 'a number of rigorous comparative studies have shown that, when well conducted, participatory methods can be more reliable than conventional surveys' (Mayoux, 1997 and Chambers, 1997).

To date the literature on PLA and PIA has only partially addressed the issue of attribution. From a scientific perspective PIA has grave problems because of the subjectivity of its conceptualizations of impact; the subjectivity of the data used to assess impact; the variables and measures used vary from case to case and do not permit comparison; its pluralist approach may lead to a number of mutually conflicting accounts being generated about causality; and, the assumption that because lots of people are taking part in an exercise means that all are able to 'voice' their concerns (so that opinions are representative) is naïve about the nature of local power relations. From the perspective of a 'new professional' (Chambers, 1997) then such a set of accounts is unproblematic, as it reflects the complexity and contingency of causality in the real world. In addition, it can be argued that PIA contributes to program goals (perhaps particularly in terms of empowering women (Mayoux, 1997) and the poor) by not facilitating the continued dominance of target groups by powerful outsiders. Why dwell on issues of attribution when efforts to overcome such problems require the adoption of IA methods that actively undermine the attainment of program goals?

13.5 THE PRACTICE OF MICROFINANCE IMPACT ASSESSMENT

(a) Knowledge creation: the methodological menu[18]

Over the last decade microfinance IA studies have increasingly moved away from single method approaches (Hossain, 1988 and Fuglesang and Chandler, 1986) to multimethod or pluralist approaches (Hulme and Mosley, 1996 and Mustafa *et al.*, 1996). The introduction of participatory approaches to IA has extended the methodological menu for data collection and knowledge creation.While sample surveys remain a common model, rapid appraisal, participant observation and participatory learning and action are increasingly used (Table 13.2). Each of these methods has a different pattern of strengths and weaknesses (Table 13.3) and this has led to a growing consensus among impact assessors that the central methodological question is no longer 'What is the optimal method for this study?,' but 'What mix of methods is most appropriate for this study and how should they be combined?' Depending on the level of resources available and the context, impact studies increasingly seek to combine the strengths of different approaches and, in particular, seek to combine the advantages of sample survey and statistical approaches (representativeness, quantification and attribution) with the advantages

Table 13.3 Comparative strengths and weaknesses of different methods

	Method criteria	*Surveys*	*Rapid appraisal*	*Participant observation*	*Case studies*	*Participatory learning and action*
1	Coverage (scale of applicability)	High	Medium	Low	Low	Medium
2	Representativeness	High	Medium	Low	Low	Medium
3	Ease of data standardisation, aggregation and synthesis (e.g., quantification)	High	Medium	Medium or low	Low	Medium or low
4	Ability to isolate and measure nonproject causes of change	High	Low	Low	Low	Low
5	Ability to cope with the attribution problem	High	Medium	Medium	Medium	Medium
6	Ability to capture qualitative information	Low	High	High	High	High
7	Ability to capture causal processes	Low	High	High	Medium	High
8	Ability to understand complex processes (e.g., institution building)	Minimal	Medium	High	Medium	Medium
9	Ability to capture diversity of perceptions	Low	High	Very High	Medium	High
10	Ability to elicit views of women and disadvantaged groups	Low	Medium	High	High (if targeted)	Medium
11	Ability to capture unexpected or negative impacts	Low	High	Very high	High	High
12	Ability to identify and articulate felt needs	Low	High	High	Medium (due to low coverage)	High
13	Degree of participation encouraged by method	Low	High	Medium	Medium	Very High
14	Potential to contribute to stakeholder capacity building	Low	High	Low	Medium to low	Very High

(*continued*)

Table 13.3 Comparative strengths and weaknesses of different methods (*continued*)

	Method criteria	*Surveys*	*Rapid appraisal*	*Participant observation*	*Case studies*	*Participatory learning and action*
15	Probability of enhancing downwards accountability	Low	High	Medium	Medium	High
16	Human resource requirements	Specialist supervision, large numbers of less qualified field workers	High skilled practitioners, who are able to write-up and analyse results	Medium skilled practitioners, with good supervision, who are prepared to commit for lengthy period	Medium skilled practitioners with good supervision	High skilled practitioners
17	Cost range	Very high to medium	High to medium	Medium to low	Medium to low	High to medium
18	Timescale	Very high to medium	Medium to low	High	High to medium	Medium to low

Source: adapted from Montgomery *et al.* (1996).

of humanities or participatory approaches (ability to uncover processes, capture the diversity of perceptions, views of minorities, unexpected impacts etc.). In well resourced studies with long time scales (e.g., Mustafa *et al.*, 1996) all of these different methods may be utilized in a comprehensive fashion. In cases where a high degree of statistical confidence is required (for example, when it is desired to 'prove' impact for policy or major investment purposes) then a large scale, longitudinal sample survey must be mounted, preferably supported and triangulated by the use of their methods on a limited scale. By contrast, if an IA is required to provide independent corroboration of the impact of a small scale program and strengthen aspects of its implementation then a mix of rapid appraisal and small scale survey is likely to be appropriate.

(b) Costs and confidence

The design of an IA must be very closely related to the budget available: this may be a platitude but over ambitious designs continue to lead to poor quality studies or delays that make findings irrelevant. Interestingly, in this age of cost consciousness, the literature on microfinance provides no specific information on the overall or unit costs of IA studies of microfinance; 'high,' 'medium' and 'low' are about as good as the data get![19]

From verbal reports it is clear that IAs adopting the scientific method and seeking to 'prove' impact cost the earth (probably US$500,000 to US$5 million, depending on the number of MFIs studied). At the other extreme high quality, rapid appraisals of the impact of individual schemes by gifted and knowledgeable individuals can produce useful findings on 'improvement' for relatively small sums (around US$5,000 to US$10,000). Between these two extremes is a vast array of different options. A reading of the contemporary literature produces the following findings.

i Studies intended to produce authoritative evidence of microfinance impact using the scientific method will be rare exceptions in the IA field. Their costs are so great that few agencies can fund them and their timescales so long that the agencies studied are likely to treat them as 'historical' rather than being of operational relevance.

ii The idea that 'qualitative' and 'participatory' assessments' methodologies are cheap needs to be challenged (Mayoux, 1997). While such approaches are much cheaper than large scale surveys, rigorous qualitative IAs will require the use of high caliber staff who are given time to prepare properly. Costs of tens of thousands of US dollars, rather than thousands, should be anticipated.

iii For studies of moderate budget (i.e. most studies) the best approach to ensuring the validity of findings will be through triangulation and using a mix of survey, qualitative and participatory techniques. The alternative, of trying to achieve a representative sample size on a limited budget, is likely to lead to severe losses in the quality of data and/or the representativeness of the sample.

iv Limited investments in project monitoring by program staff make moderate cost IA at high levels of quality much more feasible as less primary data collection is necessary (see Montgomery, 1996 and later parts of this paper).

(c) Human resources for impact assessment

In many, if not most, developing countries recruiting IA personnel who have the skills and qualities to interview, collate, analyze and write up findings is a key problem at both consultant and fieldworker levels. Commonly, different studies find themselves competing for the same small pool of people which, while it may usefully raise payments for scarce skills, puts these individuals under great strain and does not appear to stimulate a 'supply side response'. It is beyond the capacity of this paper to explore this issue, but it must be recognized as a key constraint and that efforts to build IA capacities professionally and institutionally should be a priority for development agencies if they intend to continue to emphasize the need for IA.

(d) Respondents: motivation and representation

A 'rational actor' confronted by an impact assessor asking standard IA questions ('What is your income? What do you spend your money on? How do you get on with your husband?') would soon tell the interviewer where to put his/her survey instrument. Fortunately, in the world of practice, more polite responses are the norm but the issue of how to persuade respondents to spare the time for an interview, and provide accurate and honest answers, is an important one that is rarely mentioned in IA methodological statements. Different strategies are needed for different types of respondent – program beneficiary, control group and program dropout. As a rule of thumb many researchers suggest that interviews should be concluded within one hour and that one and a half hours should be seen as the absolute maximum for an interview.

Beneficiaries are the easiest group to approach as generally they accept 'answering questions' as one of the unavoidable transaction costs of being in a program or dealing with an MFI. Motivation can be enhanced by having interviewers introduced by program officers but this has the danger of linking the assessor with field level staff and encouraging the recounting of 'the right answers.'[20] For both data quality and ethical reasons the personal introductions that interviewers make prior to interview need to be carefully worked out so that respondents understand why they are being interviewed and have an opportunity to ask their own questions before the interview begins.

Motivation is a more difficult issue with control groups as, having by definition no connection with a program, they have no incentive to cooperate. In many cases, however, the novelty and amusement value of being interviewed is sufficient encouragement (though expatriates should note that when they are working at a field site the willingness of people to be interviewed may be higher than is the norm because of the rarity value of foreigners). The problems of response increase significantly if longitudinal data are collected, as second and third interviews have much less amusement value. In such cases rewarding interviewees should be considered to promote data quality and for ethical reasons (what right have impact assessors to assume that the opportunity costs of an interview, particularly for poor people, are zero?). This can take the form of a social reward, such as bringing soda water and snacks to share with respondents (this works well in East Africa), or 'bribery' (Mosley, 1997, p. 8), where the interviewee is paid cash for surrendering her/his time.[21]

Program dropouts represent a particular problem, and a failure to pursue dropouts may have led to some IAs underestimating the negative impacts of microfinance (e.g. Hulme and Mosley, 1996). When the dropout is traceable then significant effort is merited to obtain an interview/re-interview. Where dropouts cannot be traced, or death has occurred, then a replacement respondent sampled at random from the original population, and preferably from the same stratum, should be interviewed (see Mosley, 1997, pp. 7–8).

Participatory and rapid appraisal methods that work with groups generally manage to muster respondents because of the social interaction they create. Care needs to be taken, however, to observe who has turned up and, perhaps more significantly, who has not come to the meeting (Mayoux, 1997). The assumption that participants in a PLA exercise represent 'the community' will commonly not be valid (Mosse, 1994). Additional interviews or focus groups may be necessary to collect information from people who do not turn up for communal PLA or rapid rural appraisal (RRA) sessions.

(e) The problem of 'low impact' impact assessments[22]

A final problem of IA concerns the impact of IAs on policy and practice. This depends in part on the original objectives of a study. It applies to both 'proving' and 'improving' IAs. The evaluation literature of the 1980s bemoans the limited influence of evaluation on subsequent decision making. IA has inherited this problem, as illustrated by the very limited influence of large scale IA studies (Mustafa *et al.*, 1996) on the microfinance activities of the Bangladesh Rural Advancement Committee (BRAC) and the long time lag between the World Bank's excellent studies of MFIs in Bangladesh in the early 1990s and the dissemination of findings (Khandker, 1998) to policy makers in Europe and MFI managers in Bangladesh.

A number of ways of ameliorating this problem can be identified.

i Impact assessors need to devote more time to the 'use' of their studies (and perhaps a little less time to the product itself!). Their focus must go beyond 'the report' into a dissemination strategy aimed at decision makers: bullet point summaries, short user friendly papers, snappy presentations and strategic cups of coffee are the key to this environment.

ii The timing of findings needs to be carefully considered. As a general rule of thumb the longer the length of time between data collection and findings presentation, then the lower the impact for IAs focused on 'improving' practice. The common response to initial findings presented more than nine months after completion of fieldwork is 'our program has already been redesigned so your findings have little relevance.'

iii Program managers often regard impact assessors as impractical people who have lots of time on their hands. For high cost approaches pursuing the scientific method this will be of only limited significance as the people to whom one's results must be credible are in Washington and European capitals. For the vast majority of IA studies, however, the issue of how to develop constructive relationships with program staff requires careful thought and action. Efforts to achieve co ownership of findings by involving program staff in IA design, showing respect for their ideas and opinions, and discussing interim findings are possible ways of making influence more probable.

13.6 EFFECTIVE IMPACT ASSESSMENT: ACHIEVING 'FIT'

The key task for the IA designer is to select an approach that can meet the objectives of the specific assessment at an acceptable level of rigor that is compatible with the program's context, that is feasible in terms of costs, timing and human resource availability and that avoids the problems identified in earlier sections. Wherever possible an IA methodology should be piloted before full implementation. The questions that s/he must answer can be summarized as follows.

- What are the objectives of the assessment?
- How is the information to be used and by whom?
- What level of reliability is required?
- How complex is the program, what type of program is it, what is already known about it?
- What resources (money, human and time) are available?

The range of specific responses to these questions is infinite, but for the purposes of this paper they are grouped into four categories. These categories are based on Little (1997) but their characteristics have been substantially modified. These range from impact monitoring and validation, through simple and moderate approaches to more complex approaches. They can be viewed as a hierarchy, but there is a great danger in this as it may seem to infer that complex approaches are best!

(a) Impact monitoring and validation (or, do not do an impact assessment!)

Commonly the answer to the above questions should be 'don't proceed with an impact assessment,' as a program's emphasis on 'institution building' will be undermined by IA and/or sufficient resources are not available.[23] Instead, donors could focus on strengthening the internal impact monitoring capacities of the MFI and occasionally checking the quality of this information by using external monitors for validation purposes. The greater the involvement of staff in assessing program achievements then the greater is the likelihood of findings being used (Hyman and Dearden, 1998, p. 275).

Contrary to common practice, and donor preference, building internal impact monitoring capacities does not mean creating a large IA unit within an MFI. Rather, it means helping the MFI develop its management information system (MIS) and the work of its pre-existing internal monitoring and research units to collect readily available data (outreach, repayments, dropout rates etc.) alongside 'simple to gather' types of data on who is using services, what for, why and what they like or dislike about the services. Much of this work can be done by focus groups, short interviews and rapid appraisal.[24] It is more akin to the market research that private business uses than the academic research that dominates aid financed development.

These systems already operate formally and informally in some of the large Asian MFIs and are the basis upon which their directors take many 'improvement' decisions.[25] Strengthening these systems and occasionally verifying them – rather than financing complex IAs by visiting consultants – is probably the best way to achieve the 'improving' goals of IA. The types of verification process used in Social Audits (New Economics Foundation, 1996 and Zadek and Gatward, 1996) provide a model for ensuring that internal IAs are valid.

(b) A simple approach

This seeks to provide timely information at relatively low cost about program impacts. These are the most common forms of IAs. Reliability is moderate, at best (and based mainly on triangulation), and the major objective is to test the existing understanding of impacts and contribute to improvements in program operation. The main audiences are program managers and donor 'country based' staff. The central methodological feature of such an approach is the use of a variety of methods. Usually this involves a small scale client survey, compared with a comparison group that could be rapidly identified (e.g. approved clients who have not yet received services), and crosschecked by rapid or participatory appraisal methods. If a baseline study is not available then a recall methodology would be utilized. The key variables to be studied would depend on program objectives, but for income and assets the focus would be on ordinal and nominal measurements (see Little, 1997, p. 17). For programs prioritizing empowerment goals and local institutional development, then participatory methods would be highlighted and the survey work might be dropped altogether.

Several participants in a CGAP Impact Assessment Group virtual meeting (Gaile, 1997, p. 5) argued that improving the credibility, utility and cost effectiveness of simple approaches was where the greatest gains in IA could be realized.

Characteristics to enhance the effectiveness of simple IAs include: (i) focusing on a small set of key hypotheses; (ii) using variables that have a 'track record' from earlier IA studies; (iii) clearly documented use of triangulation; (iv) methods applied consistently over time; (v) use of small sized comparison group; (vi) careful training of IA staff.

(c) A moderate approach

The moderate approach involves substantially more costs than the simple approach, yields higher levels of reliability (statistical inference rather than triangulation) and is likely to take two or three years before it delivers findings. Its focus is on both proving impact and improving programs. Its audiences would include policy makers (looking for reassurance about their agency's investments) and the senior managers of programs. The methodological 'mix' would center on a significant survey that would stratify clients and compare them with a carefully matched control group. The survey would involve at least two visits with a minimum of 12 months between them and recall techniques would not be used. Contextual and crosschecking materials would be produced by rapid appraisal techniques and carefully planned participant observation and case studies might also be commissioned. While the selection of variables would depend on program objectives the income and assets data would be extended (Gaile, 1997, p. 20) and measurement would focus on interval and nominal scales.

(d) A complex approach

The complex approach focuses on ensuring high levels of reliability with regard to the attribution of causality and has an exclusively 'proving' orientation. Its main audiences are policy makers and researchers and it is likely to be four to six years after launch before findings are available. The central method in such an approach is a large scale sample survey very carefully constructed to represent all key features of the client population. This is compared against a carefully selected control group, so that the number of households surveyed is likely to be between 750 and 1,500. At least three interviews will be conducted with each household over a period of two to three years. A much wider set of income and asset variables will be measured (Gaile, 1997, p. 23) and the focus will be on high precision through interval measurements. A set of related studies on institutional performance would be conducted, but the heart of the study would be the statistical and econometric analysis of survey findings. The budgets for such approaches are likely to exceed a million US dollars as the survey costs are high, data processing and analysis inevitably generate problems and significant amounts of high powered and high cost econometrician and/or statistician time is needed.

13.7 CONCLUSION

In recent years donors have been keen to assess the impact of their programs. The initial emphasis on 'scientific' sample surveys and statistical analyses has shifted as multimethod IA studies and most recently participatory approaches have been utilized. Microfinance programs and institutions have experienced these shifts and examples of IAs on this topic provide a resource from which this paper has sought to draw out lessons for future practice. Much further work will be needed as the claims that microfinance is a panacea for poverty reduction (most publicly through the Microcredit Summit and its follow up), and the counterclaims that caution against such enthusiasm (Rogaly, 1996 and Wood and Sharrif, 1997) demand rigorous empirical testing to find out what is being achieved and how more might be achieved.

The desire of MFIs, donors and impact assessors themselves to produce results that will verify findings about impact at high levels of statistical confidence has too often driven the design of IA studies. This can compromise quality (with small sample surveys claiming exaggerated levels of representativeness) and impact (with external, data extraction approaches making MFI staff unwilling to use findings and contradicting the 'empowerment' goals of many programs). This paper has argued that IA effectiveness should not be automatically equated with the level of scientific 'proof' that a study can claim. While all studies must pursue rigor, and this applies equally to quantitative and qualitative work, the effectiveness of an IA will depend on how well it achieves a fit between its objectives, the financial and human resources it can command and its context. There is no optimal model and different designs – characterized in this paper as 'low,' 'moderate' and 'complex' and combining scientific, humanities and participatory approaches – will be appropriate for different studies. All too often, however, donor desires for objective and external IAs (to meet their domestic accountability requirements) lead to the neglect of a key alternative: strengthening the impact monitoring capacity of the MFI itself. While striving for technical best practice should be a key goal for all in this field it would be foolish not to recognize that IA is a 'battlefield of knowledge' (Long and Long, 1992) in which different actors seek to influence the knowledge creation process so that it meets their needs.

Notes

1 An earlier version of this paper was prepared for the Consultative Group to Assist the Poorest (CGAP) in association with Management Systems International and USAID's AIMS Project. It was presented at a virtual meeting of the CGAP Impact Assessment Working Group, April 7–19, 1997. I should like to thank the participants in that meeting for their comments, those who prepared the background papers (Renee Chao-Beroff, Osvaldo Feinstein, Gary Gaile, Peter Little, Linda Mayoux, Paul Mosley and Arne Wiig) and Carolyn Barnes, Monique Cohen, Jennefer Sebstad and three anonymous reviewers for comments. Particular thanks are due to Richard Montgomery for the ideas that he has given me about impact assessment. Reprinted from *World Development*, 28 (1), pp. 79–98, 2000.

2 For a discussion of impact assessment for other forms of services to microenterprise see Hyman and Dearden (1998).

3 The impact chain model not only underpins ex post assessment but is central to most aid financed activity in the form of a variety of 'logical frameworks' that donors use to design projects and programs.

4 I use the term intended beneficiary here, rather than client, as most MFIs utilize (or have utilized) aid funds that are intended, at least in part, to benefit poor or vulnerable people and not purely self-selected clients. This is an important point as, (a) some MFIs present their client populations as intended beneficiaries when many clients are known to be nonpoor, and (b) some agencies (e.g. the CGAP) present the client populations of MFIs as 'the poorest' when they know full well that only a proportion of clients are poor and that few if any are 'the poorest', i.e. social outcasts, destitute, disabled, refugees, widows or elderly.

5 The assessment of institutional sustainability has been greatly advanced by Yaron's subsidy dependence index (SDI) which permits the assessor to move beyond simple statements of profit and loss qualified by footnotes about changes in levels of subsidy.

6 The grandest invalidation is probably the United Kingdom in the mid- to late-1980s when an unprecedented increase in outreach and profitability of institutions providing financial services for households and small enterprises created a 'bubble' which ultimately destroyed many enterprises, led to some losing their homes and impoverished hundreds of thousands of households. Also note that Mayoux (1997) has found that programs performing well in terms of outreach and repayment rates can have negative impacts in terms of women's empowerment.

7 I cannot locate my copy of a study on the USAID Anti-Poverty Lending Program! This study ably computed almost every measure of outreach, outreach growth and institutional financial health possible however, it failed to contain any information on 'who' clients were, but simply assumed they were 'the poor.'

8 Gaile and Foster (1996, Annex 1) provide a vast list of all the variables measured in 11 recent studies of microfinance impacts. The reader will also find this very useful.

9 This section draws heavily on Mosley (1997), an excellent paper.

10 This method is used widely in the medical and agricultural sciences.

11 We were not able to use this method for the Thrift and Credit Cooperatives in Sri Lanka, as the 'early' members of a cooperative are generally drawn from higher income/assets/status groups while 'late' joiners are from lower income/assets/status groups. In this case the use of a 'clients-to-be' control group would have led to an exaggerated assessment of the economic impacts of microfinance.

12 Commonly such work is referred to as 'qualitative,' but the quantitative/qualitative dichotomy is a false dichotomy. Most quantitative studies extract qualitative data from the respondent, have the interviewer immediately codify or quantify it and then use only numerical analysis. Many 'qualitative' studies transform their data into quantities at later stages of analysis (Moris and Copestake, 1993, p. 4).

13 For a classic example of such work see Rutherford (1999).

14 This issue is raised in Hulme (1997) and was debated at the CGAP Impact Assessment Group virtual meeting.

15 As Moris and Copestake (1993, p. 1) point out 'the much recommended text on data collection by Casley and Lury (1982) … included two cursory paragraphs on "quick and dirty" techniques … almost half of the World Bank's publication that superseded it (Casley and Kumar, 1988) is concerned with qualitative methods.' Studies using this approach include Hulme and Mosley, 1996; Rutherford, 1993; Fuglesang and Chandler, 1986 and Fuglesang and Chandler, 1993. For details of many recent examples see Mayoux (1997).

16 The reader wishing to explore PLA and PRA (participatory rural appraisal) is referred to Chambers (1997) and the references he provides as there is not space to more fully explore these ideas in this paper. See Mayoux (1997) for a discussion of empowerment as a program goal, with particular reference to gender.

17 See Chao-Beroff (1997) for an example of an NGO's use of participatory methods and Martyn-Johns (1996) for a comprehensive review of PIA.

18 This section draws heavily on the work of Montgomery *et al.* (1996).

19 The only report to hand that explicitly identifies absolute costs and relative costs (as a percentage of program budgets) is Montgomery *et al.* (1996), mainly in relation to natural resource and social programs. It reports that the 1994 IA of BRAC's credit program cost US$250,000.

20 At one large Asian MFI (Hulme and Mosley, 1996, Vol. 2), program field staff visited villages that had been randomly selected for survey and told borrowers to make sure they gave interviewers 'the right answers.' Fortunately, qualitative research revealed this and other villages were selected for survey!

21 This method is widespread in the United States and United Kingdom when market researchers convene focus groups to test new products. It should be noted that once interviewees in an area are paid for interviews then the likelihood of noncooperation in the future, unless fees are paid, is greatly increased.

22 An anonymous reviewer pointed out that, like most IA theory and practice, this paper is dominated by supply-side issues and neglects 'use', i.e. the demand side. This is a valid criticism especially given my earlier work which indicated that some development agencies actively 'do not learn' (Hulme, 1988) and my continued belief that the World Bank has a learning disability (Hulme, 1992 and Hulme, 1994).

23 Unfortunately donor agencies generally lack the courage to reach this decision and consultants (*mea culpa*) may have a vested interest in not promoting this option.

24 See Montgomery *et al.* (1996) for an excellent discussion of the role of impact monitoring vis à vis impact assessment.

25 For example, for BRAC in 1994 and 1995 vast amounts of technically valid data collection and analysis were occurring for the Impact Assessment Study (Mustafa *et al.*, 1996) and the World Bank-BIDS Bangladesh MFI study. The main source of information and ideas for BRAC's five-year plan (1995–2000) came from a rapid informal and focus group research exercise carried out by research officers from the Research and Evaluation Department who were 'pulled out' of the technical studies, along with discussions with BRAC.

References

Adams, D. and von Pischke, J.D., (1992). Microenterprise credit programs: Deja vu. *World Development*, 20, 1463–70.

Ardener, S. and Burman, S., (1995). *Money-go-rounds: the importance of rotating savings and credit associations for women*. Oxford: Berg.

Barnes, C., (1996). *Assets and the impact of microenterprise finance programs.* Washington, DC: Management Systems International.

Bouman, F. J. A., and Hospes, O. (1994). *Financial landscapes reconstructed.* Boulder, Co: Westview.

Buckley, G., (1997). Microfinance in Africa: Is it either the problem or the solution? *World Development*, 25 (7), 1081–94.

Casley, D. and Kumar, K., (1988). *The collections, analysis and use of monitoring evaluation data*. Baltimore: John Hopkins University Press.

Casley, D. and Lury, D.A., (1982). *Monitoring and evaluation of agricultural and rural development projects*. Baltimore: Johns Hopkins University Press.

Chambers, R., (1993). *Challenging the professions: frontiers for rural development*. London: IT Publications.

Chambers, R., (1997). *Whose reality counts? putting the first last*, London: IT Publications.

Chao-Beroff, R., (1997). *Impact assessment seen from an NGO practitioner's scope mimeo*. Washington, DC: Consultative Group to Assist the Poorest (CGAP).

Chen, M.A. and Dunn, E., (1996). *Household economic portfolios*. Washington, DC: Management Systems International.

Feinstein, O., (1997). *A transaction costs approach for microfinance project assessment mimeo*. Washington, DC: Consultative Group to Assist the Poorest (CGAP).

Fuglesang, A. and Chandler, D., (1986). *Participation as process: what we can learn from the Grameen Bank*. Oslo: NORAD.

Fuglesang, A. and Chandler, D., (1993). *Participation as process – process as growth*. Dhaka: Grameen Trust.

Gaile, G.L., (1997). *Highlights and recommendations from the microenterprise impact virtual meeting*. Washington, DC: Management Systems International.

Gaile, G.L. and Foster, J., (1996). *Review of methodological approaches to the study of the impact of microenterprise credit programs*. Washington, DC: Management Systems International.

Goetz, A.M. and Sen Gupta, R., (1996). Who takes the credit? Gender, power and control over loan use in rural credit programs in Bangladesh. *World Development*, 24 (1), 45–64.

Hashemi, S.M., Schuler, S.R. and Riley, A.P., (1996). Rural credit programs and women's empowerment in Bangladesh. *World Development*, 24 (4), 635–54.

Holcombe, S., (1995). *Managing to empower: the Grameen Bank's experience of poverty alleviation*. London: Zed Press.

Hossain, M., (1988). *Credit for alleviation of rural poverty: the Grameen Bank in Bangladesh*. Washington, DC: IFPRI.

Hulme, D., (1988). Learning and not learning from experience in rural project planning. *Public Administration and Development*, 9 (1), 1–17.

Hulme, D., (1992). Enhancing organizational effectiveness in developing countries: the training and visit system revisited. *Public Administration and Development*, 12 (5), 433–5.

Hulme, D., (1994). Does the World Bank have a learning disability? *Public Administration and Development*, 14 (1), 93–7.

Hulme, D., (1997). Impact assessment methodologies for microfinance: A review. A paper prepared for the virtual meeting of CGAP Working Group on Impact Assessment Methodologies, April 17–19.

Hulme, D. and Mosley, P., (1996). *Finance against poverty*, Vols. 1 and 2. London: Routledge.

Hyman, E. and Dearden, K., (1998). Comprehensive impact assessment systems for NGO microenterprise development program. *World Development*, 26 (2), 261–76.

Khandker, S.R., (1998). *Fighting poverty with microcredit: experience in Bangladesh*. Washington, DC: Oxford University Press for the World Bank.

Little, P., (1997). *Assessing the impact of microfinance programs on incomes and assets mimeo*. Washington, DC: Consultative Group to Assist the Poorest (CGAP).

Long, N. and Long, A., (1992). *Battlefields of knowledge*. London: Routledge.

Martyn-Johns, E., (1996). *Participatory impact assessment: putting theory into practice*. MA dissertation, IDPM, University of Manchester, UK.

Mayoux, L., (1997). *Impact assessment and women's empowerment in microfinance programmes: issues for a participatory action and learning approach mimeo*, Washington, DC: Consultative Group to Assist the Poorest (CGAP).

Montgomery, R., (1996). Disciplining or protecting the poor? Avoiding the social costs of peer pressure in microcredit schemes. *Journal of International Development*, 8 (2), 289–305.

Montgomery, R., Davies, R., Saxena, N.C., and Ashley, S., (1996). *Guidance materials for improved project monitoring and impact review systems in India*. Swansea, UK: Centre for Development Studies, University College.

Moris, J. and Copestake, J., (1993). *Qualitative enquiry for rural development: a review*. London: IT Publications.

Mosley, P. and Hulme, D., (1998). Microenterprise finance: is there a conflict between growth and poverty alleviation? *World Development*, 26 (5), 783–90.

Mosley, P., (1997). *The use of control groups in impact assessment for microfinance mimeo*. Washington, DC: Consultative Group to Assist the Poorest (CGAP).

Mosse, D., (1994). Authority gender and knowledge: theoretical reflections on the practice of participatory rural appraisal. *Development and Change*, 25(3), 497–525.

Mustafa, S. *et al*., (1996). *Beacon of hope: an impact assessment study of BRAC's rural development programme*. Dhaka: BRAC.

New Economics Foundation, (1996). *A social audit manual for small organizations*. London: New Economics Foundation.

Otero, M., and Rhyne, E., (1994). *The new world of microenterprise finance*. London: IT Publications.

Peace, G. and Hulme, D., (1994). Microenterprise and children: what are the intra household impacts of income generating programmes. *Small Enterprise Development*, 5 (1), 21–9.

Pulley, R., (1989). Making the poor creditworthy: a case study of the integrated rural development program in India. World Bank Discussion Paper 58. Washington, DC: World Bank.

Remenyi, J., (1991). *Where credit is due*. London: IT Publications.

Rogaly, B., (1996). Micro-finance evangelism, destitute women and the hard selling of a new anti poverty formula. *Development in Practice* 6 (2), 100–2.

Rutherford, Stuart, (1999). The poor and their money, Finance and Development Working Paper No. 3. IDPM, University of Manchester.

Rutherford, Stuart, (1993). Learning to lend: informal savings and credit schemes in Bangladesh. SCF Working Paper No. 5, London: Save the Children Fund.

Schuler, S.R., Hashemi, S.M. and Riley, A.P., (1997). The influence of women's changing roles and status in Bangladesh's fertility transition: evidence from a study of credit programs and contraceptive use. *World Development*, 25 (4), 563–76.

Schuler, S.R. and Hashemi, S.M., (1994). Credit programs: women's empowerment and contraceptive use in Rural Bangladesh. *Studies in Family Planning*, 25 (2), 65–76.

Sebstad, J., Neill, C., Barnes, C. and Chen, G., (1995). *Assessing the impacts of microenterprise interventions: a framework for analysis*. Washington, DC: USAID.

Wiig, A., (1997). *Credit expansion in microcredit programmes: dilemmas and feasible methods for studying them mimeo*. Washington, DC: Consultative Group to Assist the Poorest (CGAP).

Wood, G., and Sharrif, S., (1997). *Credit where credit is due*. Dhaka and London: UPL and Zed Press.

Yaron, J., Benjamin, M., and Piprek, G., (1997). *Rural finance: issues, design and best practices*. Washington, DC: Agriculture and Natural Resources Department, World Bank.

Zadek, S., and Gatward, M., (1996). Transforming the transnational NGOs: social auditing or bust? In M. Edwards (Ed.), *Beyond the magic bullet: NGO performance and accountability in the post war world* (pp. 226–40). West Hartford: Kumarian Press and London: Earthscan.

14

THE FUTURE OF MICROFINANCE

David Hulme and Thankom Arun

14.1 INTRODUCTION

In this short chapter we consider the future of microfinance – the ways in which the sector may evolve over coming years. This is not an attempt to predict what will happen – that would be foolish. Rather, we try to identify key processes that are shaping and will shape the microfinance sector. At the time of writing – against the backdrop of a global liquidity crisis, the bubble of sub-prime mortgage lending in the USA, the near collapse of major banks in the USA (Bear Stearns) and Europe (Northern Rock) and a massive expansion of the use of public finance to maintain trust in the commercial banking industry – it seems appropriate to argue that the relative maturity of the microfinance sector needs full recognition. The perception that microfinance operations are somehow riskier than the operations of the more established banking sector – mortgages, savings products for middle class people, consumer credit, loans for formal business – has clearly been proved wrong. Microfinance institutions (MFIs) are weathering the global financial crisis better than many of the trusted institutions of mainstream finance, as was the case in 1997 and 1998 with the Asian financial crisis (Patten *et al.*, 2001). Indeed, one could make the argument that mainstream banks and financial institutions would be more secure if a greater share of their portfolios were in the microfinance sector.

The key processes that we speculate on in this chapter are: the continued playing out of the 'poverty lending' approach versus 'financial systems' approach debate; technological change; regulation; and, the evolving geography of microfinance.

14.2 FROM POVERTY LENDING VERSUS FINANCIAL SYSTEMS TO COMMERCIALIZATION AND GRADUATION

The historical debate about whether MFIs should pursue a 'poverty lending' or a 'financial systems' approach (see Marguerite Robinson's chapter in this volume) is largely resolved. In most parts of the world the microfinance sector is adopting a financial systems approach either by operating on commercial lines or systematically reducing reliance on interest rate subsidies and/or aid agency financial support. This is well illustrated by the experience in Bangladesh where the Grameen Bank has shifted from its classic 'Grameen I' group-lending to the poor model to 'Grameen II' which is much closer to the financial systems model (see Hulme's 'The story of the Grameen Bank' in this volume). For observers in Bangladesh this is not a surprise given the rapid growth and success of ASA with its full-blooded, market-based approach to microfinance.

The main opponents to such a shift have not been the thought leaders of poverty lending (Professor Yunus and the lobbyists of the Microcredit Summit) but populist politicians, seeking votes, and left-wing journalists who find the idea of MFIs making profits from low-income people repulsive. The move towards the financial system approach and growth of competitive environment has put the client back at the centre of microfinance operations.

This shift in the composition of the microfinance sector will continue because of two main processes. The first, illustrated by the Grameen Bank, is of existing MFIs reducing the 'poverty lending' focus of their activities, shifting to the financial service needs of low-income households and operating savings alongside loans. To save embarrassment, such MFIs can use token programs – such as Grameen's 'Beggars Program' – to show that their heart remains with the poor even when their head (and financial portfolio) has moved to the market. Depending on the regulatory context such policy changes may be matched by institutional changes as non-governmental organizations (NGOs) and cooperative MFIs re-register as commercial banks or for-profit, non-banking financial institutions. For instance, in Pakistan, in 2002, The First Microfinance Bank was established with support from the Aga Khan Rural Support Program (AKRSP) and the Aga Khan Fund for Economic Development. The idea was to phase out the microfinance program at AKRSP and to introduce a full range of financial services to the poor over the period.

The second process is of established, formal banks and financial institutions moving into microfinance. This is happening with ICICI, Barclays, ABN-AMRO, Citigroup, Standard Chartered and others. Citigroup has publicly acknowledged the potential profits it believes it can generate from engaging in the microfinance sector. ICICI Bank in India expanded its microfinance portfolio from 10,000 clients in 2001 to almost 1.5 million customers with a portfolio of US$265 million by 2005. ICICI lends to selected MFIs at a rate of 9.5 percent to 11 percent per annum, slightly more than it charges its corporate clients, and the MFIs on-lend this money to borrower groups (self help groups or SHGs as they are called in India) at 16 percent to 30 percent per annum (*The Economist*, 2005). ABN-AMRO is investing heavily in promoting microfinance in the north and north eastern states of India where MFIs are almost non-existent. It is doing this to reduce financial exclusion and make profits. Barclays have an established relationship with *zuzu* collectors in Ghana – holding the deposits that these informal door-to-door collectors gather and permitting *zuzu* collectors to reduce the charges that they levy on clients. Formal banking institutions are also engaging in financial innovations such as venture capital funds (as with the Dutch-Ivos-Triodos Fund in India) and floating commercial and ethical bonds for MFIs (as US banks are doing for BRAC's US$75 million bonds to expand its microfinance programs in Africa). Similarly, the development of asset-backed securitization is emerging as a viable method for large MFIs to manage their liquidity and credit risks.

While this shift of focus in the microfinance sector towards financial systems approaches is set to continue it must be noted that the interest of MFIs and microfinance analysts in directly helping the poor has not disappeared. Increasingly those with concern about 'poverty reduction' have promoted 'graduation' programs that seek to provide substantial support (often financial through substantial sums of foreign aid) to ultra poor people (see Matin and Hulme's chapter in this volume, for an example). These graduation schemes attempt to develop the capabilities of poor people – in terms of confidence, skills, assets and access to support services – so that after a period of 12 to 24 months of intensive support, such disadvantaged people can gain access to microfinancial services and operate more effectively in local markets. Such schemes have moved beyond their experimental phase and are being mounted on a significant scale in several countries (Littlefield *et al.*, 2003; Hashemi and Rosenberg, 2006). Indeed, the Consultative Group to Assist the Poor (CGAP), a donor association that seeks to promote best practice in microfinance, has taken great interest in the concept and practice of graduation (Littlefield *et al.*, 2003; Hashemi and Rosenberg, 2006). If such schemes are effective then they can direct aid agency money towards very poor people but be linked to microfinance by their recognition that raising the capacity of the poor and ultra poor to access microfinancial services is a key component of poverty reduction strategies.

All this is positive, but there still remain grave concerns about some of the shift to a financial systems approach. These are illustrated by the Compartamos affair in Mexico. When this microfinance NGO became a private sector financial institution, its directors became multi-millionaires overnight. For many observers this was distasteful as people who had negotiated public grants to establish an MFI and who charged high rates of interest on loans to low-income people (under the banner of poverty-reduction) converted the resources generated by grants and high charges into private fortunes. Even the thought of leaders of financial systems approach to microfinance, such as Dale Adams at Ohio State University, was aghast at the way in which the commercialization of microfinance could redistribute assets in such a highly unequal way.

14.3 TECHNOLOGICAL CHANGE

The original 'microfinance revolution' took advantage of the technological advances in information and communication technologies (ICTs) of the 1980s and 1990s. However, often this was as a relatively late adopter with many MFIs having to convert manual records to electronic systems in the mid and late 1990s. The dramatic reductions in the cost of new ICT products – mobile telephones, palm pilots and even laptops – and the rise in connectivity through mobile phones and the internet mean that in the next decade there is enormous potential for MFIs to develop new services: services that in the past would have been economically infeasible because of high transaction costs.

These technological changes have made it easier to address two main obstacles in providing financial services to poor people – managing information and service delivery costs (*The Economist*, 2005). The challenge for MFIs is to rethink their business models and to innovate with the ways they deliver and receive services so that products are more convenient and cheaper for customers, people in remote areas can access services and security is enhanced. Until now, the predominant use of technology among MFIs has been to internally manage information. However, technology has an immense potential in other areas such as payments and credit underwriting. For instance, as mobile phone usage expands, opportunities to provide financial services in remote rural areas become feasible. The concept of mobile banking, 'M-banking.' has great promise. The South African experience shows that low-income mobile phone banking users value the service for its affordability, ease of use, and security and, it is up to one-third cheaper than the lowest price full-service account offered by South Africa's largest banks (Ivatury and Pickens, 2006).

SafeSave, in Bangladesh, provides low-income slum-dwellers with flexible financial services. On six days a week its clients can make savings, withdraw savings, take out loans or repay loans when their collector calls at their house or business. Such flexibility creates relatively complex microfinance portfolios but the use of palm pilots by collectors provides a real-time record of transactions and permits the Bank's books to be balanced, at a very low administrative cost, shortly after the close of business each day. The stage is now set for many other innovations of this type.

14.4 REGULATION

In many developing countries, governments are still struggling with how to regulate microfinance (see Arun's chapter in this volume). Many (particularly central bankers) are inclined to attempt to regulate MFIs in the same way as they do formal sector banks. Whilst in theory this will provide savers with security, in practice it discourages the evolution of MFIs and often means that established MFIs cannot develop savings products. This keeps depositors 'safe' from unscrupulous or poorly managed MFIs but means that they have to use other savings mechanisms (hiding cash in slum dwellings, buying livestock or asking a trader to hold cash). These other mechanisms are often riskier than the services that MFIs can provide.

The sub-prime crisis in the US has raised new concerns about the regulation and supervision of MFIs; in many countries the microfinance is the sub-prime market. Although the enhanced financial options can offer valuable services to poor people, there is a need to regulate the entry of bad practices and products, which could harm the financial system itself. As in the US credit market, sub-prime lenders may disproportionately target minority and lower-income people with higher-priced products offered on inferior terms. The entry of aggressive consumer lenders and their competition may encourage underwriting practices and poor-loan screening which devalues the portfolio quality. These kinds of situations and the increasing concerns of terrorism financing pose new regulatory challenges for the state.

14.5 THE GEOGRAPHY OF MICROFINANCE

Despite the phenomenal growth of microfinance over the last 25 years, most parts of the developing world remain characterized by demand for microsavings, microloans and microinsurance services vastly outstripping demand. Only in a limited number of areas – parts of Bangladesh, Indonesia, Uganda, Kenya and Bolivia – is there a competitive microfinance market where low-income people have access to a range of services and providers. Across South Asia, Southeast Asia, Latin America and Eastern Europe microfinance provision seems set to rise, through specialized MFIs and through formal banks setting up microfinance programs. However, the likely patterns of evolution in sub-Saharan Africa and China are less clear.

In Africa, relatively few MFIs have managed to reach a scale of more than 25,000 clients and provision focuses on the cities, towns and major rural trading centres. This low level of coverage is partly explained by Africa's geography: the microfinance revolution has not yet created viable models for operating in areas with dispersed populations of extremely poor people where there is limited physical infrastructure and little institutional capacity. The application of low-cost ICT-based services significantly increases the likelihood of product development for such populations and the recent upturn in African economic growth rates improves MFI prospects. However, the geographical problems of microfinance provision in much of Africa are exacerbated by the more general difficulties of institutional development in Africa, state fragility and the region's reliance on donor finance and donor ideas. As a result the pace of microfinance development in much of Africa may remain slow. We think that microfinance in Africa should focus on service provision for lower-middle and low-income households in areas where populations are dense and infrastructure is available. If effective, large-scale MFIs, led by dynamic African social entrepreneurs, can become established in more advantaged areas then they could experiment with outreach to less advantaged regions in the future. For Africa's poor and extreme poor poverty reduction policy needs to prioritize social protection (Barrientos and Hulme, 2008), primary education and basic health services rather than microfinance.

Although China has one of the fastest-growing economies in the world, the majority of the population remain in rural areas and there is great scope for MFIs. As most local authorities (counties) in China have limited experience in microfinance, the current policy focus is to share the achievements of successful, existing programs in order to encourage local authorities to increase their support to MFIs. However, HSBC opened its first rural bank in Hubei in 2007 and many more international banks and private-equity firms are expected to start soon.

One of the emerging concerns in the growth of microfinance is the uneven degree of provision of microfinance within countries (Rhyne and Otero, 2006). For example, in India most MFIs operate in the relatively developed South of the country and provision in the poorer North and East is low to non-existent. In Indonesia there is a vibrant microfinance market in Java and the Western islands but provision in the disadvantaged Eastern provinces is much lower. This regional inequality may be matched by a 'quality gap' (ibid.) and clients in low microfinance density areas may receive lower quality services at a higher price. Similarly, there are significant differences between urban and rural supply of financial services in Latin America and Africa.

14.6 CONCLUSION

The concept and practice of microfinance have changed dramatically over the last decade. Conceptually, the financial systems approach has gained ground over poverty lending and most serious analysts now view microcredit as only one of several components of microfinance. The argument advanced by Robinson in her chapter in this volume, that microfinance should seek to meet the demand of low-income people for financial services, rather than the poor and the extremely poor, widely informs present day practice. Microfinance is seen as a set of services that raises the prospects for low-income households, and some poor people, to achieve their goals – in business, consumption, education, health and other areas – and not as a magic bullet that automatically lifts poor people out of poverty through microenterprise. Microfinance specialists concerned with poverty reduction and/or extreme poverty are increasingly focusing on 'graduation' programs (see this chapter and Matin and Hulme's in this volume) that link microfinance to social protection and other services.

The microfinance sector seems set to continue to expand and diffuse through specialist MFIs and formal banks. However, the speed and nature of these processes is unclear in sub-Saharan Africa and China. While many factors will shape the future of microfinance, one factor merits highlighting in this conclusion. It is the social energy of the tens of thousands of people who are committed to analyzing microfinance and debating how additional financial services can be made accessible to the hundreds of millions of people who have very limited access to services. Few other development issues have managed to generate such passion and commitment as microfinance. Some of these analysts have it easy – they are in universities or research agencies, like us, and are paid to do such work. The majority are, however, closer to the coalface and are actively involved in planning, managing or delivering microfinancial services. It is the collective imagination and social energy of this dispersed community that has created the microfinance revolution of the late twentieth century and will take it forward in the coming years.

References

Barrientos, A. and Hulme, D. (2008), *Social Protection for the Poor and Poorest: Concepts, Policies and Politics*, Basingstoke: Palgrave Macmillan.

Economist (2005), 'A Survey of Microfinance', *The Economist*, November 5th, pp. 3–12.

Hashemi, S. and Rosenberg, R. (2006), 'Graduating the Poorest into Microfinance: Linking Safety Nets and Financial Services', *CGAP Focus Note 34*, http://www.cgap.org.

Ivatury, G., and Pickens, M. (2006), *Mobile Phone Banking and Low-Income Customers: Evidence from South Africa*, Washington, DC: Consultative Group to Assist the Poor (CGAP) and the United Nations Foundation.

Littlefield, E., Morduch, J., and Hashemi, S. (2003), 'Is Microfinance an Effective Strategy to Reach the Millennium Development Goals?', *CGAP Focus Note 24*, http://www.cgap.org

Patten, R.H., Rosengard, J.K. and Johnston, D.E. Jr. (2001), 'Microfinance Success Amidst Macroeconomic Failure: The Experience of Bank Rakyat Indonesia During the East Asian Crisis', *World Development*, 29(6), 1057–69.

Rhyne, E. and Otero, M. (2006), 'Microfinance Through the Next Decade: Visioning the Who, What, Where, When and How', ACCION International Paper (commissioned by the Global Microcredit Summit 2006), http://www.microfinancegateway.com/content/article/detail/36423 (accessed June 12, 2008).

INDEX